AN INDIAN DIARY

AN INDIAN DIARY

EDWIN S. MONTAGU

EDITOR

VENETIA MONTAGU

GYAN

Published by

Gyan Publishing House
5, Ansari Road
Daryaganj, New Delhi-110002
Phone: 011-47034999, 9811692060
E-mail: books@gyanbooks.com

Distribution Network
gyanbooks.com
India, USA, Canada, UK, Australia

ISBN: 978-93-6920-973-6 (PB)

First Published, 1930

2nd Impression 2025

Printed at: Gyan Press, Delhi.

AN INDIAN DIARY
Author: EDWIN S. MONTAGU, Editor: VENETIA MONTAGU

AN INDIAN DIARY

G. E. Franey Alan Parsons Charles Roberts M. C. Seton W. S. Marris F. C. T. Halliday

Sir William Vincent Lord Donoughmore E. S. M. Sir William Duke B. N. Basu C. H. Kisch

THE DELEGATION

[*Frontispiece*

AN INDIAN DIARY

By

EDWIN S. MONTAGU

Secretary of State for India, 1917–1922

Edited by

VENETIA MONTAGU

PREFACE

THIS diary was written by Edwin Montagu from day to day during his visit to India in 1917–18, after the historic pronouncement of August 20, 1917, in the House of Commons.

There was no thought of eventual publication : the main idea in writing it was to give the Prime Minister, Mr. Lloyd George, continuous news of how he was progressing in his supremely difficult task ; batches of it were sent home by each mail to him. Since that time, two or three other people at the most have looked through it.

Now that India is looming so largely in the public eye, I have thought it a fitting time to give this document to the world, hoping that it may help to make a little clearer the great part which the writer played in India's destinies. The welfare of India was the one mastering passion of his life : he joined Mr. Lloyd George's Government in July, 1917, only on condition that he should go to the India Office, confident in the great work which he felt he could accomplish for the cause he had so much at heart. When he resigned his office in 1922, he seemed, in saying good-bye to his work for India, to lose the greater part of his interest in life ; he was never the same man again.

The diary was dictated, usually against time, to his shorthand writer, Mr. George Franey, at all times and places, sometimes on the back of an elephant, miles out in the jungle. These week-end shooting trips were the only way by which he could save himself from a severe breakdown, which indeed continually threatened him. Whether he was the guest of honour at a vast tiger-shoot, with 1,500 beaters in a Native State, or standing up to his waist in water for the chance of bagging a few couple of snipe, he was able for the moment to forget his troubles, which had usually redoubled themselves by the time the train steamed into Delhi on each successive Black Monday morning.

He wrote impulsively, and on the spur of the moment, and the reader will continually find sweeping or hasty judgments modified or even contradicted a few pages later.

In one passage he claims, among other things, that he "kept India quiet for six months at a critical period of the War"; I hope that the publication of this diary may not only substantiate this claim, but also throw some light on an extraordinarily complex personality whom the great world never understood, but his intimate friends and colleagues knew to be passionately sincere and generous to a fault.

VENETIA MONTAGU.

GOVERNMENT OF INDIA DURING THE PERIOD OF THE VISIT

Viceroy and Governor-General: H. E. LORD CHELMSFORD, G.C.M.G., G.M.S.I., G.M.I.E.

Private Secretary: J. L. MAFFEY, C.I.E.

Military Secretary: Lieutenant-Colonel R. VERNEY, C.I.E.

Comptroller: Major J. MACKENZIE, C.I.E.

Surgeon: Lieutenant-Colonel H. AUSTEN SMITH.

A.D.C.s: T. Holland-Hibbert.
E. B. Baring.
J. Denny.
Lord Carnegie.

Council: Sir W. S. Meyer, K.C.S.I., K.C.I.E. (Finance).
Sir Claude Hill, K.C.S.I., C.I.E. (R. and A.).
Sir C. Sankaran Nair, C.I.E. (Education).
Sir George Lowndes, K.C.S.I. (Law).
Sir George Barnes, K.C.B. (C. and I.).
Sir W. H. Vincent (Home).
Sir J. du Boulay, K.C.I.E., C.S.I. (Home).
General Sir C. C. Monro, G.C.M.G., K.C.B. (Army).

GOVERNORS AND HEADS OF PROVINCES

Bengal.—Governor: H.E. The Earl of Ronaldshay, G.C.I.E. (Private Secretary: W. R. Gourlay, C.I.E.)

Central Provinces.—Chief Commissioner: Sir Benjamin Robertson, K.C.S.I., K.C.M.G., C.I.E.

Bihar and Orissa.—Lieutenant-Governor Sir E. A. Gait, K.C.S.I., C.I.E.

Assam.—Chief Commissioner: Sir Archdale Earle, K.C.S.I., K.C.I.E.

United Provinces.—Lieutenant-Governor: Sir James Meston, K.C.S.I.[1] (after February 15, 1918, Sir Spencer Harcourt Butler, K.C.S.I., C.I.E.).

Punjab.—Lieutenant-Governor: Sir M. F. O'Dwyer, G.C.I.E., K.C.S.I.

N.W.F.P.—Chief Commissioner: Sir G. O. Roos-Keppel, G.C.I.E., K.C.S.I.

Burma.—Lieutenant-Governor: Sir R. H. Craddock, K.C.S.I.

Madras.—Governor: H.E. Lord Pentland, G.C.S.I.

Bombay.—Governor: H.E. Lord Willingdon, G.C.S.I. (Private Secretary: J. Crerar, C.I.E.)

[1] Now Lord Meston.

CONTENTS

CONTENTS

LIST OF ILLUSTRATIONS

FOREWORD

The Delegation, consisting of the following members :

The Earl of Donoughmore, K.P.
Mr. Charles Roberts, M.P.
Mr. Bhupendranath Basu.
Sir William Duke, K.C.S.I., K.C.I.E.
Sir William Vincent (lent by the Government of India),
Mr. M. C. Seton, C.B., *Secretary to the Delegation*,[1]
Mr. C. H. Kisch, } *Private Secretaries*,
Mr. Alan Parsons, }
Mr. F. C. T. Halliday, M.V.O. (Indian Police),
Mr. G. E. Franey, *Stenographer*,

left London on October 18, 1917, travelling overland to Taranto, where they boarded H.M.S. *Bristol*, arriving at Port Said a couple of days later.

They spent several days in Cairo, where Mr. Montagu was the guest of Sir Reginald Wingate, with whom he had constant discussions on Egyptian and Indian affairs.

The mission sailed from Port Said in the P. & O. *Kaiser-I-Hind* on October 30, calling on the way at Aden for lunch with the Resident.

Mr. Montagu held frequent preliminary discussions on reforms with his colleagues during the journey.

The party arrived at Bombay on November 10, and this is the point at which the story opens.

[1] Now Sir Malcolm Seton, K.C.B.

I

BOMBAY—DELHI

Saturday, November 10. I am glad to get off the ship, for, as I have said, although I found it so thoroughly equipped, it was tedious in the extreme. It is really marvellous to reflect that we reached Bombay less then three weeks after leaving London, and that despite the fact that we stayed for the best part of a day at Turin, a whole day in Rome, and five days in Cairo.

The study of Reform on board the ship leads me to a belief that we have the foundation of a very fairly satisfactory scheme to work upon. My Government of India, Dobbs'[1] scheme for the Civil Service, and Duke's scheme as clarified and amended by discussion together seem to me good, provided that the compilation of the B list is satisfactory; and with my scheme of fundamental legislation I trust I shall get a little more out of Duke. But it is quite obvious that my rôle in India must be to disclose nothing of any of these deliberations, except possibly quite privately to the Viceroy, until the end, and even then I am going to work hard to let the whole thing come from the Indian Government themselves, unless I find that they are incapable of construction to such an extent that it is necessary to construct for them. But even then I shall drop hints in a pretty effort to lead them into voicing my schemes as their own. There are two dangers: (1) that I shall be regarded as having forced a policy on weaker men (if my critics only knew!), and the other is that I should be regarded as a weak, non-contributory factor, accepting the plans of other people. That danger to me is vastly insignificant compared to the other. The first danger might jeopardise my chance of carrying any plans;

[1] H. R. C. Dobbs, C.S.I., C.I.E. (A.G.G. and Chief Commissioner, Baluchistan.)

the second only jeopardises other people's judgment of me. But, after all, that does not matter in the least, and I shall have for my own benefit all these memoranda and diaries, which should be carefully dated, particularly the memoranda.

When the ship anchored, the usual swarm of small boats arrived, conspicuous amongst them the Government of Bombay launch, containing Colonel Verney, Lord Chelmsford's military secretary, the resident naval officer, my policeman, Halliday, Laverton and Lord Lathom, Willingdon's aide-de-camps. Verney brought me a letter from the Viceroy welcoming me to India, containing the usual gloomy note, and saying that the European community was no better, in fact a little worse, in its view.

The white uniforms of these officers, the bright scarlet and gold of the Government Chuprassis, of whom there were about eight, looked very fine in the sunlight, for the sky, of course, was cloudless, save for the long grey cloud on the horizon which stretches out from Bombay for miles into the sea, and is always the first thing that one sees of this town, coming from the cotton mills. The entrance to Bombay is a never-forgettable sight, but Bombay itself and one's first introduction to India is, I think, one of the wonders of the world, and must produce exuberance, enthusiasm, even to the most prosaic nature. The blue sea, the hills in the foreground, in the background, on the horizon, in the middle distance, of various degrees of blues and blacks and greys; the white buildings, the marvellous spacing, the silent, quiet crowds of foot passengers; the bright, coloured garments of the women, their stately carriage and beautiful walk at all ages, which are enough, to my mind, to repair any deficiency in beauty; the white robes of the men; the turbans of the soldiers—and all this is something which charmed me when I first saw Bombay, and is even more potent on my return. And then, of course, Bombay faces west, and the sunset as the sun sinks into the sea through purples, mauves, reds, yellows and greens, to be replaced by a black starlit night—well, it certainly could not be painted, and I cannot describe it. We spent five minutes or so reaching the Apollo Bunder. I read telegrams of welcome from all sorts and conditions of people, among whom I would mention Bikaner, Alwar, Gwalior, Bannerjea, Tilak (!) and all sorts of associations and leagues. The Bunder steps and the Bunder itself were covered with red carpet, and Willingdon, with his military secretary, Greenway (son-in-law of Brooking, the Victor of Ramadieh), the son of Greenway, of the Anglo-Persian Oil Company, were there to meet me and to introduce me to various civil servants and judges and policemen. It is a perfect God-send to me to meet, on my first arrival, an old friend like Freeman,[1] whom I have known politically and socially through the years. I feel that I can talk to him quite frankly, and the sight of a friendly face when my spirits are at the lowest and the enormity of my task is most obvious to me, is something that I have got to thank Providence for. We drove to the Yacht Club, where we all had lunch together. After lunch, Willingdon and I sat talking for about one and a half hours on the balcony overlooking the harbour. It is interesting to notice that the camouflage painting of the P. & O., with the sun behind it, is not noticeable at all ; the hull looks black, but I am told it is wonderful through a periscope. Then I drove with Willingdon to look at the new Sports Club, intended to punish the Yacht Club and the Byculla Club for their refusal to admit Indians. It is going to be a comfortable club, with good rooms and very fine opportunities for polo, cricket, lawn tennis and football. The princes are, I believe, enthusiastic, and have subscribed all the money, but it is smaller than the Yacht Club, far removed from the harbour and the main part of the town, has not the marvellous view over the harbour, and at present looks out on some rather foul-smelling water, and although Freeman's optimism is unbounded, I am afraid the Yacht Club is in no

[1] Lord Willingdon.

danger. Again I say that the social question, the fact that the civil servants are willing to work with the Indians but not to play with them, the fact that the Boxwallah will have nothing to do with them, has really brought the present political situation upon us.

Government House is in the hands of builders and cleaners, so although we drove there to look at Freeman's Kashmir stag heads—which I do not think are as good as mine—six in number, three of them very good, killed in the same valley as mine, and although we sat out and watched the sunset and talked on the roof, we were given most comfortable offices, rooms and baths in the Secretariat Building, where I read part of the afternoon letters from Ronaldshay and Pentland, the latter protesting against a charge of leakage I had made, but the protest does not convince me. Ronaldshay gives me the news that the Mohammedans of Bengal are forming a new and moderate political association as a consequence of the Moslem League's attitude with regard to Mahomet Ali. Mrs. Besant has seen the Viceroy, to demand the release of this gentleman and his colleagues. This has, of course, been refused, and, much to my surprise, and I fear to Chelmsford's anger, she has published an account of this interview in the *Bombay Chronicle*. I do not think we shall get through without taking action against her again, and I cannot but feel some sympathy with Willingdon, who says, "We acquiesced in her release, but that does not alter our opinion of her, and we wonder that Chelmsford should have seen her, when all that she was going to ask for was the release of these men about whom the Government had made up their minds." By the by, the telegrams that I received from the Moslems are ingeniously worded. They ask me to see that Mohammedans shall not be regarded adversely because they carry out the injunctions of their religion to love all Mohammedans, and then call for the release of this man. I cannot help thinking that this is a difficulty we have got into for not trying to shake their faith in the genuine Islamism of the Turk. However, there it is. I received a letter from Jaipur in the vernacular, and a request for an interview from the women of India.

And now I must record at some length my conversations with Freeman. We were both so pleased with ourselves at meeting one another that our conversation on my side was, and I think his, completely unrestrained. So far as I can gather, the policy which he is going to put forward is this : complete autonomy for the Provinces ; he would even favour their direct control by the Government of India ; complete control of all matters by the Legislative Council, with an enormous elected majority, something like sixty to ten, and no safeguard on the veto of the Governor, which he says he would freely exercise without hesitation, because the *Hukm* is understood traditionally by the Indian and would not be resented. This is a strange view from one who believes in representative institutions, for the *Hukm* policy is contradictory to responsible Government policy. This is simple constitution making, if ever you had an example of it. You see, he has been successful because he has sufficient political sagacity to do everything by negotiation. There is not the slightest doubt of his popularity, and in nearly everything the people of his Province would do whatever he liked, so that he builds a constitution upon his own experience. But you cannot build constitutions for individuals ; you have to be sure that your constitution is proof against bad individuals as well as of good instruction for good ones. His scheme would merely frighten the people into refusing him much of the powers he wants transferred to him, and I fear make the Indians demand an appeal against his veto. He dismisses most schemes other than his own as needlessly complicated, but all constitutions which have to be legally enforcible documents are complicated, or, at any rate, appear complicated on reading, but are not complicated to the people who have to work them and live with them and under them, and who are often each only concerned with one small part of it. Freeman's enthusiasm knows no bounds. He pointed me out with pride the great extensions and improvements in the outskirts of Bombay since my last visit ; he was enthusiastic about his private secretary, Crerar, and all his fellows, except at their lack of political sagacity. He showed me the beauties of the Toddy palm outskirts of Bombay island, which are certainly very lovely, and which I had never seen, with their tall, close-set palms and small, humble dwelling-houses. He is enthusiastic about the shooting, and says that he is coming to India regularly when his time is up ; in fact, he is bitten with the place for all reasons as I am. He seems to have done wonderfully with his model farm at Poona, and is selling his cattle freely to the great Indian landowners and ruling princes. Freeman wants the Indian Council appointed for only three years, in order to ensure that they are modern in their Indian experience. He even says that Sydenham is already completely out of date. A wild idea came into my head while I was talking to him which I am going to keep locked in my own bosom for the present, but which I am going to pursue, and that is to abolish the India Council and to have instead four advisers to the Secretary of State, of whom two shall be Indians ; to abolish the India Office recruitment from the Home Civil Service and to recruit everybody from the Indian Civil Service, it being an understood thing that just as a man may be allotted to a Province, and from the Province to the Government of India, so he can also be allotted at any time of his service to the India Office, and have a completely interchangeable system. I told Freeman the whole history of the Besant case confidentially. He was amazed at it, and said that the Government of India had certainly not played fairly to me in not having made my share in it quite clear. Of course they really ought to have meetings annually of all the heads of Government for an informal talk with Chelmsford. I shall suggest this. One thing seems to me to be quite clear, and that is that whatever scheme of reform we introduce, it should be a model scheme, and should be adapted quite freely, with the sanction of the head of each Province, to the needs of the Province. For instance, if Bombay wants a Freeman scheme instead of the model scheme, it ought to be free to have it or something like it. And you ought not to argue from the analogy of one Province to any other. This is the elasticity for which I have been striving, and, coupled with Roberts' scheme, on the analogy of the British North America Act, the Government of India Act containing a schedule of matters which can be amended by legislation in the Legislative Council of the Government of India, and another schedule of the matters which can be amended by legislation in the Legislative Councils of the Provinces will do the trick. Freeman's story is really one long story of the remoteness of the Government of India, and its lack of co-operation with the Provincial governments—the formality and officialdom which ride together. There is also his firm belief in the lack of training of the Indians and their lack of courage. But while others would wait for this, he is politician enough to wish to give them a chance in order that they may learn and get a real substantial chance. He warns me against appearing to give something which does not in practice work out as big and as great as it looks on paper. This is the burden of Chirol's most useful article in the *Times* which has been telegraphed out. I am very grateful to him for this. He is a little alarmed, and so am I now, at the association of Chelmsford with me all the way through. I fear that Chelmsford may make all the things too formal, and I shall have to fight him on this, if I see that that is happening. We must have informal discussions, and we must take our time. Rather than fail, I would stay a year in India and resign rather than hurry things. If a deputation ought to be followed by prolonged interviews with its leaders, I cannot confine myself to ten minutes or a quarter of an hour. I must be patient with the deputations, and I must get at the bottom of matters. I cannot be told that a quarter of an hour has been allotted to a particular interview and I must not exceed it, or see the man again. It may be necessary to talk about the weather or go and lunch with somebody with a view to getting at what he really wants and thinks. The stereotyped reading of documents and the acknowledgment of them is not good enough. It may be necessary to go out into the country to talk to some people, and I shall put these views to Chelmsford to-morrow. After all, although I did attach the most enormous importance to the announcement of August 20 as one of the biggest things in the history of India, I never really conceived the enormous importance of my visit here. If one can imagine the importance of India, then the importance of my visit becomes absolutely immeasurable. Think not only of the people of India, but of our vast interests in it, how those interests ramify into almost every home in England; think of the lives that have been spent and the destinies of English families which have been altered for all time by service to India. We are accustomed to consider as something sacred the lives laid down in this War, the wounds incurred in this War, the effect on relations by the casualties of this War. So also to us must be sacred the lives laid down or spent in India during the last 100 years, and the lives that will be spent here in future. But that is not all; that is always true. My visit to India means that we are going to do something, and something big. I cannot go home and produce a little thing or nothing; it must be epoch-making, or it is a failure; it must be the keystone of the future history of India. Why do I say this? Well, because it has shaken and disturbed to its roots a country which was rolling, as I believe, to certain destruction. The Administrator realises that he has his marching orders; he has his plan of campaign, and he has got to co-operate and is busy deciding how it shall be done, and I have got to choose between the different schemes to lay before the Cabinet. Even so far as I have gone I can best describe what I mean by two things. The first is the arrangements for my visit, with the Governor meeting me at the seashore and the representative of the Viceroy on board the ship. I leave Bombay at 10.30 at night in a special train. The manager of the railway company is told to accompany me to Delhi, to see that the train service is all right, and all along the 973 miles the line is guarded. On every station platform there are administrators, police and soldiers. The terminus of the G.I.P. at Bombay lighted with a few arc lamps was a sight I shall never forget. The whole platform was covered with red carpet. Everywhere that one could see were red carpets and palm trees, and the whole dim light was glistening with the khaki of soldiers, the red uniform of Government servants, and all the prominent officials of the place. It had all gone much too far. The special train itself has the Viceroy's saloon, with a sleeping apartment for my private secretary and my servant, and a bath-room. It has a dining saloon, and first-class compartments for all my friends. Nothing is wanting in comfort, save the presence of the dust and the shakiness of all Indian railways, which makes reading difficult and writing impossible. At the rear of the train is the special carriage of the manager, Mr. Hepper. Now all this is the reception of a king or of a viceroy, and might be dismissed with the statement that it has been overdone. I agree. I wish it had not been done for many reasons. I am not the stuff to carry this sort of thing off. For the first time in my life I wish I looked like Curzon.

All this has been done for me because I am out here to devise a new political system for India, and everybody who knows of the preparations or sees them, everybody concerned in elaborating them, makes it all the more obviously essential that the thing should be a success and that it would be disastrous if it should be a failure. So much for the official side.

And now let me say a word about the Indians. My arrival was an official secret, but it spread like lightning through Bombay. I have little experience of Indian crowds, but I have always been struck by their silence. Whether it was in the Secretariat building, or in the streets, or at the railway station, there were crowds, not silent, but cheering and clapping ; not reserved, quiet and gloomy or patient, but smiling and eager. Lloyd George on a land campaign, or when he first assumed the reigns of government after his triumph at Munitions, never got quite so much, simply because in the former those for whom he was working feared the House of Lords, and in the latter there was always the anxiety and the doubt as to whether we should win the War at least as quickly as we wanted. Would to God I could read more doubt into the attitude of the Indians, for to the British Empire and to India the crisis produced by the policy and my visit requires the ability, the tact, the courage of the greatest of English statesmen. I wish Lloyd George were here ; I wish the whole British Cabinet had come ; I wish Asquith were here. It is one of India's misfortunes that I am alone, alone, alone the person that has got to carry this thing through. Of course, my friends and colleagues are good fellows, but the responsibility rests with me. Chelmsford will do his best, but the responsibility rests with me. It is I that have got to do this thing, and I spend my whole time racking my brains as to how I am going to get something which India will accept and the House of Commons will allow me to do without whittling it down. We must wait and see. I would that I could make it clear to those at home that if the results of our deliberations are either something which India will not accept, or a niggling, miserly, grudging safeguard, fiddling with the existing order of things, we shall have defrauded, and defrauded irreparably—for they will never believe us again—a vast continent whose history is our glory, and whose hopes and aspirations, fears and tribulations it is pathetic to see. I am fearful lest in the excitement of yesterday I have forgotten something that I ought to have recorded.

I have just received Curtis's latest scheme, which I have not mastered, but it fastens on the word "responsible government," admits the fundamental importance of the pronouncement, and I think goes for the Duke sub-district scheme, with the ultimate disappearance of the Provinces.

Last night, despite the shaking of the train, I slept the sleep of the weary as I have not slept for years.

Same (*Later*). I have spent a peaceful day in the train most comfortably. This route is certainly infinitely better than the shorter route by Ahmedabad and Baroda. Particularly when we get into Bhopal and before coming to Jhansi we go through some gorgeous jungles and past many an attractive gorge. All the scenery is green or covered with vegetation ; the stations are well kept and well built. I was struck by the sight of many roughly built little encampments on the edges of the cotton fields, on the sands by the beds of the rivers, and on the clearings of the jungle, but I discovered that plague is very prevalent all the way along, and that these are the villagers thrown out of their villages. I am told that yesterday was the first day at one place on which they had not had a plague death for two months. How often in India the most beautiful things are caused by horrible causes. I saw the following birds : kites, vultures, king crows, mynahs, surprise birds, pie kingfisher, shrikes, pigeon, doves, crows, cranes.

I have read Curtis's paper through. It is far the best thing that the man has done, and I think the best scheme I have seen yet, and very well written. Many of its conclusions are those at which I have tentatively independently arrived, and others Duke has arrived at. He seems to me, perhaps, to be a little unduly wedded to the sub-provincial system, and he does not seem to have thoroughly explored the difficulties of Government of India versus Provincial Finance. I also feel that he would have great political difficulty in achieving the division of India into the twenty-four Provinces he contemplates. Already I have received a telegram from the Congress party in Sindh, protesting against the existing quasi division between Sindh and Bombay, but before I dine and give up work I want now to put the scheme as I see it on this day, November 10, before starting work at Delhi.

1. Provincial Councils directly elected on a broad franchise, partly constituencies, partly territorial, partly class.

2. A small percentage reserved for nomination by Governor ; nomination partly European, partly of cultivators to keep in touch with a territorial quasi constituency, and really to represent the interests of these quasi constituents.

3. Governor may or may not be member of I.C.S.

4. Executive Council half English and half Indian. English may or may not be I.C.S. One Indian at least to be an elected member of Legislative Council.

5. Legislative Council's wishes ultimately to prevail in all subjects, subject to reservations below.

6. In case of difference of opinion, matter referred to a Duke Standing Committee, all wholly elected, to confer with member of executive directly responsible.

7. Report of Committee to be discussed by representative chosen by Committee with whole Executive Council.

8. If the Report insists on the legislation, Government may ask Legislative Council to tackle the matter by a private members Bill with draughtsman's assistance.

9. Governor to have right of dissolution and of veto.

10. He should only appoint to the Council sufficient nominated official members to satisfy the necessity for efficient Government representation in debates and discussion.

11. Officials to have right to speak and vote as they like.

12. Government of India bi-cameral system as already described in my notes.

13. Government of India to pass resolutions, called in my notes fundamental legislation, limiting the power of Legislative Councils on certain subjects, and refusing them permission to deal with certain others. N.B.—This really enables Government of India to set up an A list.

14. Provincial Legislative Council's right to petition Government of India to carry legislation repealing fundamental legislation or increasing their powers. This legislation called in my notes enabling legislation.

15. On receipt of such petition, matter referred to Committee of Government of India Legislative Council capable of hearing witnesses.

16. Every seven years Secretary of State to appoint, by statute, enquiry into working of Government of India Act, such enquiry to deal with all cases in which Government of India has refused passage of an enabling Bill, and all cases in which Government of India suggest repeal of an enabling Bill or further curtailment of powers of any particular Province.

17. Thus Parliament will have a voice in the appointment of the enquiry, and therefore indirectly will have the opportunity of revising the working of the Indian constitution.

18. If Government of Province and its Legislative Council desires Curtis's scheme of sub-division into sub-provinces, either permanently sub or intended eventually to replace existing Legislative Council and Provincial Government, or in any way to extend the scheme described, then these are matters for an enabling Bill.

19. Frontier areas, e.g. North-West Frontier, Baluchistan, to be under Government of India direct.

20. Secretary of State's Council abolished.

21. If Stores Department kept, head to be business man, or to be absorbed in Supply Department of Home Government, e.g. old Ministry of Munitions.

22. The whole of the rest of the India Office Staff to be recruited not from Home, but from Indian Civil Service.

23. Continual interchange between two countries. (Query, also Colonial Civil Service.)

24. No Permanent Under-Secretary, but three civil servants of standing, e.g. Judicial, Public, and Revenue; Finance; Political; and a soldier for military. You may want a lawyer as well, and perhaps some of those I have described as civil servants might be outside men. These heads of departments would form an Advisory Council to the Secretary of State. Some should be Indians.

These are very tentative, and in keeping a record of the formation of my ideas, I may omit something which has crossed my mind during the day. I am quite certain that I shall have to go away and think at some time or other, and that it will be impossible to work by clock.

II

DELHI I—BIKANER—DELHI II

Sunday, November 11. We arrived at Delhi at 8.30 on Sunday morning, the 11th, to be greeted at the station by Maffey, Chelmsford's private secretary, Hailey, the Delhi Commissioner, Scindia[1] (looking much older than when I saw him last because he has lost all his teeth ; he has bought a set of false ones, but will not wear them), Basu, Vincent, and Sankaran Nair. We drove to the Viceregal Lodge across the Ridge. It is a very beautiful-looking building, standing in a spacious and excellent garden. In this garden is our camp a row of commodious tents. There are many other camps, especially the one of the Chiefs who have been invited to stay at Delhi to make my acquaintance. Nothing could be more comfortable than my own apartment—a large, well-furnished tent, with good windows and a fireplace, two sofas, two writing tables, plenty of arm-chairs. It communicates by a short passage with a dressing-room, a bedroom, a luggage-room, a bath-room and a lavatory. I give this in detail to show that it really is a small house. From it are visible all the glories of the sunsets and the sun rises. The temperature is not hot, and it is really cold at night. It is interesting to note that the order of precedence has been strictly observed in placing all the other tents. Somewhat smaller than mine, they are all exactly identical, and they are all arranged down the carriage drive, with Donoughmore's next to mine, then Duke's, then Roberts's, then Kisch, then Parsons, then Franey. You could not want a better illustration of the way things are done in India. It never occurred to anybody that I might want a private secretary near me ; all that was

[1] H.H. Maharaja Scindia of Gwalior, G.C.S.I., G.C.V.O., G.B.E.

necessary was a strict appreciation of the blessed word "precedence."

I will give now a short picture of Lord Chelmsford, not perhaps as I saw him at once, but as I see him as I write two days after first meeting with him. He has not the dignity of Hardinge or the pomposity of Curzon, but he is quite good to look at, with a fine, athletic figure, square shoulders, small hips, well-shaped head, and a graceful forward inclination of the body. Conversation soon showed that he is really a good fellow, thoroughly nice, but unfortunately cold, aloof, reserved. He seems to me to be strongly prejudiced in his views, holding them very, very keenly, but I do not seem to see that any of them are his views. They always seem to me to be views collected from his surroundings. Oh, the fact of the matter is—and it is borne in on me every moment of the day, every hour, but it is no use because nobody will believe me—the sort of man we seek to make a Viceroy is wholly wrong. He comes from the wrong class. It is not right to blame Lord Chelmsford ; it is only right to remember that that is not the sort of stuff of which to make Viceroys. They approach their problem from the wrong side ; they do the work that they are called upon to do ; they wade through files ; they think of their regulations ; and then as to the social side—precedence, precedence, precedence. Everything is divided into Government and those who are not Government, official and those who are not official, Government and the opposition. Informal discussion, informal conversation, they do not know. Political instinct they have none. The wooing of constituents is beneath their idea ; the coaxing of the Press is not their *métier*. Nothing is required of them but to get through their files, and carry on their social work according to the rule. Everything is prescribed ; everything is printed. Well, this may be all right for a Court ; it is all wrong when the Court is not Royal and is also the Prime Minister of the place. I am not at all sure that my mind is not now moving to a Royal Viceroy, with a Prime Minister appointed from home for all the work except that of a functionary. The junction of the two seems to me to be an intolerable nuisance, and it is all wrong. There is no such thing as an informal conversation, so much so that the Government never does anything except by message, resolution or Bill, and advice is never given by the non-official or the people of the country until it is asked for—and it is never asked for. I suggested a Conference of Chiefs annually five years ago. There have been only two held by Chelmsford and one by Hardinge, who objected to "annual" and only wanted "periodical." There has never been a Conference of Lieutenant-Governors and Governors. Is not that incredible in a country like this and governed like this? I have suggested one, and we are going to hold one in January—the first.

I wish I had time to elaborate what I mean, but I still say that the social side of the question is at the bottom of the political mess in which we have landed ourselves.

I have only been here two days; all the Indian Chiefs have called on me and talked to me as a friend, and I have got far more out of them than the Viceroy got in ten days of Conference. They asked for interviews; interviews were granted them of ten minutes each because it was not considered that anything but formal interviews were necessary. They have all come back unofficially, and we have an hour and a half or three-quarters of an hour together at odd times, and they talk to me as they never dare to talk to anybody else. Perhaps there is some truth in the allegation that I am an Oriental. Certainly that social relationship which English people seem to find so difficult comes quite easy to me; and we shall go from bad to worse, until we are hounded out of India, unless something is done to correct this sort of thing. The man you want as Viceroy must be a politician, and one who is going to make friends with the Indians and insist on everybody making friends, who will take his pleasure as well as his hours of business with them, and get rid of the formality which besets every operation of the governing classes in Delhi.

By the by, I see from Reuter's telegram that Balfour has made the Zionist declaration against which I fought so hard. It seems strange to be a member of a Government which goes out of its way, as I think, for no conceivable purpose that I can see, to deal this blow at a colleague that is doing his best to be loyal to them, despite his opposition. The Government has dealt an irreparable blow at Jewish Britons, and they have endeavoured to set up a people which does not exist; they have alarmed unnecessarily the Mohammedan world, and, in so far as they are successful, they will have a Germanised Palestine on the flank of Egypt. It seems useless to conquer it. Why we should intern Mahomed Ali in India for Pan-Mohammedism when we encourage Pan-Judaism I cannot for the life of me understand. It certainly puts the final date to my political activities.

Bikaner [1] came to see me at 12 o'clock, and we had a long talk. After he had gone I heard that Duke has gone down with inflamed veins of the leg, and it may be some weeks before it is safe to move him again. This is another misfortune, for his knowledge, and indeed his views, are often of the greatest possible service. He has been taken to hospital.

In the afternoon I had two hours' talk with the Viceroy, following a lunch graced by the presence of Bikaner,[1] Scindia and Patiala.[2] Chelmsford told me how he had proceeded, how he had had a Committee sitting; how he had taken my telegraphic summary of Duke's Committee as the basis, and how Meyer and Howard had worked out Finance, and how they thought we were in agreement as to general principles. I told him how we were working. I was very anxious, I said, to avoid giving him any idea as to my views; I wanted all ideas to come from him. He would not. He

[1] H.H. the Maharaja of Bikaner, G.C.S.I., G.C.I.E., K.C.O.
[2] H.H. the Maharaja of Patiala, G.C.I.E., G.B.E.

insists upon seeing the Duke Memorandum, which I must send him, but I am certain that nothing adequate to my taste will come from him, and I very much doubt if I can get Roberts or Donoughmore to go further than himself. I find myself so very lonely, and although my private secretaries are very useful for the particular function they have undertaken, no suggestions as to policy come from them. I am alone on this trip, and I might just as well have come alone for any assistance I have got so far from the others.

I saw Vincent and Basu yesterday, and I must have a talk with them to-morrow. Basu seems very reasonable, and said that the majority of the Congress would be reasonable. Vincent was very dour, and said very little.

Chelmsford told me that Mrs. Besant said that she quite realised she could not have Home Rule at once; she wanted the Congress scheme now and Home Rule after the War. It really is impossible to believe in the sincerity of a woman who seriously puts forward the view that you can have two Government of India Bills within, say, five years, and that what India is not fit for now she will be fit for immediately after the War. The whole thing is preposterous.

I understand from the Viceroy that Howard[1] and Meyer are ready to divide all revenues between the Province and the Government of India; land revenues they divide half and half still; and income tax they take 75 per cent. for the Government of India, leaving 25 per cent. to the local government merely as an incentive and for cost of collection. They assign for, I think, ten years, certain sums to Bengal, Behar and Orissa. I gather also that Meston has adopted the Curtis plan, but Pentland has said since they do not see in the Government of India scheme any sign of increasing devolution, to the Provinces they have nothing to suggest or to say. Chelmsford says that the European Association can collect, and has probably done some useful spade work, but nobody else has. The *Pioneer* is now saying that it is in favour of

[1] H. F. Howard, C.I.E., Secretary to Finance Department, Government of India.

reforms, but that our method, by my visit, of carrying them through is *opera bouffé*. They are also charging me now with trying to saddle the responsibility for the release of Mrs. Besant on to the Government of India. Really there is no pleasing them.

Chelmsford showed me a letter from the Amir, promising never to say anything or do anything as long as he lives which is not in the interests of the British Government. Chelmsford speaks very highly of Grant,[1] but he speaks highly of everybody, as one who is sincerely grateful for services rendered.

After I left him I played three sets of tennis, Alwar[2] and Chelmsford both turning up to play. Then Alwar came to my tent and talked for about an hour, and drank a whisky and soda. Very amusing to hear his contempt of the Conference which Chelmsford had just called. The agenda for it consisted of agricultural development, agricultural statistics, precedence at social functions *inter se*, and the proper way to number motor cars in Native States. Alwar set forth that somebody may have tested the Conference idea with a bad agenda deliberately to see whether any Chiefs turned up. Perhaps they all thought this, for forty-nine turned up instead of forty-three last year. Anyhow, they have determined not to have that sort of thing again. They want these Conferences made into a Council, and they have other demands to put forward. Chelmsford has asked them to draft these for our consideration, and a Committee consisting of Alwar, Bikaner, Patiala and the Jam Sahib[3] are going to draw it up. Alwar also asks again for the complete separation of the Political from the Foreign department, which would naturally follow if my scheme for a foreign member were adopted. He also asks that the Political Secretary should be assisted by four or five princes, who should be his advisers, so that the Government should not make ridiculous mistakes. Of course this would eventually develop into the fact that the

[1] Sir A. H. Grant, K.C.I.E., C.S.I., Foreign Secretary; Foreign and Political Department, Government of India.

[2] H.H. the Maharaja of Alwar, K.C.S.I., K.C.I.E.

Indian princely advisers would become actually the Political Secretary, while the Political Secretary would be their executive officer. This really is what ought to occur. If the Native States as a body ought now to have some approximation to self-government, this would be a good way, together with the Council, of producing it. The Council I would ask to sit on an agenda that they should choose themselves, subject to the discretion of the Viceroy, with the Upper Chamber of my bi-cameral Indian Legislative Council. Alwar also asks for the separation of princes who are entitled to call themselves "His Highness" from Chiefs which range down to one man, so Bikaner tells me, whose annual income is forty-three rupees and whose kingdom is a well. The proper dividing line is the eleven-gun salute.

Alwar returned again to the charge for the abolition of the A.G.G.s.[1] I quite approve of this, and put it forward five years ago. Why Baroda should be able to approach the Viceroy direct, while Gwalior has to approach him through the A.G.G., I do not understand. I would accept all these suggestions in the form I have just described.

After dinner I sat in a corner talking to Scindia. He still wants the matters that he talked to me about when I last saw here effected, his guarantees raised, otherwise he wants nothing more than the Conference made annual, not at the will of the Viceroy, but by the decision of the Secretary of State; and two Indian princes added to the Executive Council, and the Viceroy to deal only with Native State affairs. I told him that I thought this was impossible constitutionally and then he came back to the adviser idea. He told me that he was developing all sorts of industries in his State, even including the growing of medicinal herbs, and that things were going very well. He must have made a vast fortune during the War, but, poor little man, I think he has got diabetes badly, and he will take no care of himself.

Patiala, to whom I talked also last night, and who came

[1] Agents to the Governor-General.

to see me this morning, has developed into a very fine fellow, and has come to take a leading part in the deliberations of the Chiefs. He is one of the nicest men here, but there is no doubt that Alwar is far and away the cleverest of them. One is talking to a real statesman when one talks to him. He sees all difficulties in all problems.

Monday, November 12. This morning I saw for ten minutes the Begum of Bhopal, the little woman coming in to see me with just her eyes showing through a tiny square hole cut in a heavy silken cloth which covered her face. She speaks English very badly, her education in English having been undertaken by her secretary. She disapproves of the existence of Ministers, and says that she does the whole administration of her State herself, with the assistance of her three sons. She is frightfully keen on education, and jabbered about nothing else. She was wearing some hideous jewellery, which I understood was given to her by various British Sovereigns. Conversation was not very easy, but it is a curious position—this woman, alone, taking part in a Conference of Oriental Chiefs. She explained to me that she was not an Indian, but a Pathan, although she and her family had been in India for 200 years before the British occupation.

She was followed by the Maharao of Cutch, a very nice, handsome Rajput from the Bombay Presidency. Alwar had given me the upshot of all their grievances, but the Maharao of Cutch added two other things. He wanted Willingdon prolonged for another five years ; he thought he was perfect. That comes from having a man who has a little social knowledge and real friendship for the Indians. He also urged the appointment of tribunals to consider inter-State disputes and settle them. This has also been suggested to me by Alwar, Bikaner and Kolhapur, whom I saw afterwards. Some of them want it to consist of two Indian princes, or three Indian princes to advise the Viceroy, and others of two

Indian princes, a judge, and some political officers. Cutch feels very keenly because of his century-old dispute with Morvi which we can find no way of settling. Alwar and Bikaner would find it so useful, because they instance the absurdity of some of the orders passed by the Indian Government for lack of knowledge, e.g. the edict that only the eldest son of a Maharaja was to be called Maharaj Kumar, all the others being called Kumar simply. This, they say. is idiotic. The proper title for the eldest son is Yuvaraj, That differentiates him from the others, but Maharaj Kumar simply means the son of a Maharaja, and to take away the only name which actually describes what he is is only done from ignorance. So, again, they say the Government has recently put upon the Throne of a Native State the son of a Rajput by a Mohammedan woman, simply saying that they were bound to do it because they were legally married. They were legally married, but it is quite illegal to do it according to the Rajput law, a Mohammedan woman being really morganatically married.

Cutch also wants the Scindia Executive Council idea. Then Alwar came for another long talk, which was a waste of time, but very pleasant, followed by Kolhapur, the principal Chief of the Bombay Presidency (I think, on reflection, it was he who expressed his desire that Willingdon should stay), and said he was going to meet me in Bombay. Yes, I am sure it was, because Cutch is very anxious that all the princes should be under the Government of India and be taken away from the local governments. It is a comparable grievance to the A.G.G. grievance, and it seems to me it will become necessary to do it if the local governments become autonomous, but there is the difficulty of the smaller non-British territory that they will have to administer. Kolhapur thinks that no Viceroy or Governor such as Willingdon ought to be moved during the War.

Then I saw Indore, who seems to me to have gone all to

pieces. He is neurotic, ill, nervous, and refused to say anything, but says that he will tell me all sorts of interesting things if I will only go to Indore. There, he says, he can put things before me that he has not time to tell me now. When I asked him what he thought of the Conference, he simply said that he would like time to consider his answer, as he had not been there because he was ill all the time. I do not think it was very useful.

I next saw old Jaipur,[1] having to talk to him through an interpreter.

He is a fine-looking old man, with a white beard and a beautiful dress. He keeps on explaining that he is a goods train and cannot travel at a higher speed. I assured him, because I heard that he was unhappy about it, that we should certainly never interfere as long as we remained in India with the guarantees, liberties, prestige, privileges and independence of the Native States. He complained that he was old and old-fashioned. He could not dine with me ; he could not speak English ; therefore he thought ten minutes was not enough, and he would like to come again, so that I have to see him again to-morrow.

He was followed by old Kashmir,[2] who is really in his dotage, who was accompanied by Daljit Singh, who used to be on the Indian Council, and is now his Prime Minister. Poor old Kashmir, they jeered at him very much at the Conference because he fell asleep.

Another lunch, the newcomer at which was Du Boulay, but I had no chance of talking to him. Then a few seconds with the Viceroy, who asks me to see each member of his Council separately ; a short discussion with Roberts and Donoughmore, in which Roberts showed himself to be more conservative than ever about the demands of the Indian princes ; then the weary work of dictating, which I am conscious I have done very badly because I am tired. I already want two days' holiday, which I see no prospect of getting. It is not

[1] H.H. the Maharaja of Jaipur, G.C.S.I., G.C.I.E., G.C.V.O., G.B.E.
[2] H.H. the Maharaja of Kashmir, G.C.S.I., G.C.I.E., G.B.E.

that I have not the strength to go on ; it is that my work will be badly done when I have not time to think.

I end up with a summary of what I feel to be the right policy for the Native princes :

1. A Council of Princes to consist of either (*a*) all the eleven-gun salute princes plus representatives of the others ; or (*b*) representatives of the eleven-gun salute princes as well as of the others.

2. This Council to sit under the presidency of the Viceroy to discuss the general affairs of the Native States.

3. This Council to hold informal negotiations about their own affairs with one another.

4. Everybody to be invited to make suggestions as to the agenda, as well as to receive suggestions from the Viceroy.

5. Council to sit with the Upper Chamber at the invitation of the Viceroy from time to time, to discuss Imperial questions, such as co-operation in the War, etc.

6. Four advisers, chosen by the princes themselves, to be associated with the Political Secretary, and to advise, through him, the Viceroy on questions dealing with the Native States ; to sit, say, once every six months, and two of their number chosen from people who are not interested, with a judge and a political officer to sit as a tribunal in their inter-State disputes.

7. The abolition of A.G.G.s

8. Residents to be addressed as to how they are to exercise their functions, and to be reminded of the great difficulty of estrangement, and the preference for persuasion over blunt orders.

9. Political Office to be absolutely separate from the Foreign Office.

After dinner a party was given of some 100 people, and I sat on a sofa whilst various A.D.C.s brought up to me the people whom it was thought I ought to talk to, and allowed me just an insufficient amount of time in which to speak to them. I had been allowed to mark on the list of invited guests those whom I should like to speak to, but when it came to the point, I was told that it was necessary to grant a few minutes to each of the Chiefs, notwithstanding the fact that I had talked to them in the daytime.

I had the pleasure of meeting Bundi,[1] whose looks repaid me for the fact that he could not speak a word of English. His beard deliberately combed to point to every direction of the compass, and his very conspicuous make-up—died hair, painted eyebrows, and so forth—were worth seeing.

Tuesday, November 13. On Tuesday morning more Chiefs came to see me. I had a long talk with Scindia, who had learnt since I saw him last that education was at the root of everything—that the importance of education was a prime necessity. Among constructive suggestions he put before me first that there should be a Board of Education in every Province, in which Indians should have an opportunity of expressing their views. When they howled, said this sapient prince, give them things that do not matter. He wanted also that Gwalior should have a first-class Resident, by which he meant that it should not go through an A.G.G. ; but when I suggested to him that this meant the abolition of A.G.G.s, he agreed, and suggested in the same breath that his Resident, Jardine, should be made A.G.G. for Central India. This shows their constructive capacity. He also suggested that the Secretary of State should come out to India every third year accompanied by some member of the Royal Family. I do not know how welcome the representative of the Royal Family would be, but I should like to hear the views of the Civil Service about this triennial visit of the Secretary of State. It has often crossed my mind that in every Viceroyalty the Viceroy should come home to see the Secretary of State,

[1] H.H. the Maharaja of Bundi, G.C.I.E., G.C.V.O., K.C.S.I.

or the Secretary of State should go to India. I had never in my wildest moments—and my wildest moments are wild—suggested anything as extreme as Gwalior seemed to consider necessary. And then he let slip a very curious suggestion, that Residents should be rigorously punished for their mistakes. This brings me back to the universal complaint of all these princes. They are at the mercy of the personality of their Agents or Residents, and they all seem to have suffered from this in the past. They all want some safeguard against it in the future. Of course no constitution can safeguard people against this sort of thing. The best we can do is to weed out those members of the political service that are not fit for their jobs, and issue a model set of rules for Residents, which requires careful drafting, that should be their Bible and prevent mistakes. Chelmsford at least is in agreement with this—that there should be a weeding out of the service. But, like everything else, one is obsessed by the vested interest of the Service concerned and the difficulty of overcoming it.

I had a talk, too, with Daljit Singh, now the Diwan of the Kashmir State, formerly a member of Chamberlain's Indian Council—a nice, quiet, old thing, who described to me his efforts, which he thought ought to have been supported by the Government, to form a moderate party in India, and described to me his success as far as the Punjab is concerned. He is a member of the reigning family of Kapurthala. He believes that the whole problem is a problem of the employment of Indians throughout the Service, and he would rather do this than give them any political influence. It is interesting to note that although he sees the necessity for the formation of a moderate party, he feels himself helpless without the assistance of Government.

Scindia was very anxious that the Government should take part both in the celebration of the Id, the great Mohammedan Festival, and the Duhsehra, the great Hindu Festival, not that they should take sides, but that they should hold a Durbar in order to send, as he expressed it, " many happy returns of the day " to each community.

I saw also Jaipur, who simply repeated the matters concerning the princes—the assurance of their rights, non-interference of British India in their concerns, etc., etc. He also brought before me the subject of contracts entered into by the Secretary of State with railway companies, which pledged him to use his good offices to obtain rights through Native States. He said that before any contracts were made the views of the Native State Durbar should be ascertained. This seems reasonable, and I mentioned it to Chelmsford. He brought with him one of his staff with a perfect knowledge of English, to act as his interpreter. He has consistently said that his reason for seeking another interview was that ten minutes were not sufficient for him, but I have ascertained that his real desire was to see if Maffey, who came yesterday as interpreter, would come again. Bikaner tells me that he had to use all his influence to prevent his writing to Wood[1] to complain that he was not seditious and that a spy was not necessary to see that he did not misuse his power of talking to the Secretary of State. This only shows, even with an old boy like Jaipur, with his long, white beard and his pride in the fact that he is old-fashioned, how suspicious they are and how necessary it is to be on one's guard. Jaipur continually uses the simile that he is a goods train and can only proceed at its pace, while the others are express trains.

Then I had an interview with the Jam Sahib of Nawanagar, our old friend Ranjitsinjhi—in vigorous health, one-eyed after his shooting accident in England, but a coming figure among the princes. We talked about shooting, Cambridge days, and all the demands of the princes, with which he is in agreement. Notwithstanding their admiration for Willingdon, the Bombay princes want to come under the Government of India. Willingdon seems to have acquiesced, but the

[1] Sir John Wood, K.C.I.E., C.S.I. (Political Secretary, Foreign and Political Department, Government of India).

Government of Bombay overrode him. He pointed out that of the 700 alleged Chiefs, 500 are in the Bombay Presidency in Kathiawar, and the first necessity of the situation is obviously the differentiation of the real ruling princes from this small fry. One interesting thing that he told me was that he had set himself to game preservation on the English model by shooting vermin—hawks, crows, snakes, iguana lizards. So successful had he been that he hoped this year to kill a thousand brace of partridges on the limited land at his disposal.

I had another long talk with Alwar to-day, and then after lunch I was pleased to see Gubbay, who is now Controller of Currency, and who was at school with me. He is making good in every sense of the term, and Willingdon and everybody else speaks very highly of him. It was very refreshing to see him, and he spoke to me with the utmost frankness and quite characteristically. My mission was doomed to failure because it was impossible. Calcutta was in a condition of turmoil comparable to its condition after the Ilbert Bill.

After this followed a vigorous game of tennis, which is my only and weak hold upon health. Then Bikaner came to see me, to say good-bye. We went over much of the old ground again. He told me that he wanted me to settle this matter and then to come out as Viceroy, and he assured me that the overwhelming majority of a plebescite of princes and Indian people would prefer me to any other Englishman. But the achievement of settling this matter is, of course, something which is almost impossible.

Then I had a talk with Chelmsford on his return from tennis, up and down the drive. Very little transpired, but I hinted to him that I had meant what I said when I described the Viceroyalty in my Mesopotamian speech as being rolled into one person—King, Speaker, Viceroy and Foreign Secretary. He said that that was the best picture of the Viceroyalty he had yet seen. I said that there were only two solutions : one was to separate the foreign membership from the Viceroyalty. To this he objected, saying that the correspondence with the Amir, the frequent telegrams which passed between the Secretary of State and himself, the close touch in which he was with the Home Government made it impossible for the Viceroy to divorce himself from the affairs of the Foreign Office. He asked me to talk to Grant upon this matter. I said then that the alternative plan was to separate the flummery of the Viceroyalty, which made it impossible by the drain on his time for the Viceroy to deal with politics, and which prevented him, by his exalted position and the fact that it was impossible for those who saw him to separate him as a statesman from him as the representative of the King, from the Viceroy as a statesman and politician. I hinted at a Royalty as Viceroy, with a Prime Minister appointed from home to do the real business in the name of the princelet. To my great gratification he seemed to like this thing, and I feel inclined to-night to incorporate this in my proposals.

Before dinner I went to see Duke, who is sweetness itself on his bed of sickness. I put to him the plan which I have already described which I have formed for the complete subject. To my gratification, he liked it, indeed, the more I see of it the more certain I become that this is the solution of our difficulties. Tested by every representation that is made to me, it holds the field.

Wednesday, *November* 14. To-day I went up to breakfast to find that Roos-Keppel and O'Dwyer had arrived to stay at Viceregal Lodge, and at 10.30 I saw Marris,[1] who is now Joint Home Secretary, to deal with the Reforms question, and whom I took completely into my confidence. He likes my scheme, but he does not like either the Meyer Scheme of Finance or our scheme, because he is anxious that the Provinces should neither pay tribute to the Government of India nor

[1] W. S. Marris, C.I.E., who was largely responsible for the final drafting of the report.

that the Government of India should be interested in any taxes levied by the Provincial Government. His alternative is freedom to the Government of India to levy such customs duties as they like. I pointed out to him that this fear that self-government for India should lead to customs liberty was at the root of the Conservative opposition to my appointment, and I warned him that it would jeopardise any chance of getting any statute through the Houses of Parliament or through the Cabinet.

I next saw Claude Hill, and fenced round the subject for one and a half hours.

I then lunched in my tent with Basu and Roberts. I was pleased with Basu, who showed a very compromising spirit. Again in conversation I found that my scheme got over most of the difficulties. He wants a larger elective majority than the Duke Committee suggest. He wants a broad franchise and an increase in the number of the Legislative Councils, and he seemed satisfied, in regard to the difficulties as to the limitations of the powers of the local Councils, by my statutory enquiry suggestions.

He was followed by Sankaran Nair, who is really an impossible person, and I almost wish he were in England, as Chelmsford suggested. His dissenting minute consists mainly of ill-constructed suggestions, badly thought out, and abuse of the British Government. He shouts at the top of his voice, refuses to listen to anything when one argues, and is absolutely uncompromising. At the same time, he has no knowledge of loyalty to his colleagues, and consults the whole of the Congress about every minute that he writes. If he is typical of Indian opinion, I despair.

Then I went with Hailey[1] around New Delhi. I am impressed by the superiority of Lutyens over Baker. Lutyens shows distinction of architecture and novelty of idea which is very refreshing and is obvious, although the basement storey and the lay-out is practically all that has been done.

[1] W. M. Hailey, C.S.I., C.I.E., Chief Commissioner, Delhi.

I am glad to think there is a prospect, by increasing his pay, to keep Keeling, the engineer-in-charge—a wise thing—and I am sure that there will be no difficulty in this. I sympathise with Lutyens in that for some distance the view of Government House along the main avenue of prospect will be obscured, but it is too late to alter this. Hailey has not been asked to express his views on Reform, but as Commissioner of Delhi this does not seem to be necessary. He has, however, formed his own opinions, and he reiterates, as so many other people do, the difficulty of an Executive Council not depending for its life on the Legislative Council, yet compelled to carry out its orders. All half-way houses are difficult, but he would prefer the Curtis system of sub-provincial division. I am again impressed by his competence, but his optimism and the way he smoothes over all difficulties is rather specious.

Then I had a talk with Sir Michael O'Dwyer. He is a little, rough Irishman with great vigour of expression. It is quite obvious that he wishes to impress me with the fact that Indians in the Punjab believe that the announcement of August 20 appears to them to mean that we have accepted the Congress scheme, and on that basis he assures me that they have put their names to schemes in which they do not believe, and that if we could only get at the root of the matter they would show this. It is quite obvious from what he says, and from the fact that he alone of all Lieutenant-Governors is averse to an elected majority in his Council, that the Punjab must be treated separately from the other Provinces, and indeed it seems obvious that all Provinces must be treated differently. Again my scheme gets over this, for starting with a model scheme for all Provinces, it allows Provinces by means of enabling legislation to modify their own constitution.

I then had a talk about frontier matters with Roos-Keppel. I like him as much as ever, and wish I could find employment for him, for nine years, highly successful as it has been on the frontier, is too long for any man to be Chief Commissioner. I wonder if he would make a good Secretary of the Middle East Department of the Foreign Office which I have suggested in my Cabinet memorandum?

Then dinner, and afterwards a long talk with Chelmsford, whom I like more and more. And so tired out, and missing my hour's exercise, I go to bed, after spending some time in dictating these notes and writing some letters, realising that before a strenuous day of deputations I have to read a long file as to what they are going to say.

As days elapse the one thing that strikes me is that we cannot enter upon serious deliberations until the irksome task of hearing views, which begins to-morrow in real earnest and which is to be carried out here, in Madras, Bombay and Bengal, is completed. Then we must set to it *de die in diem*, and I am afraid that the date I had set myself, the middle or the end of January, for our departure looks to be quite out of the question. I know that India does not loom much at home, but here it is quite obvious that this is the one non-recurring opportunity of achieving something vital, essential, to our future existence in India. I shall, of course, determine to come home as soon as I can, and I shall continue to work at least fourteen hours a day, as I have been doing up to the present, unless my health gives out. But nobody who was not mad would spoil the ship for a fortnight or a month's delay, and I must be satisfied to come home as soon as I possibly can without now attempting to fix a date or risk all, which depends upon negotiations none the less important because they are protracted, by attempting to hurry matters.

Thursday, November 15. Ye gods, what a day! Really, I do not know what to do. I do not think we are going to make very much progress by this means. We have had our first day of deputations, and I will put down exactly what they are like. A large shamiana is erected outside Government House. At 10.30 the Viceroy and I march, preceded by an aide-de-camp, into the chamiana. The A.D.C. says as we enter, "His Excellency." Everyone inside stands up. Basu, Seton, Vincent, Donoughmore, Roberts, come in and stand in front of chairs arranged on either side of two carefully selected and perfectly equal chairs, in front of which I and the Viceroy stand. Mr. Sloan, I.C.S., lent to us as joint secretary for our work, then introduces the leader of the deputation, which is standing by this time in front of the chairs at the other end of the shamiana, some eight or nine yards from us. The leader of the deputation comes forward, shakes us two by the hand, and walks backwards to a place about half-way between his deputation and ourselves. He then proceeds to read a long address, a copy of which we each already have got, with notes on it by the Government of India. When he has read it, he bows ; Lord Chelmsford rises, and we all rise, and Lord Chelmsford says, in the coldest and most frigid of voices, "I thank you on behalf of Mr. Montagu and myself, and I can assure you that your views will receive our consideration. Now will you kindly present the members of your deputation." The formula never varies, the voice never modifies. At the close of it the leader of the deputation calls the name and description of each man, who solemnly comes forward, shakes hands with each of us, retires backwards ; and when the whole ceremony is over the Viceroy bows and walks out of the tent, followed by me. We sit down until we are called for the next deputation in about ten minutes. Was there ever such a hopeless situation ? Were ever things done more badly ? Would it not be possible to interrupt when something scandalous or controvertial is said, and ask for an explanation ? Could not some word be spoken to some member of the deputation ? A medal is worn by this man which would give one an opening ; another man one knows ; but, no, this is receiving a deputation, and I am solemnly assured by all concerned that this is all they want, and that this completely satisfies them. Well, well, well, what a world! Never will it be altered until the tenure and occupancy of the Viceroyalty is altered.

After two deputations had been treated in this way I slipped away from the Viceroy, went back into the tent and had a few words with each member of the third deputation. But I am afraid this was a most unpopular move, and I do not know if I shall ever succeed in doing it again.

The fourth deputation was from a sect called the Ahmadiyyah, which is a modern sect mainly of Mohammedans—they call themselves Mohammedans—which believes in the brotherhood of all creeds and the authenticity of all prophets. They read us a very long document drawn up by the man they call "His Holiness," the son of their founder, Ahmad, whom they regard as an incarnation of Mahomet, which was far the ablest document we have yet seen. It is moderate, almost too moderate, and it contains some absurdities, like the getting rid at once of all foreign capital. But it is awfully well written. It argues against the idea of electing some members of the Executive Council, and it argues very conclusively against the suggestion of all the other deputations and in the Congress scheme, that three-quarters of any community can hold up any Bill that it says affects the community itself.

I saw His Holiness himself, who was too shy to come to the deputation, or too holy, and who came to see me in my tent this evening. He apparently wrote this excellent document himself and had it then translated into English, which he understands but does not speak. He told me that the sect numbered some half a million, of which 30,000 were in Afghanistan and a few in England. He said it was gaining by thousands every year. They allege much persecution by Mohammedans themselves and by all other sects. He was weak in his argument about the foreign capital point. He brought up the question of the right of Englishmen to claim British juries, and demanded the abolition of it, and said that under the Penal Code an Englishman meant even a Hottentot or an American—anybody not born in India. But he had a good mind, had carefully thought out his constitutional scheme, which is very like the Duke scheme, and he really seemed to me, in his non-resisting, all-accepting, patient attitude to be rather like, if one can imagine such a thing, an Indian Quaker. Shyness or something prevented him from looking at you as he spoke. So ends the day till dinner.

Between the deputation I had some talk with the Viceroy, who seems to me to be tired out ; in fact he was too tired to play tennis to-day. Poor man, the strain on him is certainly very great. He wants me to take Meyer to succeed Holderness. He is very keen on an interchange of staff between the India Office and the Civil Service. He asked me to talk to O'Dwyer about the impoliteness of officials in the Punjab. He called my attention to the fact that in our Reform despatch we always referred to the "Letter" and not to the "Despatch" of the Government of India. I gather that this is strictly according to precedent—that we write despatches and the Government of India write letters, but it is a curious thing, which I learn is very much resented in India. Of course it would be.

I sent him last night, with a covering letter, my scheme as a tentative contribution, a landmark in my mental development. He says he has only just looked at it, but I fear he is very much depressed by the fact that it is far more complete than anything he had ever conceived in his mind. By my talks with everybody I am strengthened in believing it to be the only solution, but I fear wigs on the green when I finally produce it authoritatively.

It seems ridiculous that I have only seen Roos-Keppel for so short a time, but he really does not come into this scheme. Chelmsford does not want him for any purpose, and suggests that he might be a Governor of a Presidency. The thing that alarms me in all Chelmsford's talks seems to me to be that so little has reform sunk into his mind that he seems to think everything will go on as it is. I fear this is an incomplete account, but it is all I have time for.

By the by, I ought to record that, in my opinion, the Punjab Government has taken no trouble about this matter at all. It has not looked to see how Lord Chelmsford and I can get a representation of the true view of the Province. It has received requests from people to come and see me, and sifted them, letting those come whom they thought ought to, but they have never looked for people to come and see me and tried to see that they are representative. To-morrow I am going to see three Commissioners from the Punjab, who are all parties to O'Dwyer's submission to the Government of India, and who therefore will only echo his views. Even they never seem to suggest that it would be a good thing, knowing what a formal thing an Indian deputation is, that some members of it should see me privately afterwards. They only arranged for me to see people privately when it was asked for. This is the passive attitude which seems so ridiculous to me.

Friday, November 16. I began this morning by making the acquaintance of Sir William Meyer. I admit that it is impossible to challenge, on my knowledge, the great ability which he is alleged to possess by everybody who comes in contact with him. We began with a discussion of Lord Cunliffe's idiotic proposal that we should have two rupees in circulation of varying intrinsic value. This is a suggestion which is beneath contempt, and in the Note which Meyer has furnished to the Viceroy he is able completely to dispose of it. But he proceeds afterwards to complain bitterly of the treatment of India by the India Office, and he shows in it as great an absence of any Imperial patriotism as could be laid to the charge of any Nationalist Indian, and a complete ignorance of the dangers which lie before the Treasury which is financing the Allies. He regards everything from a very narrow Indian point of view. I took him to task severely on this, and then we proceeded to discuss Reform. He seemed to be a little resentful that we had been discussing reforms at all before we saw the proposals of the Government of India. But he still seems to think that all that is wanted is a dawn; he still seems to believe that an answer to everything is that it will come later, even when his proposals seem to be on the wrong lines. We discussed further the dangers of inconvertibility, and talked of nothing but the serious nature of these dangers. If they can be avoided, of course everybody wants to avoid them, but it may happen that you have got to choose between India and the Allied cause, and that is a choice that he never permits himself to make. He told me that people were very indignant with our fixing the value of the sovereign at 14 rupees 8 annas; he believed it would have been right to fix it at 14 rupees 8 annas and 3/16ths, or more nearly 14 rupees 9 annas. Well, I held out for that figure, but I was beaten by the City. He told me that he expected to have an extraordinary deficit on Ways and Means on his preliminary figures. I admit that his prospects are very gloomy. India is very prosperous, but unfortunately all its money is in London, and how they are going to meet this deficiency is a matter which must be taxing their ingenuity very considerably. The Treasury Bills are doing well.

After Meyer I had another talk with O'Dwyer. We got on much better on this occasion. I believe myself that he would take my scheme, provided that he was allowed to start in the Punjab on a small scale, and this I am quite willing to accept. I told him I did not think he would get off without an elected majority, and this he did not seem to mind very much. I discussed with him the manners of the Punjab Civil Service because of the complaints we had received yesterday. He said that there was notorious deterioration in the matter of the Civil Service, but he felt that we were very largely dealing with a particular and notorious case which had affected His Holiness, the leader of the Ahmadiyyah.

He was followed by Maclagan, whom I was very anxious to see—a nice, gentle fellow, very reserved and extraordinarily soft in manner. He told me quite frankly that he did not believe that Sir Michael O'Dwyer's proposal carried out the announcement of August 20, in that it hardly contains the germs of responsible government, so long particularly as it did not have an elected majority.

In the afternoon I saw the two Financial Commissioners from the Punjab, Mr. Maynard and Mr. Fagan. I saw Maynard first. He was in agreement with Maclagan, and objected to O'Dwyer's refusal of an elected majority. He would have it small ; he even suggested a majority of one, which is certainly as small as you could have it, but he wanted it. We discussed the question of making the rural franchise consist mainly of Lambadars. I pointed out to him that this was indirect election, and indeed the Lambadar is hereditary, so that it is worse than that. He said it is the franchise which would be best understood in the Punjab at present, and preferred it to a revenue basis. I think again he would like my scheme.

He was followed by the second Financial Commissioner, Fagan, who was accompanied by Thompson, the Chief Secretary of the Punjab, a very loquacious, square-headed, determined-looking fellow, whereas Fagan looked ill and was rather sour and quiet. These are two Tories of the old school, with a profound suspicion of the educated Indian, and a firm belief that O'Dwyer was going as far as he possibly could.

Next came Popham Young, the Commissioner of the Rawal Pindi division. He told me that he thought district officers were too inexperienced to leave them without a commissioner over them. It would necessitate increasing the size of the districts and putting senior men in charge of them if you abolished commissioners. This would make the district too large and deprive you of the chance of putting young men in executive control. He is a soldier ; he has done marvellous work in recruiting, having got 70,000 recruits, nearly all fighting men ; and he suddenly amazed me by throwing over O'Dwyer's scheme altogether as being insufficient, and suggesting that the Lieutenant-Governor should have associated with him a Council of two, one being an Indian, and the leader elected of a Legislative Council which should consist entirely of Indians. The Legislative Council might pass Bills and Resolutions, which would not be binding until they had been assented to by the Governor. If the Governor objected, a special tribunal would be set up, consisting of ten elected members of the Legislative Council, together with ten officials, whose voice would be final. The representatives of the Legislative Council would have to include the minority. He wants deliberately to form a party system in India. This is really a Second Chamber in disguise and wants thinking out, but he obviously is thinking of the subject and wants something striking.

Maynard came back in the evening, and I gathered from him, just as I gathered from O'Dwyer, that they both think highly of the Executive Committee idea, which would enable you to have a much larger body and get over the difficulty that on an Executive Council you would only appoint one Mohammedan or Sikh or Hindoo every fifteen years.

After tennis I had some talk with Chelmsford. He took up the attitude which he always takes up of " I wish it were possible, but I am afraid." This really sums him up in almost everything—" I am afraid it is not." We had a little talk about reforms. It is obvious that Chelmsford does not like my scheme, but it is very difficult to get anything out of him, because he never moves an inch without consulting his Council. He never expresses an opinion without consulting his Council. The whole time, charming man though he is, every document I show him he has to consult somebody before he expresses an opinion. I think I went to bed more nearly depressed than I have been yet, in fact I thought in the night it was hardly worth going on.

To add to my other troubles, Roberts suddenly—not to me, because unfortunately through the way that we are trying to do business with this ridiculous allotment of half-hours continuously through the day we have no chance of deliberation—but in conversation with Maynard, threw over the Duke-Brunyate finance scheme in favour of the Meyer scheme.

Saturday, November 17. This morning we had three of the usual deputations from the Zemindars of Agra and the Talukdars of Oudh. These collections of landlords frankly put before us, with unblushing effrontery, a desire for a landlord Raj.

After the deputations, Chelmsford and I had interviews with five of them, one of whom did not speak English. They are all very conservative ; would like an elected majority ; but would not go far with the Congress Moslem scheme. One of them suggested to me that they would like the District Officer to have an Advisory Council, but on cross-examination it was agreed that this function might be fulfilled by a wider reference to the District Board. I think this is rather a good idea.

I then wrote my mail letters, and afterwards saw Kishen Kaul, a brother of the Maharaja of Patiala's Foreign Secretary, of Kashmir. He is a Deputy Commissioner in the Punjab in charge of criminal tribes, and he agrees thoroughly with O'Dwyer's scheme. He wants nomination plus examination for the Provincial Civil Service, so that Indians can get into high positions without going to England. This seems to me to be a matter that was overlooked by the Islington Commission, or, if not overlooked, their recommendations on it are certainly unsatisfactory.

I took a preliminary reading of the Government of India scheme. This is very, very depressing, and the only new ray of hope which I get from to-day's proceedings is that the Viceroy has suggested that my scheme of fundamental legislation should be investigated by Vincent, with a view to seeing whether the fundamental legislation could actually be drawn up. He also suggests that if we have fundamental legislation we ought to have a Supreme Court for India at Delhi to decide whether matters were inside or outside the provisions of such an Act. I have always felt that it would be a good thing to have a Supreme Court at Delhi, with an alternative appeal from the Provincial High Courts to it or the Privy Council.

As regards the Government of India's Memorandum, apart from the fact that it shows no line of advance in the future, which I think is fatal, I am satisfied that it could not be accepted for a moment. I am sorry that my personality is such, that my record is such, that the difficulties of the Government are increased so much by my visit to India, for it has whetted their appetite. But any Secretary of State coming to India would have made it impossible to present such a document as this to the people of this country. They would shout derision. It does not concede provincial autonomy, or begin to concede provincial autonomy. At every stage the Government of India keeps its control, and it does not go nearly far enough in giving responsibility to the Legislative Councils. If they can go no further than this we are doomed to failure. The Viceroy actually asks me to consent to sending this Memorandum round, before we leave for Calcutta, to the Provincial Governments. If this goes round the whole thing is over. I am going to read it again to-morrow, and then try and find time on Monday to write to the Viceroy to tell him he really must push his Council infinitely further than he has gone.

Sunday, November 18. Lord Chelmsford, Maffey and I left last night at a quarter to eleven for Gagranla. We slept in the train, had an early breakfast, and an excellent but very hard day's snipe shooting. Net result, thirty-five brace. I think we all shot very well, considering it was very hot and we were up to our knees in water, having to pull our legs each time out of the mud, so that by half-past three we were all exhausted, Chelmsford and I physically, and Maffey being unable to shoot straight. It was a jolly, long gheel completely overgrown—the old bed of the Jumna. All the arrangements, including the carriage to drive five miles, and the bullock wagons, three, to drive one, had been made by a little local Nawab. Bitterns, demoiselle cranes, marsh harriers, fish eagles, big white-breasted blue kingfisher, a jackal, seven sisters, sparrow hawks, shrikes, innumerable doves were the chief birds we saw, and one cattle egret and a large heron. Two of the snipe were painted, and there was a large proportion of jacks in the morning.

The day was by no means wasted. I got far closer to Chelmsford than I have ever got before. I like him better than ever, but I cannot find any vigour or personality in him : great conscientiousness, eager desire for smooth running, complete armoury of consultation. He assured me that he was one of the majority of his Committee. He tells me that the Council were unanimous about Mrs. Besant. I am to see Tilak in a deputation, but not in an interview. He feels that the cross-examination which I submit people to is doing a lot of good. He seems hardening against the splitting of the Viceroyalty. I ventured to come closer to expressing the inadequacy of the Government of India scheme, but I would not express an opinion until I had seen my colleagues.

I forgot to record on Saturday night that we had just had

the most depressing information that General Maude was critically ill with cholera. Just before leaving late on Saturday night we heard the news that he had taken a slight turn for the better. I gather that any improvement in cholera is usually hopeful.

We have just heard that General Maude died last night. It is a horrible tragedy at the most critical moment in the Mesopotamian trouble. After consultation with Lord Chelmsford, I felt that I should send a telegram to London suggesting that Sir Charles Munro should go at once to Mesopotamia, and that Kirkpatrick, whom Chelmsford assures me could carry on here, should act as Commander-in-Chief, subject to the possibilities that the Acts of Parliament permit this arrangement. However, I saw Munro on Monday morning, and although he admits the advantage that he probably knew more intimately Maude's plans than any other living man, he feels himself, with much regret, too old for Mesopotamia, and as he is very lame and looks very old, I think this is probably true. I hear to-night (Monday) that the War Office have appointed Marshall.

Monday, November 19. A dull day, but, like so many days, not so bad in working out as it looked on paper. From 10 a.m. to 11 a.m. there were the usual stereotyped deputations, with their usual pantomine, and the usual frigid utterances of Chelmsford. There were five bodies represented, all of them Moslem, and all from the United Provinces.

First there was the Provincial Branch of the All-India Moslem League, with its Congress Moslem League scheme, subject to certain exceptions and safeguards for the Mohammedans ; then two more orthodox organisations, from the deputations of one of whom I take the following gem :

> " Without in any way meaning to discredit our Hindu brethren, by expressing our distrust of them to such an

H.H. The Maharaja of Patiala

H.H. The Maharaja of Bikaner

H.H. The Maharaja of Burdwan

Lord Willingdon

H.H. The Maharaja of Bikaner

H.H. The Maharaja of Patiala

SIX CARICATURES BY E. S. M.

[*To face page* 44

extent, our instinct of self-preservation compels us to always keep at a safe distance from them in politics while exchanging courtesies and social amenities in daily life."

These were followed by an imposing deputation of the Maulvis, the orthodox teachers in Mohammedan religion and holy writings. It was their first entry into politics, and they were impressive in the way in which they explained to us in a subsequent interview that their object was not to enter politics now, but to make sure that if changes were happening in India we should not forget the Maulvis and orthodox Mohammedanism. One man said that all would be cured if we ensured that no Mohammedan should be elected to a Council who was not orthodox. When I told him that I should find it difficult to know this, he said that the Maulvis would always tell me.

But the advantages of interviews came out in connection with the next deputation, the United Provinces Moslem Defence Association. After explaining that they had come into existence a few weeks ago to represent the more conservative Mohammedanism that was unrepresented by the Moslem League, they presented us with a scheme which was lifted almost bodily, with a few reservations, from the Congress Moslem League scheme. The chief difference was that in a Council of 150 members, 50 were to be Hindus, 50 Mohammedans, and 50 English. When we cross-examined them, they explained that they had no love of this scheme, and that they would prefer that things should remain where they were. When we asked them why they had advocated this scheme, they said : " Oh, I had come out to do something, and if something was done they wanted this sort of thing done." We asked why they did not say so, and so far as we could gather it was simply forbearance.

None of the other interviews were very interesting, except this, that the chief spokesman for the Provinces Moslem

League interview acted also as interpreter for the Maulvis. He had to listen to the Maulvis explaining why they did not like the scheme to which he had attached importance and pledged his faith. He interpreted very honestly, and when we said how painful some of the answers to our questions must be to him, he said : " These gentlemen treated the subject from a religious rather than a political point of view." The Moslem Leagues seem to be rather surprised that there had been any withdrawal of Mohammedan support from the Congress as a consequence of the Mohurrum Dusehra outbreaks, but they explained them all away as being quite temporary things.

The Imam of the Juma Masjid here in Delhi explained to us how dangerous Home Rule was, and how careful we ought to be in any reforms, but he was not very interesting.

Late to-night I saw Dr. Shija-ud-din and Moshin Shah, representing the Punjab Provincial Moslem League. The doctor seemed to me to be one of the most intelligent politicians that I have yet met in India. He saw the difficulties of most of the detailed features of this scheme, and seemed reasonable in the attitude that he thought that the leaders would take if they could be assured that their objects would be achieved by alternative methods.

This evening Donoughmore has given me a severe blow. He tells me that in conversation on Saturday night Chelmsford told him that he hoped I was not thinking the Government of India could go any further than their Memorandum, because that was the ultimate limit to which they could go. Well, all I can say is that this was not consistent with his attitude yesterday and in our conversations to-day, and he has never said anything of the kind to me when I have given him my views of the Government of India Memorandum tentatively. If really that is the case, we had better go home.

I had a long talk in my tent to-night with Meston. He complains of the lack of sympathy shown by the Government of India to local governments, and of their failure to consult them much earlier in their deliberations than they have done. He is the first man I have come across who objects to the proposals to which I think we are committed that the results of our deliberations should be submitted to the public for discussion before being introduced into the House of Commons. I and Chelmsford also think that we ought to submit them, not as the accepted proposals of the Cabinet, but as the proposals which the Cabinet desire to submit for opinion to the Indian people. He admits all the arguments against his State Council suggestions, but says there is going to be a row in any case because you cannot give the people all that they ask. It is for us to choose whether we shall have a row by refusing to give them everything they ask, but giving them something along the lines that they ask for, or to have a row because we proceed on completely new and different lines which are admittedly sounder. It is very refreshing to talk to him.

Tuesday, *November* 20. This morning I had kept completely clear, because I wanted to go up to Duke's Hospital and have a conference with all our associates. Basu, in particular, was very helpful, and shows a most reasonable frame of mind. Whether he will agree to take the same line in public that he takes in private remains to be seen. The effect of the Government of India's proposals, upon which I commented in my Note of last night, has been to rally the whole of my party to me in solid opposition, and they were very satisfactory in their attitude this morning. These people here, with whom I really have no patience, living in their seclusion and in a firm belief in their superiority, are really tinkering with the subject. They are not in earnest in suggesting a fundamental reform, and they are very foolish, because heaven save them if our tour fails. I am not going, as I have said before, to submit to the Cabinet something which I do not think is ample, but if the thing breaks down because they will not go far enough, I do not know what their situation will be. We determined to draw up a scheme of our own to circulate to local governments, on which Duke is now busy. He was most helpful to-day.

This afternoon we had two deputations, one from a body calling itself the United Provinces Chamber of Commerce, one member of which, Mr. Krishnaji, was extraordinarily interesting. They confined themselves mainly to commercial proposals and tariff suggestions. They want liberty from home for their tariffs.

Then we had a ridiculous deputation from a very large body of people called the Ahirs, who lay great stress upon their antiquity, the fact that the Rajputs were really a branch of them, the assistance they had given to the Government in the War, and the fact that Krishna was a Ahir. They are quite uneducated and very pretentious, but they say they number ten millions.

Then Chelmsford and I had a long interview with Mr. Chintamani, the Editor of the Allahabad *Leader*. He is an extraordinarily intelligent man, I think the cleverest Indian in debate I have yet seen, and his proposals were really extraordinarily reasonable. There was only one which I myself should not be prepared to grant him, namely, an elected majority in the Legislative Council of India, and even about that I am beginning to shake.

Wednesday, November 21. I have had a comparatively slack day. Monty Butler[1] came to see me from the Punjab this morning. He is very happy as a Commissioner at Attock, but is feeling very sore with the Government of India that they did not take the obvious course of putting him on the deputation to see to the carrying out of the Islington Commission Report. He is a very clever fellow, of very broad views.

[1] Montagu Butler, C.B., C.I.E., C.V.O. (Deputy Commissioner, Punjab).

I talked to him of my scheme, and he favoured it. He hates the official member.

Then I had a short talk with Meston's secretary, Gwynne. He is very nervous and shy, and I got very little out of him. Of course he favours the Meston scheme above all others.

Gait lunched with me in my tent. He had very little to say, but he also rather liked my scheme, which I put to him very tentatively.

I then had a long talk with Chelmsford. He also was attracted by my new scheme of two Chambers. He has tried it on Maffey, who likes it too. I had a long talk with George Barnes in the evening about raw hides, and I have nothing else to record save one incident at breakfast, when Meston asked dear old Basu whether he would rather be a Brahmin or a Scotsman, and Basu replied : " I would not be a Brahmin under any circumstances."

The last incident is that a small cobra about two feet long was killed just outside my tent this morning. Snakes in the cold weather are rather curious. Butler says he has been in India twenty-two years without seeing one at all.

Thursday, *November* 22. This morning I had four deputations from the Punjab, and came face to face for the first time with the Sikhs, who pleased me very much ; who presented a fine appearance, and contained many old soldiers, with happy faces, frank expressions, marvellous physique, and, of course, beautiful clothes. Somehow or other the work of becoming a B.A., LL.B., which is so prevalently undertaken in modern India, seems to destroy the personality very frequently of the man who undertakes it.

These were followed by interviews with five members of the Punjab Hindu Sabha. The Hindu Sabha is chiefly conspicuous for having adopted the main principles of the Congress Moslem League scheme, but they objected to communal representation for Mohammedans. It was an amusing feature that Mr. Sarn Das, who was a member of this deputation, had also been to a deputation the day before, demanding communal representation. We tackled him with this, and he explained that he was anxious not to quarrel with the Mohammedans. His views were against it, but if they got it, why should he appear as one who had opposed it, so he joined both deputations. I asked him whether he did not think that it would be right for me to join both the Liberal and Conservative parties in England. But this is a feature of deputations which make them almost impossible.

Next we had two men from the Punjab Chiefs Association, including Sir Behram Khan, a fine old Baluchi, who could not speak a word of English, and an interpreter. He came to tell me, oh, wonder of wonders, that he wanted no alteration in the existing circumstances, save a permanent land settlement; that all this talk of representative government was wrong. We mildly told him that he was a representative on a deputation which, but a few hours before, had asked for something very like the Congress Moslem League scheme. He said: Well, if we would insist on doing something, these were the lines to go upon very gradually, but he did not like it at all. I could not get him to understand how difficult our position was if he said one thing in public and another in private. Eventually he suggested to us permanent land settlement and provincial control of railways and of the post office.

Then came four little-educated, black-bearded, white-teethed Sikhs. One of them, Jogendra Singh, was particularly attractive. He is a writer and lives at Simla, and he had a complete scheme of ministries in some subjects and second chambers which came dangerously near my own.

Friday, November 23. This morning I had a long talk with Shafi, who was very garrulous, who explained the history of the split from the Moslem League, and stated that there would soon come into being an All-Indian Moslem Defence Association. He claimed that Husain's organisation was quite small, in fact that the deputation included all its members. We had a long argument with him about the difficulty of that part of the Congress scheme which he adopted allowing a minority to hold up legislation. He said it was only to apply to Private Bills, which certainly makes a difference, but promised to reconsider it. We had some discussion with him on the Curtis scheme, but although he said he was in favour of the formation of a Unionist Party in India, and had long favoured it, he could not agree to the splitting up of existing Provinces.

Afterwards Chintamani came back to see me. He realised that he had been rather weak when the Viceroy asked him if he called the Congress Moslem League scheme the first step what the second step would be, and he came with a long elaboration of this—the disappearance of the English members of the Executive Council, the broadening of the franchise, the control of foreign and military affairs, etc. He asked me whether I thought, if I came to a scheme, I should have any difficulty in getting it through the House of Commons. I said it depended on the scheme and on the action out here, but that we ought not to make difficulties till they arrived. I then asked him whether, if I could not get all I wanted, I should take anything. He said : "If you want only 16 annas and can only get 10, you should take 10 ; if you can only get four, you should not take anything." I told him that he seemed to have that formula at command very glibly. He said the same question had been put to him about what his Congress deputation to England should ask for or be satisfied with, and he had made the same remark. I said : Well, this proved that the Congress Moslem League scheme was not an irreducible minimum. He smiled. He told me that he was very disappointed in Meston, because, although he was a liberal-minded man, he was a bad administrator.

He reminded me that I had told him at Allahabad that Meston was a Congress Lieutenant-Governor, and on that recommendation, and Ghokale's, they had given him an address of welcome. They had now determined never to give any Lieutenant-Governor, however well recommended, anything but a farewell address.

Immediately after lunch we left for Bikaner. I have got a very comfortable, though narrow-gauge, saloon, and I have spent my time reading the Despatch on Rewards for Chiefs, which I am not going to take more than a glancing interest in, the Congress and Home Rule League Memoranda, which are very well drawn up, and Duke's draft Memorandum, in which I fear I shall have to make very radical alterations, if not re-write it. This is a pleasant prospect for a long railway journey.

By the by, the Viceroy told me this morning that Sankaran Nair had come to him yesterday, and told him that he had had a letter from Jinnah saying that he was afraid that if Mohamed Ali and Shankat Ali were not released I should be bombed. The Viceroy quite rightly answered that a message of that kind was not likely to influence his judgment. I have had many threatening letters to the same effect, and I can only trust to Providence and Halliday that all will go well.

Saturday, November 24. We arrived at Bikaner at 9.45 this morning. In spite of the luxurious bed, for some reason or other I did not sleep well : I think I had done too hard an afternoon's work. We were met on the platform by Bikaner, and went to breakfast at Lallgarh Palace. Bikaner itself has very much improved, particularly in the making of some new gardens and in the building of some very striking red sandstone, three-storied bazaars. We went after breakfast to the Fort, still, to my thinking, chiefly remarkable for its old grey glass and gold rooms, and for its marvellous Chinese tiles. We then motored out to Gujner, Bikaner driving, Chelmsford next to him, Manners Smith and I in the back of the car, together with Denny, A.D.C. in waiting on Chelmsford, and an A.D.C. of Bikaner's, who carried two loaded rifles in case we saw a chinkhana. The country of Bikaner is now completely unrecognisable. The great Indian desert is covered with bush and grass, and is not the bare stretch of sand that I saw the last time I was here. This is due to the exceptional rain, which contrasts with the exceptionally dry season on my previous visit. We got to Gujner at a quarter past one, and sat down to lunch. There was an enormous collection of people—I think there were fifty-seven—lunch being laid in the annexe to the Palace, the verandah of which had been washed away by the recent flood, which had come up over the level of the billiard-room table. The Palace is situated on the extreme edge of a great tank, the waters of which wash its walls. It is really a dip in the desert, and was nearly dry when I was here last, but now there are something like twenty-one feet of water. There is tree jungle all round, except where the Palace is, and the Maharaja has got some spotted deer (cheetal), of which he hopes to raise a stock.

Bikaner has asked Clutterbuck[1] to come at my suggestion. He is a very nice fellow ; his presence awakens memories of the happiest times in my bachelor life, certainly during my last stay in India in the jungle, and his modesty is beyond belief. I am thinking it may be possible to take a short holiday with him for, say, a week, if I get very tired. He tells me that he has already, on his own responsibility, made arrangements for this when he heard I was coming out. He is frightfully keen on industrial development and the development of the forest revenues, and is going to give evidence before the Holland Commission.

I was much relieved on the whole, because I was anxious to get a little holiday, to find that Curtis, who was expected, is so fired with his prospects of success in Calcutta that he has

[1] P. H. Clutterbuck, C.I.E. (Chief Forest Officer, U.P.).

not come. For myself, it seems to me more and more obvious every day that his attempt to confuse a geographical re arrangement of India with constitutional reform is doomed to failure.

Sir Stanley Reed, of the *Times of India*, was, however, there, and I had some talk with him. What he really wants is provincial autonomy and then firm provincial bureaucratic government, coupled with a desire to bring the Native princes into British India. He is a very willing, well-meaning, good journalist, full of pious aspirations and no definite views.

After lunch, we were transported in launches to butts built on the lake, floating on empty oil tins. They were very comfortable and roomy. Our cartridges and guns had already been placed in them, and in each there was a tray of cigars and cigarettes. Ranjit Singh, or "Jabbers," an old friend of mine, shadow of the Maharaja, brother of the Maharanee of Jaipur, controlled all the shooting arrangements, and signalled, from a specially constructed mound, with red and white flags to the various beaters. We got 270 duck, but as I occupied a butt immediately behind Bikaner and the Viceroy, where every duck could see me, I was not surprised to find that I only got 16, whilst the Viceroy got 45 and Bikaner 50. Of course, the duck all came one way, and might very well have come another. I shot quite well. We came home in the dark ; lounged about under the trees until dinner-time, while the flying foxes came out. Before dinner there was an informal investure by the Viceroy in the drawing-room, on three people whose Orders had been conferred upon them some eighteen months ago.

Sunday, November 25. We went out to shoot sand grouse, which this year was quite close to Gujner, in fact, across the water and about 100 yards up the hill. The butts were all over the place. I picked up 26 birds, firing 61 cartridges. As these birds are far the most difficult I have ever shot at, and as the shooting only lasted an hour, and I had never done it before in my life, I was very pleased with my shooting. I think the highest bag was 32.

I have worked this afternoon, and got Donoughmore and Roberts to assent to my revised Memorandum, which at this moment Chelmsford is reading. Chelmsford this evening is in a conservative mood, and has apparently, I suppose, been talking to Maffey. I tried my best to frighten him, and warned him of the impossible difficulties ahead if we did not come to an agreement. I do not know what he will say to the Memorandum, but whatever it is, if they do not produce a scheme I like I shall then have to consider my tongue free to say what I really think of the Government of India. Meyer's brain is, of course, a good one, but it is purely destructive; he is the best they have got. They have either got to take what I want or stew in their own juice when this Mission has failed. God knows, my scheme will be none too popular with the extremists, but I have felt all along that I must try and bring the Government of India with me, for the sake of the Indian Empire, if I can. I myself would go very much further. We had some talk about the relative merits of publication for criticism and publication only after we had agreed to it. I think we are committed to the former, and it is obviously what Chelmsford wants. Meston and Chintamani are opposed to it, the latter if the scheme is properly progressive.

Monday, November 26. We arrived at Delhi at 9.15 this morning, and I succeeded by omitting breakfast—of course I had my early tea on the train—in getting into the proper clothes and appear ready for the fray before 10 o'clock. It then appeared that the Congress and Home Rule League deputation had brought me a terrifically big casket representing the Juggernaut car (*absit omen*) in which their address was enclosed. *Absit omen*, too, after the deputation, in removing it from the shamiana, it was dropped and smashed. It is interesting to note this, because this is one of the sort of things one has to put up with. Although it had been made for me, engraved for me, and brought by these people from all the ends of India, the Government of India felt doubtful as to whether they should be allowed to present it, as they issued an edict that there should be no caskets presented to me by any of these deputations. I had wondered, but had never mentioned the fact, that caskets, which are so usual a feature of Indian deputations, had been absent; but, of course, I said that as this thing had come, whatever the regulation I could not refuse it, and Chelmsford agreed. Its custody, as I have said, will not be a severe tax on me, because it has been broken.

We were face to face now with the real giants of the Indian political world. We had not these dupes and adherents from the Provinces, but we had here a collection of the first-class politicians of the various Provinces. Old Surendrenath Bannerjea, the veteran from Bengal, read the address, which was beautifully written and beautifully read. There was Mudholkar from the Central Provinces, Jinnah from Bombay, Mazhar-ul-Haq and Hassan Imam from Bihar and Orissa, Gandhi, Mrs. Besant, Vesava Pillai, and so on. All the brains of the movement were there. But the difficulty is, as I have so often said, that owing to the thinness with which we have spread education, they have run generations away from the rest of India, and, whatever might be done in theory, in practice this would be only another and indigenous autocracy.

The Congress and Moslem League were followed by the Punjab Provincial Congress, with a shorter but good address; and then Mrs. Besant and the great Tilak came with their Home Rule League, and read us a more extreme and a bitter address, but one which was undoubtedly interesting and good. Of course the Home Rule League's demands are the same as the Congress's, the Home Rule League really having been started to do the propaganda for the rather old-fashioned Congress. Mrs. Besant told me that she found that Congress held its meetings near by Christmas each year, and between whiles went to sleep. It is her activity and her League which has really stirred the country up into a condition in which it is no longer true to say that political interest is confined to the educated classes. They are all seething with a desire for some change. Mrs. Besant, in her white and gold embroidered Indian clothes, with her short, white hair, and the most beautiful voice I have ever heard, was very impressive, and read magnificently. Again a casket was presented, this time quite an attractive object, an elephant tusk.

The rest of the day was spent in interviews. First came Surendrenath Bannerjea and Mudholkar. Bannerjea was loquacity itself garrulous, sedulous, but there was no sign of moderation or compromise in him. The Congress scheme was the least he would accept. This scheme really in its essence excludes naval and military matters, but on all matters of internal administration makes the irremovable Executive responsible to an elected majority on the Councils, and gives them the power of the purse, so that it is practically responsible government at one fell swoop. They would hear of no alternative.

They were followed by Jinnah, young, perfectly mannered, impressive-looking, armed to the teeth with dialectics, and insistent upon the whole of his scheme. All its shortcomings, all its drawbacks, the elected members of the Executive Council, the power of the minority to hold up legislation, the complete control of the Executive in all matters of finance—all these were defended as the best makeshifts they could devise short of responsible government. Nothing else would satisfy them. They would rather have nothing if they could not get the whole lot. I was rather tired and I funked him. Chelmsford tried to argue with him, and was tied up into knots. Jinnah is a very clever man, and it is, of course, an outrage that such a man should have no chance of running the affairs of his own country.

Afterwards we saw the renowned Gandhi. He is a social reformer ; he has a real desire to find grievances and to cure them, not for any reasons of self-advertisement, but to improve the conditions of his fellow men. He is the real hero of the settlement of the Indian question in South Africa, where he suffered imprisonment. He has just been helping the Government to find a solution for the grievances of the indigo labour in Bihar. He dresses like a coolie, forswears all personal advancement, lives practically on the air, and is a pure visionary. He does not understand details of schemes ; all he wants is that we should get India on our side. He wants the millions of India to leap to the assistance of the British throne. In fact, I may say here that, revolutionary or not, loathing or not as they may do the Indian Civil Service, none of these Indians show any sign of wanting to be removed from connection with the British throne.

And then at six we saw Mrs. Besant herself. This was an interesting interview, if ever I had one. She gave me the history of the Home Rule League, how she felt it necessary to get hold of the young boys ; how if the Home Rule League policy could be carried out she was certain that they would forswear anarchy and come on to the side of the constitutional movement. She assured us solemnly that India would have, and insisted upon having, the power of the purse and the control of the Executive. She fought shy of all the financial problems. She said she was not a financial expert. She got over difficulties in that way. She kept her silvery, quiet voice, and really impressed me enormously. If only the Government had kept this old woman on our side ! If only she had been well handled from the beginning ! If only her vanity had been appealed to ! She is an amusing old thing, in that, knowing perfectly well that the interview was to be in Chelmsford's room (because they take good care that I should never see anybody important without him), she turned up and sat in my tent, and, coming in from dressing, I found her waiting there. I told her the interview was in Chelmsford's room, and she drove me up in her motor car, and explained to me that the fact that I had not received a welcome from the Indian people was simply due to their recognition that the Government would not allow it. She implored us to come to the Congress. Oh, if only Lloyd George were in charge of this thing! He would, of course, dash down to the Congress and make them a great oration. I am prevented from doing this. It might save the whole situation. But the Government of India have carefully arranged our plans so that we shall be in Bombay when the Congress, the real Indian political movement, is in Calcutta, and now they plead plans as an excuse for not accepting the invitation which is showered on us.

I forgot to chronicle an amusing incident of the morning. After the Home Rule League deputation, Mrs. Besant and Tilak came forward to present to Chelmsford and myself copies of their memorial. Mrs. Besant asked the Viceroy if she might put a garland round his neck. He told her "No," and took it in his hands. Tilak did not ask me, but placed the garland round my neck, so that, if it gets out, it will be found that I have been garlanded by the renowned Tilak, who is only a few years out of seven years penal servitude for being, at any rate, indirectly connected by his newspaper writings with the murder of an Indian official.

Another amusing incident happened at the close of the interview with Mrs. Besant, at which she demanded our presence at the Congress. She said: "You know that I am President of the Theosophical Society, and I want to ask you two whether, if I do what they want me to do and go home, I should be allowed to come back to India." This was not a matter connected with reforms, and I was not allowed, therefore, to express an opinion, but I am bound to say I admired Chelmsford's handling of this awkward question more than anything I have ever seen Chelmsford do. His face broke into a sweet smile, and he said : " Well really, Mrs. Besant, you know that my desire is to get you safely out of India. Do you think it is likely, if I ever achieved this great end, I should let you come back ? " " Oh," she said, " then I shall not go." Chelmsford said, still laughing : " Is it human to expect the Government would allow you to come back and make more trouble for us if we once got rid of you ? " She laughed too. Then he said : " But as a matter of fact, it is against the rules for a woman to travel now." " Oh," she said, " but they will not mind my being drowned." " Well, the only thing that would make them let you go," he said, " was if I said I wanted to get rid of you from India." It was all good-tempered, and mostly chaff, and I think she went away quite satisfied.

Sir Benjamin Robertson dined with me in my tent alone. He is the Chief Commissioner of the Central Provinces, and one of the best men in the Civil Service. Of course I knew him well, for I had stayed with him for some time when I was here last. He realises that what he asked for and suggested when he was called upon to express an opinion last September is now impossible. He says there has been a tremendous hardening of public opinion, which will make it absolutely essential to go much further than he wanted then. People who were quite prepared for the administrative training provided by Standing Committees now will not look at it. He would have liked Meston's scheme of sub-provincial Councils were it not that he hates the idea of splitting up and the impossibility of two governments in the same area. I suggested to him my scheme, which got rid of some of these difficulties, and which he thought was the best that he had seen.

Tuesday, November 27. This morning we met round Duke's bedside and spent the morning there. Basu has put in a memorandum, very moderate in tone, accepting really the Duke scheme plus a second Chamber of the Government of India. We discussed it, and found ourselves in agreement. The one frightening thing of the situation was Roberts's attitude. He has been completely unnerved by these Congress people. He says that a wave of political feeling is sweeping over the country, which is true, but that they will accept nothing that we can give them ; that even if we could give them what they ask for or anything approaching it, Curzon, Milner, Bonar Law, etc., would never take it. I begged him not to consider it from that point of view, but to be prepared to recommend what he thought was right. He was almost hysterical in his profound pessimism ; had no remedy to offer, no suggestion to make, but was incurably certain that nothing but disaster was ahead of us. I, too, have been feeling recently that even my proposals fall short of what is necessary for the situation, but I wish I could see my way clearly to something more that was practicable in the present state of Indian education.

Then after lunch we saw Tilak, the politician who probably has the greatest influence of any person in India, and who is very extreme. His procession to Delhi to see me was a veritable triumphant one. He was really the author of the Congress League scheme, and although he did not impress me very much in argument, he is a scientific man of great erudition and training. It was quite obvious that he was not going to be satisfied with anything but what the Congress asks for. "We shall take whatever the Government gives us," he said, "but it will not satisfy us unless it is at least what the Congress asks."

Pandit Madan Malaviya, the most active politician in any Council, followed. He is a man of beautiful appearance, a Brahman clad in white (Tilak was also in white, with bare feet), with a beautiful voice, perfect manners, and an insatiable ambition. He is a great leader on the Legislative Assembly. He assured us also that if we did not give everything that they asked for, which they did not believe was in any way too much, which they refused to see was going too fast, there would be continued agitation. The power of the purse and the control of the Executive was essential at once. I kept on putting to him that if that was so they had much better have complete responsible Government.

After this we saw four men from the United Provinces together. It is quite true that when you have these joint interviews you do not get so much out of them, but what struck me very much was the good temper of this interview with these men, who were not, of course, leaders. Moti Lal Nehru has been a great firebrand to Meston, but even he, and more particularly Sapru and the old Pandit Misra, seemed to be quite willing to consider something less than the scheme, the difficulties inherent in which they saw, if only they were satisfied that we meant business, and that they could get responsible government in, say, twenty years.

It is all very depressing. It seems to me quite clear that as we have not touched a single one of the leaders, it is useless to count upon these lesser men, who will be swept off their feet when their leaders start an agitation again ; and I stop the day's work, feeling that we must see if we cannot go further. Indeed, the scheme that Duke suggested to-day, for an appeal when the two parts of the Budget were matters of controversy, the A part and the B part, is a step in the right direction.

I have had an interesting day, in which, of course, there has been some waste of time, and I have very little to record. In the morning I saw four civil servants, three from the United Provinces and one the Chief Secretary of the Central Provinces.

Sir Verney Lovett, who came first, and who is Revenue Commissioner, is a wise old thing who backs on the whole, rather reluctantly, not Meston's scheme, but the scheme of the U.P. Committee. He wants the Division as the unit of the State Council. He thinks it is ridiculous ever to look forward to the Provinces as a disappearing unit, and he says that communal representation must be now continued in India. I told him that a Division was, in most Provinces, a quite unnatural division of territory, and I gave him my scheme as an alternative. He asked me what I would do if my Ministry was quite unsatisfactory. I said you could dissolve the elected Chamber. He then said : "But what if you get the same lot back again ?" I said : "What would you do under your scheme in a similar situation with a Divisional Council ?" "Oh," he said, "there you would have a row in the Division ; I would have a row in the whole Province." That is true, but I do feel very strongly that you must trust these people. Everybody is looking for statutory safeguards, which make them all think that we view them with suspicion. Surely a much better way is to do what we have done in every other country, and give them a sense of responsibility by imposing confidence in them.

Then we had a deputation of Zemindars from a district of the United Provinces. They had nothing much to say, a few generalities about the improvement of agriculture, a regret that cattle were being slaughtered so quickly, and then they added a summary of the nineteen members' recommendations. I saw two of them afterwards, but I did not pursue the question far, because it was not of much importance. I am told that the whole thing is organised by one man who has very little influence, and hangs on to the skirts of the Congress.

Then a little tennis; then good-bye to Sir Benjamin Robertson ; then an interview with a fine old soldier, Subedar-Major and Honorary Captain the Honourable Ajab Khan, Sardar Bahadur, whom the Viceroy has added as a representative of the soldiers to his Council. He talked simply about commissions, the rewards of soldiers, their after-war care. I am firmly convinced that India is not doing enough in this matter, but the difficulty is that the Indian people do not regard soldiers with honour, as we do, and when they retire, being poorer than the cultivator, they do not carry much weight. We really ought to look after them, and I am going to look into this matter.

I wish I had more time. I have continually to work at a terrific pressure, because every attempt is being made to hurry me in order to get me out of the country. I cannot go now till I have finished. I do not want to appear dilatory, and I therefore have so far responded to every suggestion that I should get certain things done in time, even if it means working all night and everlasting thought.

After this I had an interview with Dobbs, who is going to administer Baluchistan. I think there is much more to be said for his scheme for Indianisation of the Services than the officials here will admit, and I am going to take the subject up again. I have asked the Viceroy to send home to Curzon his letter about Persia. It is truly sad that, owing to our desire to placate Russia—what a bad bargain we made !—we have alienated the Persian democrats. Dobbs told me that nearly 70 per cent. of the Persians openly or in secret belong to their new religion. In about the year 1857 a young man appeared, who was crucified, shot at, and finally killed by the Persians. One of his disciples then said that he was God, and that the man who had been killed was a forerunner something like John the Baptist. He preaches a sort of internationalism, and they are all deserting Mohammedanism, and these are the democrats whom we are losing. He gave me instances to show that their belief in this creed was so great that it even conquered their rapacity, which is one of their chief characteristics.

His idea of Indian Reform, apart from Indianisation, which he says is what they most want, would be to try complete self-government in a small district or area, and see whether there was an exodus from it to the rest of India. I am afraid this is impracticable. He also tells me that he had toyed with the idea of an extension of the Principalities and Native States, but had had to abandon it.

Seton is down with the fever.

We go to Calcutta to-morrow, where the programme of work is even more enormous than the half-hour interviews and deputations which have occupied all my time here. Chelmsford seems to be strengthening in favour of my scheme. It is some satisfaction to me to find that, even though I regard my scheme as much too small for the situation and many things will have to be added to it, it looks as though the work of my own brain at present is holding the field. I am quite prepared to find it will go at any moment ; I am quite prepared to discard it if I can find a better one, because I am not satisfied with it. However, this is the basis of our discussions with the local governments.

I fear there is no chance of my being home before the end of March, even though I abandon my desire to go to Mesopotamia. Of course, I will try to get home as quickly as I can.

Meyer has come out as a confirmed opponent of my scheme. I should have thought that this would have shaken Chelmsford, but all that Chelmsford says is that I must consult Meston about the drafting, that Meyer will not put his brain into it.

Thursday, November 29. My first visit this morning was from Walker, the *Manchester Guardian* man whom I had seen in London, and to whom I had given addresses and introductions in India. He is an extremely nice fellow, and has profited very much, I thought, by his visit. He had been invited by Chelmsford to dinner last night, but had telephoned before dinner to say that he had met with an accident and could not come. On investigation, the accident proved to be as follows. He had thought that the right clothes to wear for dinner were a short jacket and a black tie. On reaching Government House, he found he was mistaken. He went back and found all his clothes had been packed and taken to the station ; hence he was unable to meet the Viceroy, after coming all the way from England to do so. Strange, but there it is. This is the sort of life we lead. To-day the Viceroy, instead of sending for him, simply said : " I wish I had seen him." Walker was frightfully impressed by the seething, boiling, political flood raging across the country. He had seen much of the extreme men in Calcutta, where he had haunted the Calcutta Bar Library. He said nobody believes that we are in earnest ; nobody believes that we will do anything. They get nothing out here from Reuter, except some spikey attacks on Indians in the *Times*, or the *Morning Post*, or the *National Review*, and they believe these things to represent British public opinion about India. It amused him to discover that Lord Sydenham was a great figure out here, and that they actually attached importance to what he said, and feared him. He said they speak amiably of me, but feel certain that the House of Lords and the Cabinet will never let me do anything. When the Curtis scheme appeared, Walker asked them whether this did not argue that we were in earnest. They said : "No ; Curtis was one Englishman, but not England," and one of them significantly added : " I am not sure that I want reform ; five years of repressive government would suit me better, because then I should get everything I wanted." Well, there is a lot in that view, but it hit the nail, I think, on the head when he said : " These men are sick and tired of being a subject race. They want to hold up their heads like men, and walk their own streets free and honourably, and not as the subjects of white men animated by a keen sense of duty, but growingly inferior in their manners and consideration for them." Walker said they really want no particular scheme. The head of the revolutionary movement in Calcutta, Das, is secretly in favour of the Curtis scheme. Mr. Walker has had a much better reception than we have had. What they want is any scheme that will lead in a definite and in a short time to this freedom. He says that if in England we are governed by the Press, we are governed much more so here, and he is horrified at the feebleness of it. There is no good journalist in India. He told me that Calcutta and Bengal were really the seat of all intelligence in India. He had not been to Madras. In Bombay there was only one man—Jinnah. At the root of Jinnah's activities is ambition. He believes that when Mrs. Besant and Tilak have disappeared he will be the leader, and he is collecting round him a group of young men, whom he says he is keeping from revolutionary movements, and professes a great influence over them. What astonishes Walker is that the bureaucracy absolutely denies this whirlwind of political thought. He told me that he had had a conversation with Vincent, who talked about the corruption and graft which would result from any power being given to these people. Walker replied that if a bureaucracy happened to have been governing the United States of America they would have argued quite as well that the people were not fit for government because of these tendencies. They worship efficiency; they are proud of their own work, and they will not risk it for anything.

At 10.30 we had our first deputation—the deputation of a body called the All-India Hindu Sabha, supposed to represent more or less orthodox Hinduism, and designed to be moderate. It is really the work of Lala Sukhbir Singh. They read one of the usual addresses, explaining that they were one of the greatest people on the face of the earth, and then going practically for the Congress League scheme. Three of their number had an interview with us afterwards. Two whom I had seen before did not count, but they brought with them as their leader Diwan Madhavarao, a Madrasi Brahman of great experience, for he had been Diwan of Mysore, of Travancore, and of Baroda, and therefore is one of the few Indians with administrative experience. He was very voluble, but talked sound sense. He complained, in the first place, that we asked Indians to formulate schemes, and they were putting forward many things that were ridiculous ; that we ought to have formulated our schemes for criticism and not asked them : this was the best sort of thing they could do. But he clearly showed, although I forget his exact phraseology, that he did not attach very much importance to its workings ; he did not like it. He argued fiercely against communal representation, and said that it has served to accentuate and exasperate the feeling between Hinduism and Mohammedanism. Of course that is quite true, but to suggest that we could get rid of it now seems to me to be impossible. We are pledged up to the hilt, and we would have a rising of the Mohammedans if we did. He talked at great length about the Mysore Assembly, which had a completely elected majority, but I told him it had no power of the purse and no control over the Executive, which he agreed with, but said that was impossible because Mysore was not really a free country, and we could not argue from Mysore to British India. Of course he had brought in the analogy, not I, and ran away from it when it did not suit his purpose. He said the Indian Civil Service were determined to keep the power, and I assured him that was not so. I spoke to him very earnestly. I think he knows that we mean business, and I think he went away far happier than he came.

In the afternoon, at 2.30, I saw Patrick of the India Office, who was let go to be a soldier, but after serving with his regiment he finds himself as Under-Secretary to the Government of India under Bingley in the Military Department. It will be most useful to him when he gets back to the Military Department of the India Office ; but at the same time it is a little bit thick to let a civil servant go from England and find him a civil servant in India. He is an extremely nice boy, very much interested in India and in reform, with some views on the Secretariat, a part of the subject of which I am completely ignorant.

A very curious incident occurred whilst I was talking to Patrick. Unannounced, a carriage drove up at my tent door, from which a man descended—an old, old man with a long, white beard parted in the middle. He told me that he had come from the Maharana of Udaipur, to bring to me that old gentleman's compliments and best wishes. He told me how much the Maharana regretted that I could not visit Udaipur and go shooting with him. He had shot ten tigers during the cold weather, and only lost one, who got away. I was fortunate to remember enough that this old man had acted as interpreter for me when I was in Udaipur last. I sent all sorts of sweet messages back to the Maharana, who had sent me a present of 150 oranges, grown in the gardens of the palaces by the water, and renowned throughout India, he said, for their sweetness.

We left for Calcutta at 5 o'clock. I slept till dinner time, but really my brain is getting very tired, and my temper has almost gone. I see that the C.I.D. have got reports of how the interviews have gone at Delhi. They allege that the interviewers say that nothing is to be hoped for from Chelmsford, that he is obviously antagonistic, but they speak very well of Roberts's sympathetic manner. I suppose Roberts achieved this by never questioning them about their schemes, but he certainly has given the impression that he is frightened, I think ; and if they only knew how, when he is confronted with the conservative tendencies of the Indian Civil Service, it is difficult to get him to put his name to anything progressive, they would see, earnest and desirous of doing good that he is, how difficult it is for him to risk anything.

In the evening at dinner we were treated to some Indian

food presented to Mr. Basu, including a sweet pilau of rice and sliced fruits, which was very nice indeed ; whereby an amusing story. It is notorious that in writing about bombs the Bengali youth always use the word "sweetmeats." One day in Madras Sankaran Nair was entertaining Hardinge to dinner. Basu was asked to send some Bengali sweets to grace the dinner. Basu sent a wire to Nair : "The sweetmeats for the Viceroy will arrive to-morrow night." The C.I.D. getting hold of this, of course stopped the telegram and the parcel, and entered Basu and Nair as suspects, shadowing them for the rest of the time.

Friday, November 30. I have to-day wired home for an account of what is being done for discharged soldiers. I am getting more and more worried by a feeling that nothing like enough is being done here, mainly owing to the fact that the Indians do not welcome and honour their soldiers as we do. They really know nothing of the War.

I hear that the Madras Government has said that Indian civilians who were members of the Anglo-Indian Association, that is to say, the half-castes, must leave it because it has now become a political association, because it presented me with an address. They cannot and will not understand that civil servants in this country are, and must be more and more, politicians. I have told Chelmsford that he must stop this absurdity, and that when our scheme comes out he must be prepared to organise a great campaign on its behalf ; that it must not go by default as other schemes have ; that he must get an association formed and start a newspaper, and come down into the political field and work for its success.

I have not much to say in addition to what I have said about the train journey. I had a long talk with Maffey, and we were very frank with one another. I told him that in my opinion the root cause of the whole trouble was the profound distrust, which may or may not be justified, shown by the civil servants of the Indian and the Indian of the civil servant. The consequence is that in making any proposal or in carrying out anything, the civil servant, rather than trust to his own authority and to the righteousness of his own cause, ties himself up and everybody else with what he calls safeguards—rules, regulations and statutes. The Indian then sees that he is not trusted, and uses his powers quite irresponsibly, knowing that the Civil Service has guarded itself by its regulations. On the other hand, the Indian, irritated by this, demands powers over the bureaucracy which he does not really require, simply in order to get rid of these difficulties. I feel half inclined to suggest that we should sweep away all regulations and statutes, or most of them, give large elected majorities, do away with the officials on the Legislative Councils altogether, and say: "Now we trust you to help the Government." We have put them at your mercy for legislation, and in return you must trust them to carry out your wishes, and we shall have no statutes as to binding resolutions or any nonsense of that kind. This Indian problem is very much complicated by the fact that it is atmosphere, social and political, rather than anything definite which we have to cope with. We discussed the absolute necessity of inaugurating some assistance for the Government in order that its case should not continue to go by default because of the absurd reserve of the Civil Service. When we get our scheme published we must have an organisation to run it and to support it in every conceivable way; take the people into our confidence; invite a deputation on it to come over to England to help with the passage of the Bill; get a journalist out from England to run a good paper for it; collect funds for it, and so forth; allow the Civil Service to expound the scheme; allow civil servants to give lectures at public meetings on various points in the Government policy, and so on. Maffey agreed. Maffey also has an ingenious suggestion for announcing at once with the reform scheme the appointment of fifty Indian Indian civil servants, to show that we mean Indianisation.

Maffey told me that the question of the Congress and Bombay was one of the most difficult he had ever had to solve. If we had gone there, nothing that we said would have been read, but it would have been assumed that we were going to take their scheme. He admits that the plan of going to Bombay is thin, but he did not know what else to do.

He agreed with me that there was no drive in the Indian Government, and that Chelmsford's Asquith-like method of summing up and always reflecting the opinion of his Council was not suitable to a Council composed like this one. They were all very fond of him and very loyal. It certainly differs from the time when I was here last, when all the strong men like Craddock, Butler, Fleetwood-Wilson and Carlisle were all quarrelling like cats. These small men stick together. He told me as an instance that Lord Chelmsford had written quite a good speech for his Legislative Council full of fine language, a frank and manly expression on reforms, a statement that he and his Council were responsible for the release of Mrs. Besant, and that he would shield himself behind no man. He showed his speech to the members of his Council in turn, and by the time they had finished with it they had criticised nearly the whole of it and nothing was left. Chelmsford meekly adopted all their suggestions. This is really a typical instance. I told Maffey that I had heard of Bikaner showing his speech at the Conference of Chiefs to his brother Chiefs, and of Mrs. Besant being compelled to submit her Congress oration to the Committee, but the idea that a Minister's speech should be edited by his colleagues was to me completely novel.

Chelmsford tells me that on his Council Meyer is hostile to my scheme; Claude Hill can be persuaded; Vincent and Du Boulay prefer it to anything else; Lowndes likes it; Barnes will accept it; "Sankaran Nair likes it," says Chelmsford enviously, " because it comes from you and not from me." But, of course, they do not mean the whole of my scheme, and part of it without the rest is no use.

Roberts tells me that an All-India Mohammedan deputation came to see me at Delhi. They had been told they must only talk about reforms. Their address included a request for the release of Mohamed Ali. They were told to cut this out ; they refused and went home. Oh, if Chelmsford had only argued with them, it is very likely he could have pursuaded them, and now they have gone away disgruntled. Roberts told me that two of them had been to see him. They said they did not greatly care about the internment of Mohamed Ali, but they were convinced that it was part and parcel of a determination of ours to interfere with the Khalifa, and even to propose that contemptible old man, the King of the Hedjaz, as Khalifa. I immediately thought I would wire to Balfour asking him to make an emphatic statement that we had no intention of interfering, but Chelmsford characteristically said he could not sanction such a telegram without asking Grant. Good God ! As a matter of fact, Bob Cecil seems to have made the statement yesterday. If only they would advertise this throughout India, but of course they won't.

An amusing incident to show that the hordes of servants, who, poor things, find that time hangs heavily on their hands, must try and please one. I tried to go through the train to see Mr. Basu. As I started down the corridor, servants thronging the passage, seeing me coming, they opened the first door, with a loud crash, that seemed handy. The result was I interrupted poor Donoughmore's afternoon sleep. I explained that I did not want to see him, and that it was the officiousness of the servants ; and went on to find that the next door was thrown open for me, with the same result on poor Duke. I then refused to go any further until I had explained that I wanted to see Mr. Basu. They all agreed, and assured me it was all right, and took me along two carriages, kicking from the way the coolies who were taking their afternoon sleep in the corridors, and then landed me in the post-office car, and introduced me to a young Babu, whose name they assured me was Basu, the man whom I was looking for.

III

CALCUTTA

Saturday, December 1. We arrived here this morning, and were met at the station by various civil servants, Ronaldshay and Gourlay. I breakfasted in my room, and wrote a few mail letters, and arranged business. I do not think it is possible to describe Government House, Calcutta. Built, it is said, in imitation of Kedleston, it contains a central block and four wings, rather like a Maltese cross. No wing communicates with any other. The ground floor, which is under an enormous flight of steps, is exactly like a railway terminus. Above this floor comes the dining-room floor, separated from a small drawing-room, with a silver throne, by a huge gloomy parade, as it were, paved with grey marble and pillared. Above this again, and occupying the space occupied by this gloomy, lofty parade ground, the dining-room and the drawing-room, is a huge ballroom. The floor of the wing giving off from this is occupied by me, Parsons and Franey. The floor of the wing opposite is occupied by Chelmsford and his staff.

I went to see Chelmsford this morning and told him of the arrangements I had made, which met with his approval.

Ronaldshay then came and talked to me. We found ourselves much in agreement about the fact that it is British ascendancy and subject race feeling which is at the bottom of everything. He is fast becoming a Curtisite.

After lunch, Chelmsford and I interviewed two civil servants, a man named Monahan and another named Stevenson-Moore.

After that we played tennis—grass courts—a very different game from what we had been playing at Delhi; but whether it was because of the sun, or whether it was because of the railway train, I collapsed in the middle. I went upstairs, had a bath, and immediately afterwards had my first introduction to the great Curtis. We spent an hour together. At last here was a person unprejudiced, keenly interested, properly equipped. I spoke to him with complete frankness, and although, of course, he prefers his scheme, he is quite prepared to see mine adopted. I am bound to say that he convinced me that an official majority is a thing which cannot be tolerated. I wish he sometimes made a joke ; I wish he sometimes viewed things from some other attitude than that of Curtis, the empire-builder.

A new subject that he raised with me was the English Press in India, and its habit of vilifying the Indians. He wants them proceeded against. It was a satisfactory talk. He did not convince me that you could practically sub-divide the Provinces now, but of course our two schemes are so similar that it really does not matter.

Next I had a talk with Sinha, who is really on the whole the greatest gentleman and the most loyal and attractive Indian I have known. It was a long and very friendly talk. He tells me that the Bengal request for Standing Committees plus binding authority for those Committees on some subjects in not more than three years' time was a compromise made between him and Ronaldshay to please Wheeler.[1] Wheeler seems very reactionary. He tells me that Nair tells him that the Government of India will do nothing. I think Nair is wrong, and I told Sinha not to lose hope. I outlined my scheme to Sinha, and told him it was coming before the Government of Bengal. He said that he thought the scheme would meet their requirements. He warned me that the new responsible Governments would probably make a mess of many of the things entrusted to them, but however inefficient they were, he wanted them to try. He hoped it was not too late, although things in India were very, very

[1] Sir Henry Wheeler, K.C.I.E., C.S.I. (Member, Bengal Executive Council).

serious and growing more serious every day. I wish I could get the damned bureaucracy to realise this, but we are literally sitting on an earthquake.

I then felt too tired to do any more ; I send a note to ask for dinner upstairs, and went to bed.

Sunday, December 2. I started with Holland-Hibbert at 8 o'clock this morning to get a day in the country, away from all worry, and a shoot. We started two cars together, Maffey and Verney being in the other one, along the same road, and we dropped them at the twenty-eighth milestone from Calcutta, where their host was to meet them for a quiet shoot. We went on to the forty-second milestone, where our host was to meet us. There seems to be a fatality about my shooting with Dods of the Hong Kong and Shanghai Bank. He has the reputation of being the biggest snipe shooter in the world, and he has two records which, I think, are not equalled by any other gun to his name, namely, 131½ couple in a day, and 101 snipe to 120 cartridges. We had bet with Maffey that we would get 42 snipe to every 28 they got, based on the mileage from Calcutta. We had timed our arrival beautifully, for we were due at 10, and we got to a pontoon bridge six miles from our destination at a quarter to ten, to find that they were moving the pontoon bridge on that morning of all others, and we could not get across it till 12. I noticed with interest that the whole of the arrangements of removing, re-mooring, repairing the bridge were in the hands of Bengalis, apparently labourers, without a foreman or anything, and they knew what they were doing, although possibly they worked slowly, fetching one plank at a time. Everybody seemed able to swim. We met an old, old Bengali coming up stream in a boat. He spoke English, and told me he was going to inspect some fisheries. He informed me that Mr. Montagu and the Viceroy were coming to shoot there next Sunday ; that Mr. Montagu was a keen hunter and had hunted with

Babu Mukerjee last time he was in India, and had written to him to come again. Dods told me that I should not find him what he was five years ago ; that Mukerjee had gone all to pieces, and that the shooting is bad. I finally joined my nice little host at 12 ; went off two miles on an elephant, and started shooting with him at one. Unfortunately, we went to the most distant and the smallest place first. In expectation of my arriving at 10, the shikaris had been sent off at half-past 9 and could not be recalled. It would have been full of snipe at that time of the day, but the villagers were all over the place when we got there. There were rice fields on the edge of the most beautiful lake in the world ; the vegetation and the palm trees were lovely. We saw three snakes—one python, one small, harmless snake, and, I think, a cobra. Holland-Hibbert's party also saw a cobra and a fish-hawk going away with a snake. There were no jack snipe about ; they had not arrived yet. The pin-tail snipe was not in yet. The snipe we shot was the common English snipe. I do not think we missed more than three all day, but we only got ten couple. Holland-Hibbert and Dods's cousin got nine couple. I have not yet heard what Maffey got. We raced home to Dods's tent as fast as the elephant could carry us. Of course, if I could have ridden a horse we should have got much more ; the elephant is so slow. Dods is now on the Committee of the Zoo, and spends most of his spare time in getting birds caught for the Zoo. He is a most interesting person, and we had many talks on ornithology, and a few words on the isolation of the Government of India. Dods has incited me to go and shoot flying foxes at the Zoo before breakfast on Tuesday morning, a novel experience. Apparently the flying foxes are there in such numbers that they are spoiling the trees.

We reached home at 8 o'clock, speculating whether we should be in time for dinner, to find that the doctor, alarmed at my escapade of yesterday, had ordered dinner for me in my room, with a bottle of champagne. After dinner I went to bed.

Monday, December 3. I suppose I must keep up this wretched practice, so boring to me, and so difficult to discharge efficiently, of recording my proceedings. I do not think I give a thought, waking, and, I fear, sometimes sleeping, to anything but Indian reforms, except for the hour a day which I try to keep for exercise. I read my papers before breakfast, and begin the serried series of deputations and memoranda, copies of which for yesterday and to-day are appended to these notes.

To-day began with four formal deputations. Here it is not necessary to go to a tent. We have a large room with two thrones on the first floor, the drawing-room at nighttime, and certainly under Gourlay's management these formal deputations go very quickly.

One of these deputations was from the Anglo-Indian Association, which really repeated very much the same tale as we had heard from the All-India Association, this being the Bengal branch.

The other three were interesting. One was from the Bengal Chamber of Commerce, and contained the leaders of the great movement which so forcibly protested against my visit, headed by Sir Hugh Bray, all English ; and another was the Calcutta Trades Association of retail traders, equally English and even more prejudiced. Sandwiched between them came the British Indian Association, a more or less conservative body, headed by the Maharajadhiraja Bahadur of Burdwan, the best type of conservative Indian.

After the deputations we had a joint interview with five representatives of the British Indian Association. Burdwan spoke very well, and came out of cross-examination very well. He frankly confessed to differing from his Committee on the separation of the Judicial from the Executive, merely because he thought it would weaken the hands of the British Executive, for he has a fierce love of the British connection—not a passive acquiescence, but a firm belief in it. He it was that was called " a pot-bellied swashbuckler " by Keir Hardie, and retaliated with the far better abuse of calling Keir Hardie " a white surdar coolie." He is a large and very rich Zemindar, and wishes to be made an independent Chief. He has great courage.

After they had gone came the Bengal Chamber of Commerce. Their address had been far more reasonable than their public utterances would have led one to expect. They came in, I was told afterwards, very nervous, and Chelmsford stood up to them nobly, and therefore I was encouraged to enter into controversy with them ; warned them of the trouble they had been laying up for themselves by taking no part in politics ; assured them that it would be necessary for them to do so in future, and told them that they must assert their position and must rest their claim to protection on the vindication of their case to the Indian people rather than for ever on the Government of India, which they abused. Chelmsford told them that he was glad to have been instrumental in bringing them into political life. We asked them of what they were really afraid, and why they resented my visit : explained to them that no alterations were to be attempted until after the War, but that we were preparing for alterations, just as we were doing in Ireland and in reconstruction generally ; asked them how they dared assert that they were not going to be consulted about our plans when they had read the announcement of August 20. They told us that they could not control the Press, and were very annoyed at being saddled with the responsibility for it. Considering that the Press subsists on their advertisements, and that the Editor of the *Englishman* is a member of their Association, this was a bit thick. One of them, the most reasonable, Ironside, who accepted the Curtis scheme, told me that their real indignation was based on the fact that when he was in England in October of last year Islington had told him that an official Committee sitting in London had hammered out a scheme, which was then cut and dried and ready to present to Parliament ; that he had asked whether the Bengal Chamber of Commerce would be heard, and was told that it was now too late. I asked them whether they really believed that this could be true, and that Chelmsford and I were really going through a solemn farce, having a scheme all the time in our pockets. They said they accepted my assurance. I am communicating with Islington, and shall see these gentlemen, or some of them, again on Friday.

Then we had a deputation of the Anglo-Indian Association, with whom we did not do much business ; and then I left to drive through Calcutta to a lunch with Basu at his own home.

The whole of our party went. Gourlay, a man much loved by the Indians and private secretary to Ronaldshay, also to Carmichael, the best type of Indian civil servant, and Maffey, Chelmsford's private secretary, were the only others.

We lunched in an enormous shamiana, of great heat, for there was only one thickness of canvas, and that very thin, between us and the sun. I sat between our host, who is still increasingly optimistic, and Burdwan. I must say that if you take the large assembly of Indians, something over 100 who sat down to lunch, together with the Indians who were too orthodox to eat with us, but whom I saw afterwards in the drawing-room, it was a wonderfully representative crowd. Extremists, Conservatives, Mohammedans, Hindus, revolutionaries, were all there. Old Mati Lal Ghosh, Editor of the *Amritsa Bazar Patrika*, the Maharaja of Dharbunga, the Maharaja of Burdwan, Sinha, Gupta, Bannerjea, Rajendra Mukerji, Sarbadhakari, Mehta, Das, were some of the more prominent figures, and my old Cambridge friend, Prosanto K. Sen. Any number of snapshots were taken and then a group ; and after lunch a young woman played and sang that harmless, wailing song, "Bande Mataram" ("Hail to the Motherland"), prescribed once as illegal, and therefore made enormously popular with the Indians. Basu turned to me and said: "We always stand up when this song is sung; do you mind?" Of course I said "No," and we all stood up. I do not think Maffey will ever forget it.

I came home at 3, after a lunch warranted to kill anybody who eat it. Cooked on the European principle, the menu would have to be seen to be believed. Dish followed dish; meat followed meat; sweet followed sweet. Well, well, abstinence secured my survival.

Then the Calcutta Trades Association met us. We talked to them again on the necessity of Englishmen joining in political life, but we did not do much.

A game of lawn tennis, and then Burdwan came for a private interview, with a memorandum which he had furnished. He is the first man who has suggested a Royal Viceroy, in which I thoroughly believe, and a Second Chamber, in which I thoroughly believe. Altogether it was a very Montagu-like suggestion.

And, finally, an enormous dinner party. Sixty-one people sat down to dinner. We all assembled in a small room first, and had to go through the pantomime of presentation, first to Ronaldshay and Lady Ronaldshay, and then to His Excellency and Lady Chelmsford. We filed in to dinner. I sat between Lady Ronaldshay and Lady Bray, the wife of Sir Hugh Bray. I talked to her a little. She is a plucky woman and spent the summer in Calcutta (Sir Hugh Bray is a cousin of my old friend, Edmund Bray, now in Mesopotamia), and we knew many friends and places in common.

Tuesday, December 4. This morning I got up early and went to the Zoo, and shot away as many cartridges as I liked at those huge bats, the flying foxes, night herons, cormorants and crows that were disfiguring the Zoo. I sat on a bridge

E. S. M. Bhupendranath Basu

CALCUTTA

Caviare Frappé
Thon des Castronomes
Olives

POTAGE

Consomme Tosca

POISSON

Beckti Froid Sauce Tartare

ENTREE

Filet de Boeuf Grille aux Champignons
Saute de Volaille Marengo
Legumes
Choux-fleur a la Creme Petit Pois
Viandes Froids
Jambon
Dinde Farcie
Galantine de Sarcelles
Bosse de Boeuf
Selle de mouton
Salade

ENTREMETS

Corbeille de Meringues a la Chantilly
Tarte de Fruits a la Victoria

GLACES

Bomba a la Brasilienne
Casata a la Palermitaine

Fromage Dessert Cafe

Luncheon Menu chez Basu

[To face page 82

across an enormous piece of water, and the things flew along at varying paces. It was quite good shooting. Meanwhile, the animals did not seem to care in the least, some of the big storks immediately going to collect the wounded birds. A pair of tapirs swam about in the water and dived quite unconcerned.

I came home to breakfast, and began at 10 with four deputations, the Central National Mohammedan Association, a conservative body which had little to say; the Bengal National Chamber of Commerce, an Indian affair headed by Burdwan; an Indian Association got up by Bannerjea; and a Marwari Association of native bankers or moneylenders; and then began interviews.

The first was with the Bengal National Chamber of Commerce, headed by a man called Raja Hrishikesh Saha, whom we ragged properly for continually subscribing, on various deputations, to views in which he did not believe. He had a private interview afterwards, when we continued the ragging, and listened to him droning away on local self-government, on which he was quite interesting.

Then came five members of the Indian Association, which amused us very much, because all five seemed to differ, old Bannerjea, the most vocal, the most loquacious, always flying off into perorations and fine sentences. More particularly Dr. Sarkar and a Mr. Sen were extremely extreme, and I think will be satisfied with nothing we can do, but would be satisfied with what I would do if I had my own way.

Followed lunch, at which I sat between Lady Chelmsford and Holland-Hibbert; and then an interview with a man called Nath Ray, who had nothing much to say; old Sarbadhakari, who was more interested in Calcutta University than anything else, and who is a very cautious moderate; and then R. D. Mehta, an old Parsi, who has sent in an extraordinarily good memorandum on Montagu lines, but who came out badly in cross-examination.

Chelmsford is hardening again, and I am getting more extreme. I think I must give him a fillip, and so I am sending him a few memoranda I have circulated to my colleagues. I cannot get these people to trust any Indians really. I will not be content with anything short of provincial autonomy and complete control of all services by a responsible government unless they will accept my scheme of Enabling Bills and Statutory Enquiries.

I had a few minutes with Sir William Duke. He told me that he had seen a policeman, Clarke, of Calcutta, whom I am going to see if I can only find time to see him and strength to listen to what he says, who believes that you ought to hand over the police to something approximating to British Watch Committees. I told Duke how I was moving forward. I rather think, as I write now, that I am quite prepared to give full responsible government, subject to very little fundamental legislation in the Provinces. I must see Curtis again before I leave, God knows when, but I think on "Our Day," but I have determined not to go to the races.

Then we had a long interview with Moti Lal Ghose, the charming old Editor of the *Armitsa Bazar Patrika*. He is a fine old boy, gentle in his manner, with a strong sense of humour, a devout Brahman, a fierce politician, thoroughly bitter, with a profound disbelief in public of our good intentions, though accepting them in private. He reminded me that five years ago he had told me that our Indian Empire was slipping away from us. He spoke fiercely of malaria, and expressed the belief that it is only the people themselves that can prevent the appalling death-rate, the frightful enlarged spleen condition, the decimation of the Bengal villages. Moti Lal Ghose has abandoned the Congress League scheme, and goes for complete responsible government in the Provinces, with the Congress League scheme for the Government of India. He is in a great hurry, and I begged him to be a little more patient—ten years was a long stretch in the life of a man, but very little in the life of a country.

Then followed one of the most appalling dinner parties I have ever been at in my life—sixty people, all men, Indians and English. Owing to the fact that one or two of the guests did not turn up, the seats were far enough apart almost to allow a lady to sit between each of us, if the ladies had been there. Conversation was, therefore, very difficult. I had sent Chelmsford my notes to my colleagues on the official majority question just before dinner. He told me that he did not sympathise with me at all, and that he wanted his official majority; that as I admitted it was only a matter of method, he hoped we would not quarrel about that; we would choose something to quarrel about of real substance. I said very little, shortly, that if he preferred a dishonest method, as it came to the same thing, and if we agreed about everything else, morality would not impress me. He then said that his inclination was to leave the Government of India alone, as we had enough to do in other branches. I said then I was afraid we should quarrel, because I should never consent to that, and the matter dropped. He is obviously hardening a lot and showing his teeth. Well, I shall show mine. The sooner we come to grips the better. But as every day goes by I am more inclined to accept complete responsible government for the Provinces.

After dinner we were joined by a few of the old stagers, like Dharbunga, who did not eat with us, and we sat talking till 11.

The two Tagore painters were there. They told me that they are embarking on larger canvases now, which are really new to India, except for frescoes. They are nice, interesting people, but I was not allowed to speak to them long before they were snatched away.

Wednesday, December 5. To-day we have had the usual

weary round—deputations from various Moslem bodies this morning, the Moslem Association, the Moslem League, and so on, and this afternoon we have had two deputations from Assam.

The Moslem Association pretends to be more conservative than the Moslem League, but submitted an appendix to its suggestions, which was really just as extreme. They were very nice people, and explained that we were to take no notice of the appendix, which really did not represent their views.

The Moslem League was very, very vehement, and I had a long and interesting argument—because he was a very intelligent man—with one of their members, Aminur Rahman, who is certainly very sincere, and does not see any of the difficulties of the Congress Moslem League scheme. He certainly helped me to come nearer to responsible government.

Thursday, December 6. I spent the morning with the Burmans, nice, simple-minded people, with beautiful clothes. Complete loyalty ; no sign of political unrest. They wanted nothing but the spread of education and separation from India, largely because they were afraid of Indian immigration and Indian domination under a Home Rule scheme. Strangely enough, they are all dependent on Indian coolies for the cultivation and harvesting of their rice, the Indians coming into their Provinces for harvesting, much as Irishmen do at home. They have one representative on the Government of India Council, who is quite useless and out of place ; in fact, there is no community between the two countries. On the other hand, India must naturally protect its frontiers, and railway communication between the two countries must be assisted by India.

An influential-sounding deputation, headed by an Indian called Mehta, was to have come on behalf of the Burma Provincial Congress Committee, to ask for the Congress scheme. He himself admitted, although he brought 5,000 signatures to the petition, that it was only for India he wanted it, and not for Burma.

Then I had an interview with a very intelligent Indian Civil Service man named Keith, who is Revenue Secretary in Burma. He explained much of the reasons why the Burmese wanted separation from India ; said that they were quite self-supporting, but had not enough money for revenue ; their settlement was atrociously bad ; and gave many instances of Government of India interference with their affairs and refusal of their demands. The Legislative Council of Burma contained only two elected members, who were both Europeans. The Government of Burma had expressed an opposition to panchayets. One of the deputations objected to this, and Keith objected that they were willing to reconsider it. I asked Keith, a brilliant idea having struck me, whether it would not be a good opportunity of cutting away from the Morley-Minto Reforms altogether, and I put before him, on the spur of the moment, this scheme : Cut Burma adrift from India ; re-name the Viceroy the Governor-General of India and Burma ; take the Burmese representatives from the Indian Legislative Council ; give Burma the whole of its own revenues, minus a contribution for Imperial defence, and then give it a complete Curtis constitution—Punchiats, District Boards, State Councils, at present mainly, if not entirely, nominated, with a *magnum concilium* instead of a Legislative Council. He promised to go away and discuss this with his Government.

I lunched with Sinha, and I am bound to say it was one of the pleasantest parties I have seen. Here was the modern Bengali at his best—Gupta, Sinha, Mukerji, Bose, Lady Sinha, Lady Mukerji, Lady Bose, and two pretty, attractive young daughters of Sinha's and their husbands. Lady Sinha is very nice, but nearly blind. It was a friendly, merry party, which I was torn away from to go back to two interviews. The first was with Rai Jadu Nath Mazumdar, who asked for votes for women, and had a complete scheme with a second chamber at the top ; and he was followed by a man called Manilal Singh Roy, who was particularly interesting on village unions and local government. He had much experience of these matters, and rules the district with a rod of iron.

Then followed a garden party of 2,000 people in the garden here, where I spent my whole time shaking hands feverishly. I had a word with Cooch Behar.

Then followed a long interview with Mukerji, who is an extraordinarily nice fellow, full of the social grievance ; of the farce of the existing Legislative Councils ; who liked my plan very much indeed, and suggested what seems to me a good idea—before I leave India a final conference of representative Indians at Delhi to discuss matters, say five from each Province. I think that would be a good plan.

I dined quietly with Marris at the Bengal Club. He is a very nice fellow, and I growled and grumbled and explained the difficulties of the plan which I thought we had come to. He expressed the view that the Indian civil servants were very sorry that their day was done ; recognised that it was inevitable, and were willing to go ahead. He said the Government of India was not as bad as I thought it was, that Meyer was the weak spot. Cleveland [1] was dining at another table, and we had a bit of a talk after dinner. He is full of joy at his own skill, both with criminals and also with crocodiles, of which he has got sixty in the last few weeks. He is very proud of the C.I.D., and absolutely ignores the political difficulties which result from it.

Friday, December 7. In the morning I went to the Zoo before breakfast. The gardens are beautiful ; the birds are good ; the collection of Indian snakes is very good ; and the way in which the barefooted but nimble keeper walked in among the poisonous snakes was very exciting.

[1] Sir C. R. Cleveland, K.C.I.E., K.B.E. (Director, Criminal Intelligence, India)

After breakfast we had, first of all, three deputations, a formal one from the European Association, Curtis's organisation, and the Bengal Provincial Congress Committee. These were purely formal. Afterwards I had an interview with the Hill men. This was interesting. They put a scarf over your hand before they shake hands with you. This is the only "swag" I have got recently, save a history of the Karens given me by the Burmans. They only wanted to be left alone and to be separated from India in case it got Home Rule. They were very nice people from the Hills, mainly Mongolians.

By the by, I must record an amusing mistake by the Viceroy when he was dealing with the Buddhists, as he thought, of one of the Burman deputations, who asked for compulsory education. He began to expatiate upon the virtues of the schools he had seen, when one of the deputation said, in a very quiet voice: "I beg your pardon, my lord, we are Christians."

They were followed by an interview with the Curtis deputation. As these people have got really the only workable scheme yet evolved, they were very interesting, and I wish I could have had longer with them. What interested me was that both Colonel Pugh and P.C. Mitter, who spoke on their behalf, repudiated the sub-division of Provinces and wished the State Council area to be equal to that of the Provincial area, so that the Curtis scheme has now become my scheme. Hurrah! This is progress, and I am not in the least alarmed that despite the independent and spontaneous development of my scheme before I had seen Curtis or any of them it will lose me the pride of authorship.

Next we had the European Association, representing the European community, one of whom was the Editor of the *Englishman*. They had very poisonous references in their memorandum to the inconvenience of my visit, but I chaffed them unmercifully, argued with them, congratulated them upon their entry into politics, said I was glad I had achieved this, read them extracts from their own newspapers and stigmatised them as untruths. Altogether it was very successful and did a lot of good.

They were followed by the old father of Burdwan, who had very little to say. He is a Conservative of the old school, a nice old fellow. He wished for the development of local government, and said that panchayets never had more power in his district. Out of his conversation I learned what I ought to have known before, that despite the fact that salt is a monopoly of the Government of India, they had never developed their supplies and were still importing salt. Consequently there had been a great rise in its price. Oh, how we have misused our opportunities by sloth.

After lunch, old Gooroodas Bannerjea, the old retired judge, who had very little to say, came to see us ; and then Ashutosh Mukharji, who has been put upon the University Commission. He is a very clever fellow, of course, and everybody anticipates that his cleverness will succeed in making the Commission nugatory. Old Rajendra Mukerji last night said that Ashutosh only cared for arts, and the numbers of B.A.s and the endowment of research ; and all the other people would listen to him, although they believed they would not. He talked about the University Commission, and explained how careful he was to let the Commission see everything, so that he could not be accused of guiding them. He spoke strongly against my scheme and the Curtis scheme, because, he said, you could not possibly separate departments. He had nothing to suggest in answer. Of course, he is right that there is room for friction in every plan, except complete responsible government.

I spent the afternoon going through the draft of the letter to local governments with Duke and Seton. We have added a paragraph about the Government of India. I have renewed my protest against this letter going as a formal document with a view to publication. The Cabinet told us that our conversations were to be informal. I do not believe the Government of India has any *locus standi* at the present moment. By making it a formal document, you run the risk of making everything formal. These Indian officials do not understand informality, with the necessary result that we shall have to continue to draft answers, rejoinders as safeguards for our own position, e.g. we must answer Meyer on Brunyate.

After that I had a talk with C. B. Das, an extremist, but a most sensible fellow. Chelmsford, Curtis and I have, between us, absolutely blown the Congress Moslem scheme out of the water and the intelligent people are all discarding it. They all realise you cannot make an Executive responsible to a legislature that they cannot control. For that reason they want to leave the Government of India responsible at present, but they are demanding, as Moti Lal Ghose did, complete responsibility at once for local governments. Das argued this very strongly. He originally was a great advocate of the Curtis scheme; now absolutely repudiates it. He is certain there will be no popular enthusiasm; he is certain that it cannot work; he is certain that the Indian civil servants would have it in their power to prevent it working, and mean to do it. It is really completely a question of confidence. I argued with him; I implored him; I saw him privately, and he added: "Well, give us Standing Committees, a new electorate, decent Legislative Councils, and no power for five years, promising us it all in five years in your Act of Parliament. I would rather have this than steps that I know will not work. The half-way house is no good; there is no intermediate possible between responsible government and complete irresponsibility."

He attracted me enormously, but his distrust is based on the police and the way in which the C.I.D. is used. He told me of the prohibition of English histories, of the way that everybody is trying to get confessions from the internees, and so on.

Afterwards Hornell[1] came. He has agreed to stay on five years more, but he is deeply, deeply, deeply depressed. He also says that Ashutosh will wangle the University Commission, and that education in Bengal is a farce, that there is no drive anywhere in any Government—red tape, regulations, prevent any development.

Saturday, December 8. This morning the Bengal Landholders' Association came. They asked for a Second Chamber for the Government of India ; they want complete responsible government in local bodies. Fazl-ul-huq came to this deputation. He prefers the All-India Moslem scheme. Girija Nath Ray Bahadur was their leader. He assured me that the Curtis or my scheme would not work, and so on ; also of his distrust of the Civil Service and the police.

Then old Gupta came along, a keen believer in the Curtis scheme ; does not believe in any of the bogies ; thinks that immediate responsible government in the Provinces is quite impossible.

After lunch I went with Gourlay to see the three brothers Tagore and their pictures. Goganindra has gone in for caricatures *à la* Max Beerbohm. They are all under Japanese influence. Some of their paintings were lovely. One of their pupils, Bose, has done exceptionally brilliant work. They have a beautiful collection of old pictures, too. Raobindra, the poet, has come out as a politician because of the horrors of the internees.

The Council meeting, which was to consider the draft letter to local governments, sat from half-past two, and at 6.45, when the Bishop of Calcutta and the other missionaries came to see me, I had to receive them alone because the Viceroy was still in Council. The Bishop harangued me about the necessity for progress and going slow. He smiles com-

[1] W. W. Hornell, C.I.E. (Director, Public Instruction, Bengal).

placently at everything, and says that nothing will work. Holland would hand over the police to the Curtis Governments, keeping education as a reserved subject, because he is afraid that they will never educate the oppressed classes.

When I had finished with these, I was suddenly startled by being told that the Viceroy wanted to see me. He told me that he had got everything through Council except that they would not have the paragraph about the reform of the Government of India, but had agreed that he should write that part as a private letter, which I should draft. I told him that this was another argument in support of my case that the document ought not to have been one from the Government of India at all, that it was a breach of faith with me, and that the Government of India had better make up their minds once and for all that there were only three courses open to them: either to agree to reform the Government of India; to refuse to reform the Government of India, and so to differ from me; or to convert me, because, as at present advised, I would not go home without a scheme for reforming the Government of India, which I believed was indefensible in its present form. Chelmsford immediately said that they were by no means unwilling to consider it, but they had not considered it yet, and would not commit themselves to mentioning in a document from that august body a scheme affecting their own organisation which they had never pompously considered. Well, well, he kept in the last paragraph which promises a further address on the subject, and I have drafted him a good letter to the heads of Governments.

By the by, for the last two days, in accordance with conformed plan, I have been receiving telegrams asking me to "soothe afflicted hearts" and let loose Mohamed Ali. They number now well over two thousand. It must be good for the revenues of India!

Then to the Bengal Club, where I dined as the guest of Sir Hugh Bray. We had quite a merry dinner party. I sat between Bray and a fellow named Outram, and after dinner sought refuge from the ordinary ordeal of presentation in a game of bridge, in which I succeeded in taking out of Donoughmore 70 rupees. Bless him, I wish it had been from the Chamber of Commerce rather than from a member of my own party. Most of the rest of the party, with the exception of the austere Roberts, sat down to poker. Thousands of rupees changed hands, and they played a bold game, betting heavily on nothing. After all, I think the party was a success, and I came home and went to bed.

Sunday, December 9. On Sunday morning I started off to shoot, going to Habra in a motor car with Finch-Knightley.[1] When we got to Habra we were met by a policeman named Shaw, who had been sent out from Calcutta to see that I came to no harm. He walked in the boiling sun with us all day ; he had no gun or interest in the piece. Frank Carter, the boxwallah, was in charge of the business. He is a very nice fellow, one of the nicest men I have met out here, who is easily moved to guffaws of laughter. We motored some five miles more, where we were met by Babu Mukerjee, the large landowner on whose estate we were to shoot. He is the man whom I shot with five years ago. He has got much older since then and seems to have been very ill ; he cannot do much walking. He had a son-in-law with him and three elephants : the son-in-law is rather like an elephant. We got on to the elephants and went two miles across country, through tobacco and rice fields, until we got to a river where Mukerjee had his tent. He told me that he had written to me when he heard I was coming to India, to ask me to shoot with him. I was much touched by this. When we got across the river we began to shoot. Then two more miles on the elephants, and more shooting. Total bag for the day, 18½ couple—very pleasing. My cartridge average came out to 9½ couple with 32 cartridges, and I was quite

[1] A.D.C. to Lord Ronaldshay.

pleased. I also shot a green fruit-eating pigeon and a hare. Mukerjee has turned out to be a very good big game shot. He goes every year to Assam, and has got 80 tigers to his own gun in his lifetime. He was surrounded by the usual swarm of nephews and brothers-in-law, and there were hordes of naked villagers living on air and refusing food. Malaria all over the place; poverty horrible. We said good-bye to these people, and it was significant that although all of us, including Carter, carefully shook hands with everybody that looked like a relative of Mukerjee's, the policeman only shook hands with Mukerjee himself, and that very grudgingly, and disregarded all the other proferred hands.

Then home. Out to dinner at the Calcutta Club with Gupta.[1] Enormous horde of Indians, all very cordial in their reception. I sat between Gupta and the Maharaja of Cooch Behar. Gupta told me a new story of discourtesy. His two young children, with their ayah, had been turned out of a first-class carriage by an Englishwoman, who would not ride with them. Of course, it was an awful nuisance for her to have his children in her carriage, but in England we have to grin and bear the sight of brats.

Monday, December 10. I got up early and revised the draft of the private letter to heads of Government on the Second Chamber. I told the Viceroy also about a conversation I had had with Frank Carter about the Boy Scouts. Here, again, with our customary folly in these days, we are laying up trouble for ourselves. The Baden-Powell organisation absolutely refuses to have Indians in it. The Indians are demanding Boy Scouts because of their new military desires and ambitions. It is obviously impossible to refuse them, so we have to recognise a separate organisation. At the moment when we are complaining of the divorce between the two races; at the moment when we have a chance, by proper organisation, to keep the future generations together, we are

[1] Sir Krishna Gupta, K.C.S.I.

making it impossible. By these absurd segregations we are losing the chance of bringing the boys together.

I then went off to see Ganeshi Lall's shop with Balfour.[1] His collection of Jaipur and Lucknow enamel, his beautiful Indian pictures, his glorious jewels, his marvellous old embroideries and fabrics simply made my mouth water more than I can say. However, I knew it was no use buying stuff that you could not use except under glass, and I contented myself with buying some stuff for dresses—the best of his pieces were beyond my means—and a little piece of Jaipur enamel. I could have spent three years' income in that shop without getting half what I wanted.

Then home to my first deputation, the association to safeguard Moslem interests. Nothing particular about this.

Then after lunch great fun. Mr. Jones, a Welsh radical who now edits the *Statesman*, came along. I began, very mildly, asking for his political views, and then read him extracts from his own paper. "What are the principles on which journalists act in India?" I said. "Do you ever verify your facts? Is it one of your traditions that it does not matter whether a thing is true or not so long as it gives you a text for a leader?" A dirty pocket handkerchief came out of his pocket, and he mopped his brow, and said: "I should like you to be more explicit." I said: "You tell me in this article that I quote of October 17 that I ordered the release of Mrs. Besant. Why did you say that? Had you any papers to prove it? Who told you that I had ordered the release of Mrs. Besant? Why did not you believe what I and the Viceroy had said?" "That was my inference." "Have you ever corrected it, knowing it was not true?" The dirty handkerchief came out again. Next statement. "You say here that I had persuaded Lloyd George that it was necessary to do something in India, and that the desire for reform came from me. Have you read His Excellency's speech in the Legislative Council? Do you know that he

[1] A.D.C. to Lord Ronaldshay.

invited Austen Chamberlain here? Do you know that he sent a despatch home in November, 1916? Why do you make these statements which are not true? Do not you realise that Indian journalists copy the lead of British journalists? Have you no idea of editorial responsibility?" Nothing but muttering and murmuring and handkerchief.

Then I went to Burdwan's garden party, which was much like other Indian garden parties, except that there was a man who shot at strings of suspended apples with a bow and arrow and succeeded in breaking the string every time, blindfold or seeing; an old boy who split beans on a small child's nose with a large and sharp sword; a party that danced in a fire; a vanishing lady, and so forth; ending with the most appalling comic sketch by two third-rate music hall artistes, one of whom impersonated Charlie Chaplin. The whole entertainment, or part of it, at any rate, was a commentary upon some aspects of British rule in India. Here was the representative of the King and all the society of Calcutta looking at a thing that would not have been tolerated on the pier at Brighton. Well, we amuse them with conjurers and third-rate performers, and they retaliate in all solemnity by amusing us with the same thing, and it is polite for the Viceroy to clap heartily. What must they think of us in their minds?

I drove back with Chelmsford and had a row with him about the Boy Scouts. He said he could not interfere; the Government had washed their hands of the whole matter; it was the Boy Scouts organisation itself that would not allow it. I said that was not the case, that both Carter and the Commissioner, Pickford, whom I had been talking to to-day, wanted Indians in, and said it was a great mistake, and that the Baden-Powell organisation in England would not let them. I told Chelmsford that I believed it was not a case in which the Government could wash its hands of the whole matter, that we should regret it in twenty years' time, and that he certainly ought to take steps at once to bring about this reform.

The letter to local governments has gone.

We had this evening a deputation from the Loyalists' League, Monghyr. It was a small thing, arranged at the last moment, in order to present an address to me, and it is the first league I have seen whose object it is to preach the Government cause and defend it against anarchists and seditionists. I wish there were more like it. It is a model of what Indian associations ought to be.

I went down to dinner, not feeling particularly cheerful at the prospect of a feast of seventy-four. The long-expected mail arrived just as I was going in to dinner, but all I could rescue out of it was a letter from Lord Sydenham full of stuff of no use. Franey brought me news just as I was going in to dinner that there was nothing else but official packages. He followed with a note saying home letters had been found.

For some unearthly reason the Ronaldshays turned up to go round their seventy-four guests about a quarter of an hour before the Chelmsfords appeared. I had one disturbing *contretemps* in entering the room, being told that it was my duty to stand next to Lady Sinha, whom I was to take in to dinner. I made a bee-line across the room to get near her for the ceremony. I said : " How do you do ? " to her, and she, poor blind lady, mistaking me for the Viceroy, proceeded to courtesy low. She was loudly reprimanded by her husband. The whole audience tittered ; she did not turn a hair. I felt uncon.fortable, and finally could stand it no longer, so complaining of the heat of the room, I walked out to wait with the A.D.C.s outside.

After dinner I found myself placed between the Lord Bishop of Calcutta, who discoursed on snakes, and the late Canon Allnutt, of Delhi, and on the other side by the Admiral.

After dinner I talked a little more about Boy Scouts to Carter and about the Zoo to Dods, and I had an interesting talk with the policeman, Plowden, about Cooch Behar and the growth of the anarchist movement, which he says is growing and spreading among the Mohammedans. Then I had a few words with the Persian Consul-General, who denies the story of the growth of the new religion in Persia that Dobbs told me about in Delhi. He himself said cynically : "There is no room for new religions ; if I lose my old one, I never want another."

Tuesday, December 11. Back to the weary round in the morning. It was Dharbunga's day, a proper prelude to "Our Day." He had got up three deputations, and he read long addresses from all of them—All-India Landholders ; All-India Orthodox Hindus ; Bihar Landholders. They all wanted official communal representation. When I asked them how I was to define in an Act of Parliament an orthodox Hindu, they said an orthodox Hindu is one who believes in caste. When I said : "Which caste?" they said : "Oh, just say orthodox Hindus ; that will be sufficient." Ye gods, what children they are ; and they are all anxious rather to get protection than to stand on their own legs and fight their own battles. I talked to them rather severely on this line. I told them I had heard that they were stampeding to the Congress extremes because they were afraid the Government was going to be stampeded ; that they were to believe no rumours about our policy until they heard what our policy was, and that they were to remain patient and loyal to the Government. They took it very well. Of course, old Burdwan was there and Chitnavis, the original mover of the resolution asking to be taxed for the War. Altogether I shook hands with Dharbunga during the morning, coming and going, fourteen times. He will not do anything himself. He wants Conciliation Boards between the Hindus and Mohammedans to manage the festivals. I asked him : Why appeal to the Government to do it. He said the Government must do it. Cosimbazar was a member of this deputation also. I think they will take Curtis.

Our next friends were the All-India Conference of Indian Christians. These people are going on fast ; they number three and a half millions now, and will soon have four millions, but they have four times the literacy of any other people in India, and the talk of communal representation for them, with their mixed electorates, is the most flagrant demand I have ever seen. We must beware of this system which Morley introduced, for it is fatal to the democratisation of institutions and causes disunion between the Hindu and the Mohammedan, and we must not extend it more than we can help. Their leader, Das, is a pathetic example of what a man can do belonging to an unpopular sect by appealing to mixed electorates.

At night Sinha came to talk to us for an hour and a half. He was extraordinarily impressive and entertaining, and I really think his diatribes against official majorities, and his plea that if the Government of India could not get its Legislative Councils to assent to its legislation it would be infinitely better to pass the matter by ordinance impressed Lord Chelmsford. He gave a complete scheme of his own from village councils, which, by the by, he said would take at least three years to establish. He wanted the two Governments, the Ministry and the Executive Council, to sit in the same Legislative Council, but I think we argued him out of this. I told Chelmsford, when he had gone, that if he would give me the whole of Sinha's scheme I wanted nothing more. The worst of Chelmsford is that although the cross-examination which goes on in his presence does him a world of good, when he gets back to the reactionaries, heaven help us.

Wednesday, December 12. This morning I had to see Clarke, the Commissioner of Police in Calcutta. He is very interesting ; very impressed by the feeling that the people are against us on the police, and suggests that the watch and ward functions of the district police should be subordinated to watch committees so as to show the people that we intend to train them for transference of the police. The one trouble is that they want police for a different motive to the one for which they want education. They want education because they love it ; they want the police because they hate them. They want to control education to make it better ; they want to control the police to make them worse. However, there is much in Clarke's suggestion, and I sent him to see the Viceroy.

Then, having refused to see the races because I had come to Calcutta to work, I had Curtis to lunch, and he stayed with me till 4 o'clock. He is a strange mixture of impossible inhumanity and soundness. He wants to abolish the jury system for Englishmen in this country, which, he said, was possible in Rhodesia, and to arrange for the same treatment for Colonials in India as Indians get in the Colonies by statute. He also wants separation of the Judicial and the Executive. He is still angry with Chelmsford, whom he saw before lunch, and refused to make peace with him, but says he is going to dismiss it from his mind till after the War. He then told me that he could not discuss his quarrel with Chelmsford because he would not like to say anything on the matter without the presence of Chelmsford. Poor Chelmsford ! He tried to hold out the olive branch, but it was no good. There is no doubt that Curtis and I see thoroughly eye to eye and he is going to be most helpful, and he is a valuable acquisition because he holds in the hollow of his hands the *Times* and Lord Milner.

So ends Calcutta. I like Chelmsford more than ever. Fatigue cannot stale the courtesy of his manner or the inherent honesty of his character. Whether he will ever be got to express any opinion of his own, or to get over the difficulty of deferring to everything that is said to his officials, I do not know. Ronaldshay is alive and he has some driving force. I am going to devote my whole attention to obtaining support for my scheme, because I believe I cannot think out anything better than I have got, and I believe it is perfectly straightforward from beginning to end. I see my way clear all the way through. I am going to set out my scheme as it stands to-day now.

MAIN PRINCIPLES

1. No advance towards self-government can be possible which does not attach responsibility to the Indians for the votes they give and the speeches they make.

2. It is far better to use honest than dishonest devices, and it is better not to give with one hand and take away with the other, or practice any fraud upon the Indian people.

PROPOSALS

1. Complete system of Village Unions, District Councils, unofficial, with the dawn of local self-government Civil Service.

2. A completely elected Legislative Assembly with a Ministry responsible to it in charge of the B subjects.

3. A Legislative Council consisting of nominated officials and members delegated from the Legislative Assembly.

4. No official majority in this House.

5. Governor to have power to pass legislation in emergency by ordinance, which shall hold till the next statutory enquiry. See below.

6. Standing Committees to be associated with the members of the Executive Council.

7. Executive Councils to be only two in number.

8. For framing the Budget, joint sittings between the Executive Council and the Ministry.

9. This procedure to be adopted in all cases of dispute, i.e. if the police wish to close a school for sedition, Ministry to be informed of it, with power of taking it for decision in the joint sitting.

10. Joint sittings not to be by vote of majority. Unless an agreement is reached, Governor to decide.

11. Executive Council only to consist of two members.

12. Ministers to be allowed to vote their own salaries.

13. Communal representation to continue and to be extended to landholders and Sikhs and European communities, but to be taken away from Chambers of Commerce. Universities to remain.

14. Government of India to have two Chambers.

15. Power of ordinance as in Local Councils.

16. Ruling princes to be invited to sit for Imperial purposes.

17. This will not appear so strange as it is now, as in growing federation Provincial autonomy becomes more complete, until it is found that nearly, if not all, the functions left to the Government of India concern the Native States, i.e. Customs concern the people of Bikaner when they smoke imported cigars.

18. Government of India to allow Provinces to tax anything except a certain number of heads.

19. The Brunyate[1] scheme of finance adjusted to smooth away inequalities, e.g. the contribution from the United Provinces.

20. Burma to be separated from India, Viceroy becoming Governor of India and Burma.

21. Burma to have all its own finances except for a contribution for Imperial defence, and no member on the Imperial Legislative Council.

22. The Meyer scheme to be turned down because it does not really proceed on provincial autonomy lines.

23. Enabling legislation through the Government of India every five years.

24. Statutory enquiry every ten years only, to consider whether ordinances passed either by the Imperial Government or the Local Government shall remain in force, and cases where Enabling Bills or Disabling Bills have not been passed.

[1] J. B. Brunyate, C.S.I., C.I.E. (Member of the Council of India).

25. Judicial and Executive to be separated.

26. Officials to be allowed and to be ordered to speak in Councils and to explain Government policy in the districts.

27. A new organisation of Indians to be collected, assisted in every possible way by the Government, for propaganda on behalf of our proposals, and to send a delegation to England to assist us.

28. A conference at Delhi of the nucleus of such an organisation.

29. If I fail to get Chelmsford's assent to all this it will remain for me to decide how far I can compromise. On this I shall take the advice of Sinha and Curtis. Then, if we still differ, I shall go home and fight it, and if I fail, resign.

30. If I succeed in getting the Government of India to assent to all this, then I am going to ask the Prime Minister to relieve me at once of my office, to remove Lord Islington, and to make me Under-Secretary of State for India until such time as the Bill is through Parliament.

31. This only if he will consent to appoint as my successor Sir S. P. Sinha, giving him a seat in the House of Commons.

32. This idea, which came to me in my bath this morning, seems to me the most brilliant that has ever entered my head. It will teach the Indian civil servants that a British statesman who, however undeservedly, has reached Cabinet rank, finds nothing derogatory in assisting rather than controlling an Indian. It will fire the imagination of the Indian, and it is just the sort of thing that Lloyd George's dramatic sense will accept. However, all that is very much in the future.

33. I think three members of the Executive Council of the Governor-General should be Indians, and that all statutory restrictions upon his choice of colleagues should be removed. It is a matter for consideration whether there should not be an Attorney-General.

34. I still adhere to the opinion that the functions of the Viceroy should be split in two.

Thursday, December 13. The first night on the train (Wednesday) we played bridge. This morning I mainly devoted to my mail, but I had also a very long talk with Vincent. He expressed some alarm lest, if the War news continues bad, things in India will pass from our control; but on politics, although very sticky, I found him better than I expected. Abolition of trial by jury he is quite willing for; separation of Judicial and Executive, he is quite willing for; recruitment of India Office by Indian civilians, he is quite ready for; appointment to Civil Service in India by nomination and examination and a Civil Service Board to arrange it, not a Government concern, he is quite ready for. He likes the scheme of the United Provinces Committee best, but seemed to be quite pleased when I said we could do different things in different Provinces, and he liked my Burma scheme. He said we need not worry about finance; the Government of India did not like Brunyate's scheme nor Meyer's scheme, and would be quite prepared to accept anything that could be devised to harmonise the two.

I then told him that I must have a Second Chamber in the Government of India, as at present advised. If the Government of India stuck to their insistence on an official majority in the Upper House, I should very much regret it, but if I got everything else I would agree to it. Further than this I was prepared, if we could hammer out a good scheme for the Government of India, to say in our report it was a matter for the consideration of the Cabinet whether this scheme might not be left over until the other scheme had been carried, but I should do this with great reluctance. He is very anxious to have a Foreign member, and did not at all dislike my idea of an Attorney-General outside the Executive Council of India.

After he had left I had a talk with Chelmsford, who said Vincent was very pleased, and said that he was quite convinced now that I did not intend to thrust my views down the Government of India's throat. I replied : " Most certainly not ; that is quite right I intend to persuade you to accept them." " Yes," said Lord Chelmsford, " but he says that you show every disposition to be willing to compromise." " Oh, he is quite wrong there," said I ; " I can only compromise on things I regard as non-essential. Vincent said that Roberts was very depressing, and that Donoughmore disliked the Government of India. I said I did, too, as a machine."

I do not think I recorded the fact in Calcutta that Roberts suddenly came to the conclusion he must attend the Congress. I told him either that he would have to leave because he could not sit through certain speeches, or he would be accused of sitting through them when he ought to have left ; either that he would be regarded as our emissary, in which case we would frighten the moderates into thinking we were accepting the Congress scheme, or he would be regarded as differing from all of us in wanting to accept it, which was not the case ; in any case, we were Chelmsford's guests, and must not do anything of which he disapproved. Chelmsford has had a talk with him, and he has abandoned the idea.

In the afternoon I finished my mail, and had some talk with Duke, Roberts and Donoughmore, also a little conversation with Chelmsford about borrowing powers for the Provinces. I hope I am converting him on that. He says he sees no reason why we should not borrow for other things than railways and irrigation if we have a sinking fund. Duke says he does not like my scheme because of the incapacity of the Bengalis. Roberts tried to describe to us a scheme of his own which I could not understand, but which he is putting on paper.

Last night I thought of a modification of my own scheme. If we had a free hand we would sub-divide Provinces, and thus get over the difficulty of two Governments, one of which would be regarded as Indian and the other as English in the the same area. We cannot have that. A brilliant idea :

let us group them. Let us divide India into, say, four Presidencies, each Presidency presided over by a Governor, with an Executive Council and a Legislative Council for the transaction of A subjects, Law and Order, things in which the Government of India are interested, and the Budget of the whole area, with no powers of taxation, but with the right to allot the amount of money to be spent on the B subjects. Under him would be a series of Provinces, presided over by Lieutenant-Governors, aided by Executive Committees or Ministries responsible to an elected Assembly, each with a secretary at present from the Civil Service. Thus you might have the Presidency of Bombay, with a Lieutenant-Governor of Bombay and a Lieutenant-Governor of Sindh ; a Presidency of Bengal, with Lieutenant-Governors for Bengal proper, Bihar, Orissa, Assam ; a Presidency of Madras, with Lieutenant-Governors of Madras, the Central Provinces (query Ceylon) ; a Presidency of Upper India, with Lieutenant-Governors of the United Provinces and the Punjab. As A subjects became B subjects the Presidencies would disappear. After all, there are some advantages in larger areas for Police and Law and Justice. It is only in developmental work that you want small areas.

It is just worth recording that to-day at lunch-time a deputation appeared on the platform, anxious to extend a welcome to Chelmsford. Indignation reigned supreme. This must be a plot of Basu's. How could we receive a deputation without the consent of the local Government? Roberts got his head boxed by Chelmsford for daring to suggest that he should go and speak to them. I said nothing, because it is no use tilting against pinpricks, but I looked pained ; and after lunch Chelmsford actually went and spoke to them. It really is a heartrending sight to see at every station that we stop at the nearest the crowds can approach is two fields off, where they look and watch. I cannot for the life of me see that, in a country where the police are everything, the risk in little country stations would be very great of allowing people to come and cheer, and attempt to make the Government more popular with the people. Contrast this with the Prime Minister's visit through England. Here everything has been done to keep the Viceroy aloof from the people, and, of course, and possibly rightly, to see that I did not interfere with his position in the country.

IV

MADRAS

Friday, December 14. We arrived at Madras to-day at half-past one, and drove to Government House in motor cars. Pentland met us at the station, and we were cheered through the streets by the nearest approach to a welcoming crowd I have yet seen. Poor things, the people of India expect a great deal. Some are apprehensive, and hope that their apprehensions will not be realised, but most of them, in fact, everybody that shakes hands with me, believes that a new heaven is going to dawn upon earth, and I do not see that anything that we can do will be satisfactory to them.

Madras has produced no contribution whatever to the discussion of the matters we have to deal with. The Government of India letters and circulars are answered on half sheets of notepaper; the whirlwind rages round them; political storms wax and menace, and they remain obstructive, angry, sullen, effortless.

Nothing can exceed the beauty of Madras—the blue sea, the white buildings, the white-dressed people, the rich green vegetation, Government House itself set in a park, in parts English-like, with great spreading trees and lawns, in parts tropical, with groves of palm trees and herds of black buck feeding on the grass, and the sea beyond—the most lovely thing you can possibly imagine. And the dining-room on the first floor on a great verandah right open to the air, with great pillars and green blinds, white and green ceiling, and tables spread on the black and white marble floor—it is a dream place.

In the afternoon I wrote a few mail letters that were remaining over, read a few papers, and then played tennis. After tennis we had a conference, when I think I convinced my colleagues about my Enabling Bill process, got their assent to framing a scheme for the reform of the Government of India, and discussed franchise a little bit.

Then dinner; about twenty-one guests. I sat between Lady Pentland and Lady Cardew, wife of the senior member of Council. She is very interested in birds. She first drew my attention to the brilliant amethyst-coloured honey-eaters, like humming birds, and about the same size, that collect the honey from the flowers under my verandah. She talked about snakes. She seems to have had many adventures with Russell's vipers.

After dinner I talked to the Indian member of Council, a very tame creature, who has been up and up and up in the provincial service: his name is Rajagopala Achariyar. I also talked to the Collector of Madras, who is a Mohammedan, Aziz-ud-din, a loyal, well-trained, well-drilled person, who interested me because he has the habit of taking off his turban with a low bow when he speaks to one.

Saturday, December 15. I had a talk with Chelmsford about the procedure at Delhi. We are to have a week of confabulation ourselves, and then to meet in Joint Session with the Government of India. When the Lieutenant-Governors come we are to have an agenda for each day, so as to confine the discussion, and a sub-committee on finance, consisting of Duke, Meyer and Meston. He talked to me about the difference between himself and me—I had *adlati*, he had colleagues; I was really independent. I told him I did not wish to point out how lonely I was, and that really his description was not accurate, because the Government of India did not really come into it at all. I was here to discuss the matter with him. He was quite right to try and carry the Government of India with him, but the time would come with us when he would have to decide whether he would back

GOVERNMENT HOUSE, MADRAS

Standing.—(3) Lieut.-Col. Austen Smith (Surgeon to Viceroy), (5) J. L. Maffey (Private Secretary to Viceroy), (6) M. C. S., (7) E. B. Baring (A.D.C. to Viceroy), (8–9) A.D.C.s to Governor of Pondicherry), (10) C. R., (11) R. Verney (Military Secretary to Viceroy), (12) F. C. T. H., (13) W. Holland Hibbert (A.D.C. to Viceroy). *Seated.*—(1) D., (3) H. E. M. Martineau (Governor of Pondicherry), (4) Lady Pentland, (5) Lord Chelmsford, (6) Lord Pentland, (7) E. S. M., (9) F. W. D. *Seated in front.*—(2) A. P., (4) J. Denny (A.D.C. to Viceroy).

[*To face page* 110

up transient phantoms or make a good scheme on his own. He agreed, but said he was right to carry them with him if he could. I said : Certainly ; that would aid matters very much indeed, but I felt he was being coerced by them, and he must remember that Meyer would soon be gone and Meston take his place. I do not think I did much good, but I warned him of the position in which he stood.

Later I saw Gillman,[1] who is quite progressive. He has, I am afraid, no weight with his colleagues, or they would never have tackled the question in the way they have done. He is in favour of the Curtis scheme, and would divide the Telugu portion of the country in the north from the Tamil country in the South, and have two State Councils.

He was followed by Sir Clement Simpson, head of Binny's, who are doing an enormous business in the manufacture of cotton khaki for the Indian Government. He was a very excellent fellow, but he had no political views, and I do not know why he came. I could not get him to complain or to say anything, and, unfortunately, I have no newspapers here to know what the Madrasi people have been saying about the situation. I entered into an explanation of why we had tackled the matter during the War, but all he wanted was a permit for a school teacher to come out.

Another lunch, much like yesterday, and another meeting with my colleagues, when we came to the conclusion that it was better not to have a week's sitting alone and then a week with the Government of India, but meetings interspersed in both weeks.

Then a garden party at Guindy, a lovely place about seven miles from here, to which we drove amid cheering crowds. It was not very exciting, but it was a most charming place, and I am glad to have seen it. I had some talk with a few Indian judges, and so forth.

The great feature about this place is the terrific influence and the fear that everybody entertains of the Brahmans.

[1] H. F. W. Gillman, C.S.I. (Member, Executive Council, Madras.)

That is the great feature in which this country differs from any I have yet visited.

Sunday, December 16. Got up at 6, and motored thirty miles along the Chingleput Road ; then turned off, and had the most glorious day's shooting that I can ever remember. It was a perfect and divine holiday, and cleared my brain. The game was snipe, but if anybody had seen us shooting, I would have defied them to tell the sort of game we were likely to be getting. We were right away from human habitation ; great blue lakes among lowish hills ; the hills were thickly covered, and the plains between them too, with bushes about three feet high, sometimes higher, making quite a creditable reserved forest used for firewood. It was just rough jungle with a few trees among it, and the hills were scarred in places where the bright red rock showed. It is in this jungle that the snipe are found. We walked mainly in line, with a lot of coolies who shout and make noises. The snipe jumped up at all sorts of distances and places, dash down the hill, backwards and forwards, are most difficult and sporting driven shots, and worth any ordinary marsh snipe ten times over. The bushes which usually found themselves between you and the snipe increase the difficulty of the shooting. As I think snipe shooting is the best fun in the world, this dry snipe shooting is a superlative form of it. We walked all day till about 4, with twenty-five minutes interval for lunch, from 8 o'clock in the morning. It was not too hot ; the scenery was beautiful, the shooting was difficult ; there were enough birds ; there were delicious flowers ; glorious butterflies, particularly one jolly fellow with a bright red lower wing and sooty black upper wing. The guns were Verney, Maffey, Holland-Hibbert, and myself, and we killed forty-four couple of snipe, three partridges and a quail. Our hosts were three business men—Campbell, Walker and Partridge—who made the most splendid hosts, ran the whole thing for us, but carried no guns. Such hospitality is almost incredible.

Monday, December 17. This morning we began the weary, weary, dreary round. We had some discussion on Saturday about the prohibited deputations, which had really been crowded out because there was not room for them, and the two most important ones are to be put in. But they are the same series of things. The addresses are all to be found among my papers ; people who want the Congress League scheme and people who do not.

In the evening there was a dinner party. I do not know what I am to do about these dinner parties. I cannot keep awake after dinner ; in fact, after I had yawned three times in quite a nice woman's face, she asked me if I found Madras a sleepy place. It really is most inconsiderate that, after days such as we are having in Madras, even worse than the Calcutta days in my opinion, in a hot climate, it did not occur to somebody to give us an occassional evening off, as could easily have been worked, by giving a dinner party to twenty-eight people one night instead of fourteen on two successive nights. The dining-room is big enough in all conscience.

I had a long talk in the afternoon, in the presence of the Viceroy, with Welby, of the *Madras Mail*, who was also at dinner. He is a far abler man, I think, than any of the other journalists I have seen. Frankly he admitted that the Mrs. Besant incident had made him determined to resist all reform ; that his was a daily newspaper ; he did not think much what he wrote ; that if he had been editing a weekly he might have watered down some of his language.

At dinner I sat next to Mrs. Whitehead, the wife of the Bishop, a very clever woman, very much loved in Madras. She confirmed my impression that during the past five years the change which has come over Madras is simply appalling. Then it was a peaceful country, inhabited by men and women on amiable terms with one another, differing from the whole of the rest of India in being happy. Now the English hate the Indians ; the Indians hate the English, and this new violent opposition of the Brahmans to the non-Brahmans has become the guiding principle of the place. Unfortunately, all the non-Brahmans are so afraid of the Brahmans that they do what seems to be everybody's habit since Lord Morley gave the Mohammedans separate representation—they ask the Government for protection instead of organising themselves and fighting for it. Here, if anywhere, is room for representative institutions, because here is a party—a religious party, it is true, but a party—but nothing seems to be done, and nothing will be done whilst communal representation is extended and exists. Of course, the causes of this are partly Mrs. Besant and partly the fact that there is no government.

Tuesday, December 18. I went out this morning before breakfast with Donoughmore to the Aquarium, which contains some most beautiful coloured fishes, particularly a black and white striped fellow, with bright yellow fins, but it is really very badly run, because the seas round Madras must be full of the most wonderful medusæ and hydroids, and there is nothing rare or extraordinary in the collection. There are only about ten tanks. Then I went to see the Zoo, which is beyond words bad. There is nothing worth seeing, and the cages in which the animals are kept are almost ghastly. Pentland described them as better than when he came here, and it appears that the cages are new.

After breakfast we had Indian Christians, Catholic and Protestant, and landed proprietors, Zemindars, etc. We were made to waste our time by having three separate interviews with three separate bishops. Not one of them was of any importance. The most interesting was the Indian Bishop of Dornakal, but he had very little to say, except to talk about the conscience clause in missionary schools and the depressed classes. Waller, the Bishop of Tinnevelly, is a much more interesting man. He explained the Brahman position by the fact that there were no intermediate castes between the Shudriyas and the Brahmans, the Kayasths and the Kashastriyas of Northern India being absent. He thinks that the solution of the conscience clause would be to allow the missionaries to decide whether they should have a conscience clause or not. The head of the Roman Catholic Church, a Dutchman called Aellen, who has been here for thirty-seven years, and looks like the Master of Trinity, tried to talk to us about the difference between the canon law and the English law. His insistence upon putting this in had prevented a joint address. They all want communal representation for the Indian Christians, with the exception of Waller, the Bishop of Tinnevelly, who admits that it is a bad method. I will not have any more communal representation. It was designed, mistakenly, I think, to give protection to backward communities. The Indians ought to stand on their own legs ; they are thoroughly well-educated and intelligent. I talked very severely about this to two of them who came to see us in the afternoon, a barrister-at-law called Devadas and a man called Hensman, also a man called Abraham Panditar Avargal, who has a strange history. A civil servant who had been out here invested all his savings in four enormous gold bricks, which he built into the wall of his house. When he retired and went to England he left them here. On his death-bed he told his daughter about them. His daughter came out to India to find them, fell ill and was nursed by Panditar. On her death-bed she told him about the gold bricks, and his fortune depended upon his having found them.

We had an interesting deputation from the women, asking for education for girls, more medical colleges, etc., etc. One very nice-looking doctor from Bombay, Dr. Joshi, was present, the deputation being led by Mrs. Naidu, the poetess, a very attractive and clever woman, but I believe a revolutionary at heart. She is connected by marriage with Chattopadyia, of India House fame. They asked also for women's votes. The woman who drafted the address, Mrs. Cousins, is a well-known suffragette from London. Cousins himself is a theosophist, and one of Mrs. Besant's crowd. Mrs. Besant herself was there. They assured me that the Congress would willingly pass a unanimous request for women's suffrage. Immediately they had gone we interviewed the Coorg Land-holders' Association, who want very moderate reforms in Coorg. They were fine old savages, with knives and axes bristling in their belts. I asked them if there were any women landholders in Coorg. They said : Yes. I asked if they were members of their association. They said : No. I asked why. They said it had never occurred to them. I argued in favour of women's suffrage, and one man blurted out fiercely : "Yes, but women are women," which seemed to him to conclude the whole subject.

Dinner party in the evening, followed by Indian music. Wednesday's programme looks even more dreary than any of the others, and it includes a garden party.

I had some talk last night with Chelmsford on the subject of the reform of the Government of India, which he says is the only difference between us. I have everything to lose by differing from Chelmsford, but I cannot leave the Government of India untouched. It is not because I said that I believed it was bad ; it is because I felt it was bad. I felt it before I came out ; I feel it more so now I am here. The dead hand of the Government of India is over everything, blighting it. It is worse than anything, except the Government of Madras. I cannot leave it alone, nor do I think the Government of India can decently refuse to consider itself. It will look so very vulnerable to think that they were willing to touch everything except themselves. Their only chance, living at Delhi as they do, is to be surrounded by a really representative collection of people from all over India. This can only be obtained by enlarging and liberalising the Legislative Council. You cannot do this and keep official control without a Second Chamber. Therefore one is led to a Second Chamber. A Second Chamber has the incidental advantage of incorporating into the fabric of the Indian constitution something which ought to spread and extend, and be the machinery for incorporating the princes sooner or later. Further, the Legislative Council as it stands is not meant to develop ; Morley said so. We want to sweep away this dead wood and make something that is intended to develop. In addition to this, there is no argument in saying you must wait and see how the Legislative Councils of the Provinces work, for there we are trying to begin transferring the power from English to Indians, and the Government of India we intend to keep as it is, only in a more suitable condition. I am going to address Chelmsford on the subject.

I had a letter to-day from Mrs. Besant, saying that things were happening in England about which she wished to speak to me. She wanted, further, to have some talk with me because, as President of the Congress, she would be leading the Indian political movement during 1918, and she was prepared, within limits, to modify her policy ; but she wanted to talk to me first, and she could not do it in the presence of an official by whom she was likely to be interned when I left. I showed the letter to the Viceroy, who agreed that I should see her, and I have fixed up a meeting after she has seen Lord Donoughmore to-morrow afternoon.

Wednesday, December 19. The morning began by my seeing Stokes, who breakfasted with me. He is a friend of Seton's, and is a collector of a district here, and has been in the Government of India. He seems to be, therefore, a little more alive than most Madrasis ; but I could not get much agreement with any policy out of him, and I do not think he was much more hopeful than anybody else.

The deputations were mainly from non-Brahman Associations, who talked about the necessity for communal representation and a dyarchical system. What strikes me as so astounding about these non-Brahmans is that although they are vigorous enough to object to the influence of the Brahmans, they lie on their stomachs and appeal to the Government for help instead of fighting ; and although there is the beginning of the most promising party system here, they want to spoil it by the horrible extension of communal representation.

Then followed the Moslem League, and, of course, after that the non-Moslem League Moslems. Each said that the other was non-representative ; each said that the other ought to be disregarded and ignored.

Then came the Ulemas of Madras, who summed up their policy, in answer to His Excellency's question : " Can you tell your views shortly to the Secretary of State and myself ? " by saying : " We does not want Home Rule." Then a delightful old man, with a beautiful beard and a fine profile, told us that he had studied the Khoran and all the Commentaries, the Bible and the Holy Books, and he could find no sanction for the Congress Moslem League scheme in them !

And then I saw Mrs. Besant. She told me that Lord Sydenham had been telling lies about her in England, and that she proposed to take action against him, but that she did not wish to do anything to embarrass me : did I object ? I asked her whether she wanted me to plead with her to spare Lord Sydenham for my sake ; if that was her suggestion, my answer would be that it did not seem to me to be worth while. She then told me that she did not much care what scheme we adopted, provided that it led automatically to complete Home Rule within a short time. I urged her to use her influence with the Congress to put that test to any scheme that was submitted. She said she would, but they would take anything which gave them elected majorities and the power of the purse. I told her that the power of the purse meant everything, and she said: "Not with reasonable people." I said I could not defend a policy in the House of Commons on the ground that it was meant for reasonable people, and I reiterated that the sole test which she ought to apply was whether it led assuredly to self-government. She then said that there must also be some restriction of coercive legislation, that she never knew when and how security was to be demanded for a paper and for what reasons. My own view is very strongly that if the Government would only explain themselves, see these people more often, not merely warn them, but argue with them as we have been doing in our interviews, that they could do a great deal of good. It is the unexplained *hukm* that is out of date. I do not think I did much good with Mrs. Besant, but it was well to have seen her, and she has been pouring more stuff into me since. She wrote to me in the evening and told me that she did not come to the garden party because she had not been invited; that she had called at Government House when she was released from internment in order to let bygones be bygones, but that the officials were petty. If I had been Pentland, I think I should have asked her to the garden party and sat her at tea between the Viceroy and myself: it would have been a pretty revenge.

I told Mrs. Besant that I should tell the Viceroy all she had said, and she said: "I like your Viceroy; he seems a good man." I told him this also.

Then followed an interminable garden party of 850 people, grossly mismanaged because I was left to be stared at by everybody and quite unable to find anybody to talk to.

By the by, I asked Mrs. Besant whether she was going to say anything about social reform, and she said: "No; it was no use talking about social reform, because the English could not do it without interfering with religion; there would be time to talk about social reform when they got powers." She promised to send me her Congress address to Bombay.

At the garden party a fine old Zemindar from the south came up and showed me a locket he was wearing of blue enamel, with diamonds, containing a lock of hair of George I, and a portrait of his ancestor, given to him, I think, in 1790, by the East India Company. He asked me to take it back as a present to the King-Emperor. I told him the King-Emperor would much prefer to know that he wore it. I had to shout to make him hear, and a crowd collected. He seemed much gratified when I promised to tell the King about it. I came away from the garden party as quickly as possible, disgusted with the fact that the A.D.C.s, generally from ignorance, had left me absolutely in the lurch. It is no use asking a man at such a party to whom he would like to talk; they ought to introduce him. I seized a soldier by the hand and asked him in desperation if I had ever met him before at one time in the afternoon. He replied: "I am certain you have not."

There was an auction in the banqueting hall after I had gone, and the Queen's presents that I had brought out and a musical-box chair presented by the young Sinclair, and included in the sale, fetched the top price of 1,500 rupees. Four hundred rupees was realised for a card bearing the Buckingham Palace crest and saying: "From the Queen," and 520 rupees for the first rupee note issued in this Province. By the by, I hear that these rupee notes are going very well.

After the garden party two men came to see us who had nothing much to say of great interest. A man called Reddiyar was scathing on the subject of Mrs. Besant's lead to the Home Rulers. I was very tired, and went away to prepare for dinner. I sat next to Lady Pentland (who discussed with me Zionism, the disappearance of old Liberalism, the wickedness of Nationalism), and Mrs. Phillips, the wife of a judge. Donoughmore and Roberts dined at the Cosmopolitan Club, where they delivered speeches which appear to have been very amusing. Donoughmore brought the house down. He is very popular with the Indians, and is really very good-natured with them. He told them that he had come to India to help to make a constitution for them, but his own constitution was being ruined by having too much to eat. They are never likely to forget this *mot*. There may be some great fun out of this, because I asked Maffey to write me a letter protesting in the name of the Viceroy against speeches being delivered by my party, and I have called upon them for an explanation. I hope they will not learn about the joke. It will upset Roberts very much.

I have not had any talk yet with Pentland ; I really must before I leave here. I am quite sure that he is talking and acting under restraint, and I think I shall have to ask him what he would prefer to do—to stay on or to go home. I am certain that the Government of Madras is an impossible institution.

Thursday, December 20. This morning I went before breakfast to the Victoria Technical Institute. I bought a few yards of stuff, but most of the attractive things had already been purchased by other members of the party. Then I went on to the Aquarium, and looked at the fishes again, and home to breakfast with Roberts. He has produced his scheme, which is a variant of the dyarchic double Chamber scheme, and is not uncompromising.

Then we started the day's round with an address from the Andhras in favour of a Telugu Province ; a short interview with Subba Rao—they are all Congress men—and then I met one of the most interesting men I have come across, a man called Achariyar of Salem. He is really a great man. He was a member of the Municipal Council, and was sentenced to ten years rigorous imprisonment for a Mohammedan-Hindu row that occurred in his time. The Government dismissed him from the membership of Council. He appealed ; won his appeal and was acquitted ; brought actions for perjury against the witnesses and got them condemned ; sued the Government for wrongful dismissal and got damages. He is an astute thinker ; he objects very strongly to all forms of imprisonment without trial. I think he is on the right lines in these things. He objects to provincial autonomy, and wants a development of the Government of India, with a Parliament of 300 people, subordinate administrators, but with no sovereign powers or Legislative Councils, and the annexation of Ceylon. He is the most vigorous thinker that I have met, even though some of his ideas are impracticable.

An interesting feature of the deputation from the Andhras was the inclusion in a deputation largely of Brahmans of one punchayet.

After a short interval with a man called Sarma, who was not in the least instructive, and simply a Congress League man, I at last met Srinivasa Sastri, Ghokale's successor as Savant of India, and a thoroughly sound man. He argued in favour of the Congress Moslem League scheme, but finally said he would accept any scheme which fulfilled four conditions :

1. There must be elements of progress and a guarantee of progress in the scheme itself.

2. The step must be substantial and not hedged round. There must be no humiliating stipulations as to fitness.

3. That India should have fiscal liberty. I said that the principles must be settled by an Imperial Conference. He agreed.'

4. Absolute equality between races.

I am quite sure he is on the right lines, and I am quite sure it would aid matters if we could only get rid of the Judicial and Executive. I am quite sure, also, that the Government must issue a public declaration to the Governments that they must work the scheme and that the civil servants must not obstruct. Chelmsford and the Government of India want to do as little as they need. I think it is absolutely essential that they should do as much as they can. Grudging giving has always been the bane of Indian administration. I am going to tell Chelmsford so.

Sastri is much in favour of a conference at Delhi of non-official Indians. He says he is quite willing to serve with Basu in choosing them. They should be moderates, because a time is coming when we shall have to declare war on the extremists. He is anxious that we should invite a deputation to England.

After he had left, two men came, one a Home Ruler and the other in favour of the Curtis scheme.

After lunch we had Ramaswami Aiyar, who is one of the cleverest men I have ever met in my life. He would do brilliantly at the English Bar. He was opposed to Mrs. Besant in her case against the *Hindu*, but has since become her legal adviser, and she has got him heart and soul. He was very extreme, but very, very, very able. He tied us completely into knots. He is so anxious that the absurd representations against the Brahmans should disappear. Even although he is a Brahman himself, he would fix the maximum number of seats that the Brahmans should win in Madras, but he would not have separate representation. I am sure his method is better, but I see no necessity for either.

He was followed by Subrahmanya Aiyar, an old ex-judge, who had written a violent letter to President Wilson in which he asked Wilson to interfere to get Home Rule. I pitched into him with great violence for saying in his letter that British officials voted themselves "exorbitant salaries and large allowances ; they refuse us education ; they sap us of our wealth ; they impose crushing taxes without our consent ; they cast thousands of our people into prisons for uttering patriotic sentiments—prisons so filthy that often the inmates die from loathsome diseases." I spoke to him so harshly and so violently that I fear he will never have a good word to say for me again, and this is the man who edited my speeches !

But it was a disgraceful paragraph ; and when he describes the Indian civil servant as being so subtle and clever that he would put into the shade a syndicate composed of Machiavelli, Li Hung Chang and Abdul Hamid, he really showed how ridiculous he was ; and he is a judge with a pension. I told him that he ought never to have served a Government of which he thought like this. He is very old and infirm, and perhaps I treated him rather harshly, but I was angry.

After him I went to the Cosmopolitan Club as a guest of the Indian member of the Executive Council, and had tea with a lot of people. I had a long talk again with Sastri, who is going to be most helpful ; and came home to see the Editor of the *Hindu* and the financial expert of the Congress party here, the Editor of the *Swadesamitran*. They neither of them understood the Curtis scheme, as their pamphlet showed, but one of them produced a pamphlet which, if true, contains the most crushing indictment of the Government of Madras for disallowing all sorts of legislation and resolutions, and therefore bringing this crisis upon themselves.

They were followed by the Diwan of Mysore, who came to speak to me about the Cauvery Arbitration, and also about his desire to associate princes with the Second Chamber. He is quite right. Chelmsford objected, but I am sure Chelmsford is wrong.

Hurrah for a holiday ! I was permitted to accept an invitation to dine at the Madras Club with Gillman, and I went there. Maffey, Verney, Bernard Hunter, Mr. Justice Todhunter, Gordon Fraser, Walker, who went shooting with us, and Sir William Vincent were the chief other guests. It is an enormously big building, rambling over many acres. The cooking is excellent, and it was very pleasant to hear "God save the King" being played upstairs at Government House as we went out to dinner in short coats and black ties. Welby was also one of the guests. Really, these people who talk about the authority of the Government having gone as a consequence of Mrs. Besant's release will one day make the Indians believe it. Bernard Hunter talked of forming a new Indo-European Club. He is very anxious to see a State bank for India ; thinks the rupee notes are going fairly well ; and has just shown his business foresight by buying all the whisky in Madras for the Club when he read that the Americans had stopped manufacture. After dinner we played a little mild bridge ; I came home at about 11, and so to bed. An interesting day.

Friday, December 21. This morning Pentland came to breakfast with me. He told me that he believed we ought not to talk politics to these people at all ; we ought to play with them, humour them on politics, and discuss with them industrial development, education and social reform ; that there is no necessity for doing anything ; that he could not understand why we thought differently ; that nobody in Madras wanted the announcement ; that the whole of his Council were unanimous ; that even the last Council agreed with him. He actually said there was no difference of opinion between him and Sivaswami Aiyar, the late member of the Executive Council, who is an out-and-out Congress scheme man. He talked about the Brahmans bitterly. He assured me that all respect for the Government had gone ; that people used to consider all officials, from the Viceroy downwards, as sort of gods not to be argued with or challenged. That had all disappeared ; we were playing with fire ; danger was written everywhere ; that he does not know what to say or how to think ; he has no confidence to express an opinion ; he does not know what to say. The position is very difficult ; authority has gone, he is not prepared to say whether for always, but, at any rate, for the present. He told me that the theosophical papers were writing violently blackguarding the Government and the history of British Government in India for neutral consumption. I asked him why they were not answered. He said he was not prepared to commit himself to any opinion on that; there should be something done about it, but they had not been answered. He told me that Mrs. Besant, at an interview with him before her internment, had read from a paper. He asked her what paper it was. She said the Congress League scheme. She asked him if he had not seen it. He replied: "I have not seen that paper." She then spread all over India that he had not seen the Congress League scheme. I asked him why he did not deny it. He said he did not choose to, but that was the sort of libel that went on! He assured me that constitutional questions were impossible here. I told him that the Viceroy and all his Government differed from him in his views. He said he did not like that expression of opinion, but he was told that the Viceroy's Government was a very weak one. Ye gods, when one reads of the resolutions and Bills which these people have disallowed; when one realises how they have brought the whole thing upon themselves, I did not know what to say to him. It was almost oppressive. We shall simply have to ride over the Government of India. Pentland has certainly behaved extremely well to the Viceroy and myself, if he thinks all this. He told me that everything in India was a public document; that the Government of India letter will soon be public property, and that it will be said that we formulated schemes whilst we were pretending to hear opinions. That is obviously the line which the Government will inspire the *Madras Mail* to take. It is a warning.

Chelmsford tells me that he spoke to Pentland about my suggestion that he ought to have asked Mrs. Besant to the garden party, and he said that most of the Europeans would have walked off the ground. I wonder! Have they no more humour than we have?

By the by, I asked Maffey to write me a letter on behalf of the Viceroy protesting against the fact that Roberts and Donoughmore had made speeches at the Cosmopolitan Club.

I got the letter and asked them for notes in reply. It is almost impossible at the present stage to discover whether Roberts has seen the joke : Donoughmore, of course, did. Roberts has certainly impressed Maffey with the belief that he takes the thing seriously.

After I had finished with Pentland, the Advocate-General of this Presidency, Srimivasa Aiyangar, came to see me. He assured me that nobody really expects the whole of the Congress Moslem League scheme, and if they are certain that it will develop, they will not much mind. He thinks the Curtis scheme is the best. He tells me that there is great bitterness against the Government, but he had nothing very much to say.

At lunch we were honoured by the presence of H.E. the Governor of Pondicherry, the French Settlement in India, who could speak only French. Things are very harmonious in Pondicherry because there is no colour feeling.

After lunch we had a long talk with Dr. Nair, the leader of the non-Brahmans. He does not object to the Curtis scheme, but only if he has communal representation, on which he was very fierce. He said for a time, at any rate, it was essential ; that the Brahman officials worked against his candidates ; that even judges of the High Court had canvassed against him ; that he could fight against dead odds, but he could not fight against this sort of thing. He was most eloquent, rather impressive, and a very vigorous personality, but he has obviously got a bee in his bonnet, because he explained that the Home Rule movement was financed by German money. His sole authority for the statement seemed to be that once they were poor and now they were rich.

Chelmsford rather alarmed me by telling me that he wanted to agree with me on how we were to deal with agitation when I had gone home. I am quite sure you cannot permit these extreme powers to be used by these people, because people like the Government of Madras would misuse them at once.

After all, the right answer to agitation is defence, not internment; explanation, not tacit acquiescence until the pot bubbles over. Besides, if we present a scheme for discussion, we must be prepared to modify it if discussion convinces us, and therefore agitation will run again.

I came home and had another talk with the attractive Ramaswami Aiyar. He wished to assure me that they used violent language because they were goaded to it by the Madras Government; that until he talked to me and Lord Chelmsford, he had never had the opportunity of speaking frankly as man to man on political matters with any man in high office. Is it not amazing? He said there was no doubt about the social difficulty. Did not I understand what sort of government we had? Did not I see how there were Indians and English, with the Indians segregated at one end and the English at the other? They were sensitive people, and they could not help resenting the feeling of inferiority which they were made to feel when talking to English people. He was keenly sensitive about the accusations brought against the Brahmans, and he was awfully angry at the efforts made to get rid of deputations by this Government; e.g. he said he had himself, in answer to the accusation that the Home Rule movement was a Brahman movement, been among the non-Brahmans, and had got 800 signatures to a petition, men of substance, to whom he had spoken on the subject. He got them to present a petition, which had been refused until the very night of my arrival. What other interpretation could be put upon it, except that the Government of Madras wished to show me that there was no non-Brahman share? He then talked about the split between the Moslem League and the new Islam Association. He said that the Prince of Arcot had signed the Moslem League representation and had then afterwards resigned without explanation; that he had formed his own association and presented an address nine days after the last date upon which addresses might be presented, and that the Government of Madras had accepted it. He is a lawyer; he wants both sides of the question argued; and the petty way in which they have tried to exclude him has grated upon him. I asked him point blank what he would accept. He accepted Sastri's four criteria, and I am afraid he would never accept periodic enquiries. What he wants is a time limit, and there is much more in this time limit than people really believe. He pathetically said that their confidence in me was everything, and he begged me not to be persuaded to desert them.

By the by, the *Bombay Chronicle* and similar papers have been fools enough to suggest that I am being imprisoned and dragged in the trail of the Viceroy. I see that the Calcutta correspondent of the *Madras Mail* talks about my refusal to see people in Calcutta and keeping myself confined in my room. Could any man ever have crammed more into the twenty-four hours than I have done? I am here for a purpose; I have no time for anything else, and it was only under protest that I went to the exhibition this afternoon.

The evening was occupied by another dinner party, and I sat next to Lady Pentland. She told me that Lord Pentland, as she called him, was the only man she had ever met whose actions were always dictated by an infallible sense of right and wrong, and gave me an opening to express my regret at the pain I had been instrumental in causing them both, and to say that although I admired the admirable courtesy and restraint with which they had treated us, I had felt myself that restraint, and felt sure that they were wrong in thinking that their authority had been impaired. I was now much better able to understand the situation, and although I would still support the action which Lord Chelmsford had taken in answer to my suggestion, I saw now why it was so difficult for the Government of Madras to understand it. If we had questioned their decision to intern Mrs. Besant, then their authority would have been outraged. We had endorsed it, but we had regarded her release as a separate problem, and, as Lord Crewe had said in the House of Lords, I think, only to be contemplated when some political occurrence made an alteration of the circumstances. We had believed, and did believe, that that political occurrence was to be found in the announcement of August 20, but now that I saw how the officials of Madras agreed with Lord Pentland in attaching no importance to the announcement, and regarded it as a mistake and thought that, even now, it entailed no action, I could easily understand why they thought that the Mrs. Besant release was a reversal of their policy. She assured me that she found from experience that Lord Pentland's judgment was always right. I said that I had no doubt whatever in my own mind that it might be necessary to intern Mrs. Besant again ; that even then the fact that we had released her unconditionally would not alter my judgment as to its being a good thing to try. She said she was glad that they had not resigned ; but I am afraid I did not do much good.

Saturday, *December* 22. After an early breakfast we had our last remaining interviews. We began with a native clergyman, now at a large college, named Ponnayya, who dealt chiefly with order in schools, and said that as he was backed up by the University Senate, whose warning against strikes had been successful, there was no difficulty in enforcing order. He does not want violent changes.

Then there followed a very interesting and very attractive man, the Rev. Macphail, of the Madras Christian College, which I remember particularly as one of the best colleges in India. He had been mined on the *Mongolia*, and had lost three fingers of his right hand in getting into the sea, and had been ten hours in an open boat. He is a member of the Senate of the University, and thought that the danger of the colleges from strikes was over. The great trouble has been caused partly by Mrs. Besant's propaganda and partly by the fact that the head of the school was an untouchable, and his influence was resented by the Brahmans, but he was being supported and had really scored a victory. The demand for fiscal liberty he talked about very much, and the difficulty of granting it.

He was followed by Mr. Kandaswami Chetti, Editor of the *Social Reform Advocate*, who claimed to be the man who had started the Curtis scheme of dyarchy and was a thorough supporter of it, but an opponent of Home Rule or of Brahman influence.

Then there came Diwan Bahadur Deskika Achariyar, who was Chairman of the District Board of Trichinopoly, and is now Municipal Chairman of Trichinopoly. He also wanted compartmental transfer, but wanted a Second Chamber nominated. He did not understand the grievance of the non-Brahmans. He has a great record of public service, and during the four years he had been Chairman of the District Board of Trichinopoly he had made many non-Brahman appointments. He told us an amusing story of a co-operative credit society managed by a village committee, two of which were Brahmans, two non-Brahman caste Hindus, and two Panchamas. When they met in deliberation they all sat on different levels so that the air from one did not pollute the others! They discussed business freely together, and the Panchamas usually carried the day. This contrasted very well with Macphail's story of having seen in a west coast town a Panchama approach a store kept by a Brahman, put his money on the ground outside the shop, and shout out what he wanted. The shopkeeper came out and took up the money and put down the goods, which the Panchama removed. Great difficulties apparently are occurring because Panchamas are forbidden to use roads which are paid for by the municipality. Achariyar has under him some Taluk Boards which are presided over by officials. This has at present led to no friction, but he thinks that the Taluk Boards must also have a non-official system.

Afterwards we saw a delightful, courteous, old man, Venkataratnam Nayudu Garu, principal of a college at Pittapur. He had not much to say, except that he would accept the Curtis scheme, but he wanted communal representation. He was a delightful, loyal, old man, who began his interview with a prayer for Chelmsford's and my health, for long life to the King, and the continued existence of the British Raj.

Then we went down to the harbour and saw the damage done by the cyclone. It just shows how dangerous it is to take things on trust. Admiral Gaunt has sent home and supported a request by Sir Francis Spring for a steel caisson to repair the damage. Spring's request was pathetic. It contains these words : " It seems to me that a very disproportionate outlook is indicated when, for lack of a paltry 230 tons of steel—as I said, only one-fourth the weight of one trawler—the very existence of a port of the importance commercially, and potential importance strategically, of that of Madras is subject to the risk of being wiped out of existence." I quote also the last paragraph : " Meanwhile I am sitting here helpless, with my valuable specialist foremen and engineers half idle, just trying, in what may conceivably prove a quite futile manner, to keep the damaged breakwater from cutting back further. Had the caisson arrived as expected in September of this year, the damage would have been made good, once and for all, by the end of April, 1918. Now, at best, it will be a year later, and, unless something is done on the lines suggested for expediting the manufacture and supply of the caisson, *anything* may happen, even to the wiping out of the port." His appeal had been fervently supported by Pentland. When I got there and saw it, I discovered that they were busy at work with a temporary erection independent of steel which would make the harbour safe for a year, and might make it safe for twenty years. These sort of appeals for priority vitiate the whole reception of all India's claims, and I could not help feeling and speaking very severely about it. I could understand Spring's anxiety. He has grown up with the harbour ; he wants to go home and feel that it is secure. He helped practically to build it on the flat coast of Madras. Now he has a 200-acre harbour protected from all winds, but it will have to be much extended, as the sand silts up from the south. This will take place, he calculates, in about sixty years, by which time he hopes the debt will have been amortised. It has grown much since I was here last, and was well worth seeing. I should think there must be few of its kind. Spring claims to know the Indians very well, and has forwarded a scheme with his views on reform, which I have not yet read.

After seeing the harbour, we went to the fort, and saw the interesting old church, with its records of reminiscences of the Duke of Wellington, Milton, Clive, and so on.

Then home to lunch, and a considerable meeting with my colleagues. We agreed to send the House of Lords scheme and the scheme for Governors and Lieutenant-Governors for the consideration of Chelmsford. We had some talk about the conference at Delhi of non-official Indians, and made a little progress. Seton is to write a memorandum. I am convinced that unless we form a nucleus to support us, we shall never get our scheme through. There is great agitation already about a scheme which asks the Indians to be treated as schoolboys, getting a little more each time their schoolmasters say that they may have it. Of course, that is not my meaning. I do not doubt their ability to work representative institutions. Other countries have done it, and I think Indians can ; but until they have learned the customs, conventions, traditions, and uses which are inseparable from representative institutions, and which cannot be embodied in any Act of Parliament, the transfer of powers of law and order to them will lead to anarchy, revolution, bloodshed and starvation, which has resulted in Russia. It is this use of power which they must be taught, which they must learn by experience, and which we cannot risk. I cannot see that there is anything offensive in telling them this, and I have asked Mr. Franey to make a note of this for use when I come to begin the writing of the matter for our report. A nucleus of people who will support us, provided our scheme conforms to certain principles which we shall announce, is essential, otherwise I do not see how I can assure the Cabinet that our scheme will be worked by any section in India.

Then we went to the station, said good-bye, and started off for Bombay, the last place where we shall receive evidence. On the train I had some talk with Chelmsford. I told him that Halliday had told me of an article in *Capital*, pointing out that I had completely won the hearts of the boxwallahs in Calcutta and restored their confidence, but that they feared that the influence of Charles Roberts on the way home might lead me astray again !

I had some talk with Chelmsford about our report—assuming agreement what we were to say in our report. Marris is to set to work to draft the skeleton. I had some talk with Marris about it, and he is now closeted with the Viceroy. I raised some of the matters I wanted included : Chelmsford objected to none of them. I want to lay stress on the social difficulties ; upon the possible necessity of geographical re-arrangement ; upon the position of the Indian Civil Service, both in order to save them from scurrilous attacks and to give them the guiding line of what they must do in the future. I want to say something about fiscal systems, and I am going off with Franey into the jungle to write this stuff the last week in January or early in February for Chelmsford's approval. All this, of course, pre-supposes agreement upon our recommendations. I am quite certain that in all those services which Indians do not control we have got to use the Standing Committee thoroughly, so that we shall see control with the co-operation of, and not without explanation to, Indians—Standing Committees in the Legislative Councils, Standing Committees from the District Boards associated with the district officers, and so on.

All this pre-supposes agreement about what we are going to do, and that depends upon :

1. Their application on the agreed principles ;
2. Their taking my Enabling Bill scheme ; and
3. Reform of the Government of India, which does not look any more promising.

I leave Madras with a very heavy heart. It seems to me hopeless. Here, if anywhere, officials administrate and do not govern ; here, if anywhere, they refuse to explain themselves and hold themselves aloof ; here, if anywhere, they misuse powers, either their Press Act or their powers to disallow resolutions and Bills. Here they have caused their own situation. Madras is not the same place that it was five years ago. Brahmans and non-Brahmans, English and Indians—all have been set at loggerheads. We must have a vigorous Governor for Madras. Pentland does not know what is going on in his own Province. How can he know? He never discusses politics with these people. After all, as Ramaswami Aiyar told us, no Viceroy touring has ever given opportunities to people to give their political views. Willingdon, I should think, was the only exception, to apply this to Governors. It has had an enormous educative effect on political creeds. I know they will accuse me of breaking faith with them if I agree anything with the Government of India, and that makes it all the more necessary why, after this education, I should not desert them. I cannot hope that they will not say I have not broken faith with them, but I want particularly to try and avoid it having any justification in fact.

Pentland, thin, whiskered, in tightly-buttoned frock-coat,

large gardenia-like flower in his buttonhole, saw us off on the platform, looking what he is—an early Victorian Governor in post-War India.

Sunday, December 23. I am confirmed in my belief that the reasons which make self-government impossible in this country now are not really distrust or unfitness or lack of ability or want of character. Unfortunately, there are some people, many people, who agree on this fact that self-government is impossible now, but agree because they despise the Indian, and it must be quite clear that we do not agree with them. What we want, as I have said before, is a growth of those conventions and customs and habits of representative government, without the acquisition of which democracy cannot stand, without the cultivation of which representative institutions are an expression of something which does not exist. Now it is, I hold, a tenable proposition that rather than wait for the growth of these conventions, which no Act of Parliament can produce, but which Indians have as much chance or certainty of acquiring as any other nation, we might give them a chance at once to work out their destiny. Chaos, revolution and bloodshed will occur, but the result years afterwards might be a more vigorous, more healthy, more self-created than the plant we have in view. The only trouble about it is that India, the most invaded country in the world, would soon once more be despoiled by a still vigorous Germany, or an ambitious Japan, and England would certainly reconquer the country rather than permit this to occur, and then the delicately-nurtured plant of education, still now in a critical condition, would have absolutely disappeared.

That is why we must stick to the first alternative, the policy of August 20, but for heaven's sake do not let us go on narrowly and steadfastly cultivating some fields through multitudes of harvests while we leave the jungle uncultivated and unexplored. As I have said before, our opportunities in India which we have taken are equalled only by the opportunities which we have missed. Cultivation of the co-operation of the people is the chief one that we have missed. Avoidance of wounding their pride is part of this plan ; spreading wide our boon, so as not to produce a favoured few, is another one.

Chelmsford tells me that he thinks he will have to take action about Mrs. Besant's speech, and promised to tell me what he is going to do when he has made up his mind. Perhaps it is as well that I should not know. I had thought of writing her, regretting the strength of some of her language, but I fear it will be no good. There will, of course, be an outburst again of anger at her release, and jeers that my visit has not produced a calm atmosphere, and that she has violated her pledges.

I had some talk with Basu. He is a wicked old man because he does not read the documents that are given to him, and I had to explain over and over again plans that he ought already to have found in his papers. He does not like a separate Cabinet, nor does he want responsibility to the elected members, because he does not feel that until a party system is evolved any useful purpose would be served. I think we shall have to be very careful in our nomenclature. What we are really going to do is to have one Cabinet with two Committees, one Cabinet with members in two Houses, the two Houses having different functions. It is really the Congress scheme of elected members of the Executive Council, only although they are quasi-elected in the sense that House of Commons Ministers are quasi-elected, they will not be responsible for the decisions of the Executive Council, although sitting with them for some purposes. Of course nothing will be said about their being dismissible by the Legislative Assembly ; they will be appointed for the lifetime of a Council. Basu urged that they should not be paid so much as previously ; I assented to this. Basu urged that the two Houses should have power of legislating on their own subjects independently, but should make recommendations to one another on each other's subjects, either by legislation or by resolution requiring the assent of the other House. I assented to this. Basu tells me that when he was a boy, about forty-five years ago, although his village was only thirty-two miles from Calcutta, it was impossible to go from one place to the other without great risk of life, and he knew very respectable men who went the greater part of the journey stark naked in order to show the dacoits that they had no money on them. He told me this story to emphasise the fact that the young men of to-day forgot the many things that they owed to British rule.

We lunched at Shahabad, in Hyderabad territory, with old Farrideeonje. Before arriving, Fraser, the Resident, came to see me, and we spent about a quarter of an hour in the train together.

V

BOMBAY

Monday, December 24. We reached Bombay at 8.30 this morning, just as I finished dictating my diary for the previous day. We were greeted by Freeman, and drove through small crowds to Government House. I think Government House, Bombay, is one of the most beautiful spots in the world. A long, heavily-wooded drive leads to a collection of the most beautiful little bungalows, with white walls, large verandahs, red roofs nestling round what is called the State Bungalow, with its big dining-room and ball-room. The Viceroy and I occupy one bungalow. My bedroom is in the centre part of it, and round the rectangular building is my dressing-room, my bath-room, my breakfast-room, my sitting-room and my office, all tastefully furnished in Lady Willingdon's favourite mauve and white. It is up on a height, and outside is the sea, facing east, with sea sunsets that have got to be seen to be believed. Donoughmore is even nearer the sea, lower down, and Parsons is on the same level as myself. The warmth, the lack of formality of the greeting of Lady Willingdon and dear old Freeman ! How Lady Willingdon keeps her vitality I cannot understand. It is a wonderful thing. She comes to see if we are comfortable at all hours of the day ; she alters the disposition of our luggage, and objects to our buttonholes. But aloofness is reduced here to a minimum, and I wish this spirit could be conveyed everywhere. Naturally, Willingdon has had no trouble with his people, but so much depends upon personality, which cannot always be reproduced.

We went to the Durbar Hall to receive deputations at ten,

after a hectic breakfast, all talk, and a round of visits to one another, conducted by our hostess. Lady Willingdon's and Donoughmore's affectionate embrace reminded one of other scenes and other places. Nothing could have been more comfortable or more expeditious than this wearisome reception of addresses. We received no less than ten formal addresses before lunch in the greatest comfort. Between each we retired to our little sitting-room, and actually found that we each had a little lavatory on either side of it in a tent adjoining that of my *adlati*. The addresses were marked by the extraordinary cleverness with which they were drawn—a very high level indeed. The majority were Congress League schemes, the usual problems of communal representation, and one of them actually suggested proportional representation worked out in detail. This came from the non-official members of the Legislative Council, the first Legislative Council that has presented us with an address. It is due to the influence of one man, R. P. Paranjpye, who was a little my senior at Cambridge. Paranjpye was senior wrangler, and is now head of a college of about 1,025 boys at Poona. He is a member of the Congress, but not a Home Rule Leaguer, and he is doing his best to keep his boys from politics. We could make no impression on this deputation, who demanded the Congress Moslem League scheme. Jinnah was as able as ever, but failed to impress the Viceroy. He certainly impresses me. To my amazement, the Viceory told him, in the presence of the deputation, about Nair having said that bombs would result if Shaukat Ali and Mohamed Ali were continued in internment, and then refused to discuss it. We did not do any good, but we had one and a quarter hours with them, followed by some Mohammedans, who professed allegiance to the Moslem League scheme, but did not seem very happy about it in cross-examination.

Then a game of tennis. Lady Willingdon is very good,

but it was far, far hotter than I had found it at Madras, and I could not play more than one set.

In the evening I had a talk with Paranjpye, who showed us his scheme of proportional representation. Of course this is a way out of many difficulties, if they will only accept it. He said there was only the choice between proportional representation and an extension of communal representation. As regards Mohammedans, he wants them to have their separate electorate, with proportional representation in it.

Afterwards we had a long talk with Curtis. I tried to show the Viceroy some of the difficulties of the Curtis scheme in Curtis's presence. It only serves to strengthen my opinion as to the merits of my own scheme, which will, of course, as I have often said, be regarded as Curtis's scheme.

Out of this interview, and a little talk that Chelmsford and I had together on our verandah in our dressing-gowns when everybody had gone to bed, I modify not my scheme but the nomenclature of it. Really the Governor shall have one Ministry working in two committees, one a committee for A subjects, working in the Upper House, and the other a committee on B subjects working in the Lower House. The Budget and things common to both shall be decided by joint sittings, the Governor deciding on points of conflict between them. This really goes very near, except for the two Houses, to the Congress scheme with half the members of the Executive Council elected, except that neither is responsible for the decisions of the other, and, of course, the B Committee cannot hold office if it loses the confidence of the Lower House. It is agreed between us that the Governor should be constitutional as regards B subjects but interfering, the last word being with the B Committee.

Curtis wants to root out all the civil servants, and to allow them to start with civil servants of their own as soon as they have formed it. I am sure they are not fit for that yet. I do not think Curtis was very pleased with these modifications, but we are going to have another talk with him on Christmas evening.

The dinner was large, and I sat between Lady Willingdon and Mrs. Carmichael, the wife of one of the members of Willingdon's Council, whom I had dined with when I was here last.

I have just been cheered by the news of a mail on Saturday, which will not give me much time because the outward mail goes on Sunday.

I had some talk with Carmichael, who prefers the Meyer scheme to the Brunyate scheme, but likes neither and loathes all change. He is more like Madras than Bombay. Freeman is an enthusiastic believer in my idea of a small meeting of people who are to form the nucleus of a supporting organisation to be supported by the Government, and to be a go-between between the Government and Indian public opinion, and to send a deputation to England. Chelmsford also is liking it, and I suggested a civil servant to be deputed to keep in touch with them. He suggested Marris. I said I wanted Marris to come home with me, and I suggested Gourlay. Chelmsford is anxious as to the reception of our scheme, because he has had a letter from Curzon asking that nothing new should be sent home !

Christmas Day, December 25. This morning is Christmas morning, a lovely, coolish day, with the sea looking more beautiful than ever. There has been a great interchange of presents. Lady Willingdon has sent me pictures of herself and her husband ; Lord Donoughmore has given me Stewart Baker's book on Indian Ducks, which I love to possess ; Alan has given me a cigar case, and Lord Chelmsford a cigarette case with the Viceroy's initials on one side and my own on the other.

I have had a long talk with Jinnah. He began by referring to Shaukat Ali and Mohamed Ali. He assured me that he believed in the good faith of the Government, and their anxiety to release them, and their belief in the evidence which prevents them doing so which Mohamed Ali and Shaukat Ali say is forged. He said that he advocated their release, either on the assurance of people like himself and Mahmudabad, or their trial by a secret court, or the publication of the evidence against them. He assured me that he had not meant to threaten, but only to tell us, as was his duty, the consequences that were likely to occur with the growing feeling and belief that they were innocent men. I told him that I had no jurisdiction in the matter, that I would not interfere and I would not discuss it ; that I always believed it was right for the Government of India to explain all their actions and to satisfy public opinion of their reasons for taking them, but I should go no further than to say this, that I was quite certain that in this case they were acting rightly in finding themselves unable to do this.

He then urged me to have a conference at Delhi at which I would take leaders of public opinion into my confidence. I should think he gets this idea from Basu. I seized the opportunity to say that I could not have people there whose motives were revenge or love of agitation, and I asked what guarantee I had of my confidence being respected. He asked me : Did I believe in him ? He said he had never abused anybody's confidence about Mohamed Ali and Shaukat Ali, and that I might rely implicitly upon his assistance in all matters, provided he was satisfied as to the scheme. Could not I even now give him some indications ? I then told him that, in my belief, Curtis was on the right lines, but that the objections to Curtis were :

1. That he confused reforms with geographical re-distribution ;
2. That he did not make sufficient machinery for avoidance of friction between A subjects and B subjects ;

3. That he sketched no certain plan of development from a system under which in some subjects the Indians get more than the Congress and Moslem League scheme and in others much less to a system under which they get as much on all subjects as they do on some. I believed that I should be advocating the best scheme for India if I could get over these difficulties.

He assented, with two additions :

1. That Curtis's scheme did not touch the Government of India ; and
2. That something would have to be done to put this on a better footing.

I asked him whether this difficulty would be removed if, keeping the control of the British Government unimpaired, a beginning was made in what was to develop into an Indian Parliament for all Indian affairs, coupled with Provincial autonomy. He said that he had hoped for more, but was quite prepared to accept this.

He then begged that, in order to make the thing more acceptable, something should be done with the outstanding Indian grievances ; their existence was a reason for asking for constitutional reforms which, if they were swept away, would not be so eagerly demanded. I asked him what the grievances were, and he said :

1. Arms Act.
2. Fiscal liberty.
3. Judicial and executive.
4. Abolition of racial distinctions.
5. Modification of coercive legislation.

I said with regard to the latter that we had too much to do to make it possible for us to go into detail in regard to it , that it was quite out of the question to look forward in the near future either to relying entirely on the ordinary processes of the law as we knew it now to deal with the undoubted anarchist conspiracies which existed, or to make it possible to give India complete liberty of the Press. He agreed, but thought there might be an exploration made under which the views of Indians could be heard on some of the provisions, and at any rate the use made both of the Press Act and the Internment Act. I said that nothing could be done in either of these directions to modify the power of the Executive during the War. This closed the conversation, with an assurance that he was at our service at all times, and that the scheme which I had outlined would completely satisfy him. I said that I would remind him that I had given him no scheme ; that I had merely taken him into my confidence as to some of my beliefs ; that everything I had said was guarded by " ifs " ; that our discussions, when we had finished the evidence, would reveal to me how far these " ifs " could be realised. I know how excellent Lord Chelmsford's judgment is about men. I wish I could believe that Jinnah was anxious to do everything in his power to help us on these lines. After all, roughly sketched like this his policy is so like mine.

Christmas morning I spent in writing. In the afternoon we motored out some twelve miles to a large artificial lake at Vehar, which produces some of the water for use in Bombay. The road there was very lovely through jungle, and the lake itself is extraordinarily beautiful. Some excitement was provided by the fact that we had rifles, and crocodiles were seen, but anybody who has ever shot these animals must realise the futility of proceeding after them with people talking at the top of their voices in creaky rowing boats. We had tea and came home.

We had some talk with the police, who are very anxious for a definite announcement of policy and the stopping of all agitation for alternative plans.

A small Christmas party, with a little bridge afterwards, and then a long consultation with the Viceroy on the subject of Persia ended the day. The Germans have put us into rather a quandary by pledging themselves and the Turks not to invade Persia, and promising to withdraw Russian troops. It seems to me always so disastrous that Great Britain has been forced by Anglo-Russian diplomacy into a position of hostility to Persian democrats. The historic part of Great Britain is to befriend national aspirations. I am not sure that in the East, at any rate, we have not forgotten this, and our policy of disruption and control over Persia must react upon Indian opinion. I would, therefore, withdraw our troops. We can always send them back again if there is any sign that the Germans were breaking their word, and I think anyhow that the risk must be run. But the Government in England are financing and assisting the counter-revolutionary party in South-East Russia. It makes it impossible, therefore, apparently to withdraw our troops from Persia, for Persia and Mesopotamia must eventually, one would hope, unite with this effort if it is successful, although I should have thought from here that it bore very small chances of success ; and if I am right in believing that it involves our keeping troops in Persia, the German ruse of putting us into a quandary will have been successful. The Government of India agree, but I think their telegram was a very bad one, and I re-drafted it. I am not sure it is much better, but there it is.

Wednesday, December 26. The morning of the 26th was spent in ten more deputations. The feature which has been remarkable in Bombay is the very high level of these addresses. They are very well drawn, very carefully prepared, and far better than anything else I have seen. No wonder, in my opinion, that people are inclined to go further in Bombay than they are anywhere else. I would especially mention the address of the Bombay Presidency Association. If it were not for the one difficulty of their finding men, I would not have the slightest hesitation in giving Bombay complete responsible Government—not the slightest. But it is interesting to note that even people who are more or less extreme in policy do not like any responsibility. They want power to make their resolutions binding on the existing Executive, but they do not wish to take over the work of the Executive. I sympathise with them. I think they are genuinely afraid, although Chelmsford will not listen, that we are trying to force responsibility on them in order to show that they are no use. On the other hand, I do not see how they are ever to learn to exercise responsibility unless some responsibility is given to them now.

It was not a good day for our scheme, because so far as I could see nobody would look at it. Sir Dinshaw Wacha and Mr. Samarth, who came in the afternoon, were nice people, but they were genuinely afraid of responsibility. So also were the respresentatives of the Deccan Sabha, headed by a nice old Parsi named Wadya. Altogether they said, " Give us the power to pass resolutions, to influence Government ; we will use it in a spirit of sweet reasonableness, but we are not fit for responsible government." And yet when anyone else argues that they are not fit, people like Jinnah say that you are insulting their nationality.

I am beginning to wonder whether I shall not modify our scheme by putting both halves of the Government into the same Chamber instead of two. However, that will be seen when we get to Delhi.

I went for an hour in the afternoon to the race meeting. It was very pleasant ; it is so nice to do these things in beautiful weather, and I investigated the inside of, and learned the mechanism of, the totalizator. It has a tremendous advantage, it seems to me. Not only is the machinery highly ingenious and almost securable against breakdown ; not only does it work here without any friction, but it has the advantage over the pari-mutuel of disclosing to the public how the betting is going. It makes it necessary to bet in ready money ; it gives the proper odds instead of odds bookmakers can afford. It destroys all the paraphernalia of bookmakers and the sordid side of racing, added to which it gives substantial profits to the Government, or in this case to War charities, and certainly has much to commend it. If only we would not at home pretend that betting did not exist or that it was curable !

Dinner was at the Byculla Club. A dinner of some one hundred people in a very pleasant building with an attractive dining-room, remarkable for the fact that it is so conservative that it has no punkahs in it, but only coolies waving fans. It was pleasant enough. I sat between the chairman, Sir John Heaton, a judge, and Mesant, the engineer of the Port Trust.

Saturday, December 27. We started this morning with an interview with the representatives of the Deccan Ryots' Association, with their demands for many forms of communal representation, and their general support of the Congress and Moslem League scheme, which did not go very far when we examined it. On the other hand, they were full of fear of a Brahman autocracy.

Then we had Rai Bahadur Dougre on behalf of the depressed classes. He was a very nice fellow, taking a great interest in the depressed classes. He is a caste Hindu, and he brought with him two untouchables, who struck me, although one did not speak English, by their extraordinary intelligence. He thinks that communal representation for them is necessary, and I believe he would make a very useful moderate man of the kind that I am looking for.

There followed Mr. Setalvad, the Vice-Chancellor of Bombay University, an extremely clever lawyer and a very nice fellow, who argued extraordinarily well. We put before him the whole of our scheme, and he has gone away to think over it, I think favourably.

After lunch we saw the Parsis, who had nothing much to say ; the Talukdars and Sardars of Gujarat, who want to be made ruling princes, and claimed that their history allows of it ; and then we had a long talk with Chandavarkar, who I think would also support us. He is a most impressive and very nice fellow, and has done splendid work for the depressed classes. I did not put to him the whole of my scheme, but I propose to do so before I leave Bombay.

Then we saw Rahimtulla, who, of course, is trembling on the verge of the Executive Council. I did not find him as clever as people say he is, but I am perfectly prepared to take their verdict in preference to my own.

In the afternoon I drove round the Port with Freeman. He is rather unhappy about our scheme, which he thinks goes too far.

In the evening there was a quiet dinner. Freeman and his wife went to a show at the theatre, and we played bridge and went to bed early.

I find that Chelmsford is a much more eager convert to my scheme than I am myself. I am a little doubtful about it, because some people really feel that they are not fit for any responsibility yet. However, I am sure it is the best going.

Friday, December 28. I have had to-day the most strenuous day I have had in Bombay. I got up early and drove with Freeman to see the Parel Institute, which I had seen five years ago. Leston is still in charge, and it is a most interesting show. It is here that all the anti-plague vaccine is made for India, and it is the biggest research laboratory that they have got. They propose to add to it eventually a Pasteur Institute. Situated in old Government House, it is now being used largely for enteric cases in order that all people who have had enteric in the Mesopotamia area can be examined to see if they are carriers of enteric. They are all, of course, convalescents, and I wandered round and talked to some of them.

Then we saw experiments being carried on with regard to bilharzia, for fear of its being imported from Egypt, but apparently at present the snails which contain the worm are not the same species, and the worms they contain have not the same results. One of these snails contains a parasite which, if put into a glass with a few fish, acts so quickly that it kills the fish in twenty minutes. We saw some experiments on guinea pigs, and some experiments that were being tried as to the best rat poison and the best form of rat trap. Leston seems to me to jump at conclusions on statistics compiled from too few experiments. You cannot tell what proportion of rat traps are good, I should have thought, from just one hundred traps ; the next one hundred might give a totally different proportion. We also saw again the fascinating performance of extracting venom from snakes by making them bite into a glass basin and then feeding them on egg flip and putting them away for a week. I cannot understand why there are not more accidents. It is only bites from Russell's viper and the cobra which can be cured, but the cure is certain if taken in time. The poison is mixed, injected into a horse, and the serum obtained from the horse is potent against either snake ; but if the serum is prepared from only one poison it is not. The Lauder Brunton tube is a very doubtful experiment. Potassium permanganate does not always act, and the wound caused by the lancet may be more poisonous than the snake bite itself.

Back late to breakfast, which we had hastily, and then dealt with various Mohammedan deputations.

The interesting part of the discussions occurred when we came face to face with the separation of Sind. The Sind

Provincial Conference, which came on behalf of the Congress Moslem League scheme, wants the abolition of the Commissioner of Sind pending the creation of a special Province. They do not want a special Province at present because of the expense. The Sind Mohammedan Association, which is conservative, wants Sind separated as soon as possible and meanwhile the Commissioner kept. It is undoubtedly true that Sind gives more funds to Bombay than Bombay gives to Sind.

A large luncheon party was the next strenuous effort. I sat next to Mrs. Egan, an American journalist, who has been to all the theatres of War, and is a great admirer of British rule and British achievements in Mesopotamia. She was even in Constantinople, and told me that all the population wanted the victory of the English at the time, and hoped we should get through to Constantinople. She told me a lot about the Philippines, in which she had lived, and said that responsible government there had been an appalling failure, and we ought to take an object-lesson from it. The backward tribes there are still administered directly by the American Bureau.

Keatinge, the Director of Agriculture, wants our scheme, and would welcome an Indian member presiding over agriculture, which amused me, as Freeman, who presides over agriculture himself, says that he could never get on if anybody but himself had that department; an Indian would be quite impossible. Keatinge struck me as very promising.

But I had a severe blow when we saw Stanley Reed[1] in the evening. Sir Stanley Reed, to whom I described my scheme in detail, objects to it altogether. He wants complete authority on all subjects by the Legislative Council, subject to the veto; my scheme would produce apathy and would not strike any imagination, and has no chance of success. The only subject he would reserve would be the police. As,

[1] Editor of the *Times of India.*

therefore, there is nothing in principle between us but the details of the A and B list, I cannot understand his vehemence, but certainly as Reed is the only progressive journalist in India his opposition is very, very sad.

In the afternoon I went to tea with Sir Sassoon David and old Shapoorji Broacha. They are two delightful old men, living very humbly. I said to Shapoorji, " Are you still in business ? " He said, " Yes, I cannot see any more, so I work." " You must be making a lot of money ? " " Yes," he replied, " all India is." Lady Willingdon tells me that whenever she asks them for money they give it. Shapoorji has put a special fund apart for assisting distressed Europeans home. He has made all his money, he said, by the kindness of the Europeans, and he wants to help them.

Then Lady Willingdon, who came to fetch me there, drove with me to see Lady Ali Shah, the mother of Aga Khan. She lives in a very nice house on the sea, and she has the most beautiful Persian china I have ever seen in my life. I am the first male that she has seen socially except Lord Willingdon. She sat very nervously, holding Lady Willingdon by both hands, but she is a dear old lady, and she and Lady Willingdon seem to be the greatest friends, kissing one another at intervals. She asked for news of her son, whom she longs to see out here. She is very fond of his son, and I cannot think why he does not bring him out. She hears from him by telegram every week, but she is quite ignorant of his serious illness. She rode down from Baghdad through Persia, taking with her, as a condition of the permission to come, bundles of leaflets which she promised to distribute, but which she burnt. Of course she is a great figure in Mesopotamia and related to the ruling people of Persia. Her courage is extraordinary. She was really most delightful to me ; presented me with a large basket of flowers, and one of those decorative necklaces of tinsel—all the old courtesies, and I enjoyed my twenty minutes there very much.

Then came Reed, whose interview I have already described, and we ended up with a dinner party on a large scale at which I sat next to Mrs. Palmer ; but overwork had at last told, and I had hastily to leave the table to avoid an impending fainting fit. However, a long night in bed has done its work, and I am all right this morning.

Saturday, December 29. This morning I did not go to the Zoo as I had intended, for my health made me think it was desirable to take it easy ; so I did nothing till I saw a certain Mr. Standen, who is the Commissioner of the Berer Division. He is in favour of territorial reorganisation of India in order to avoid linguistic difficulties and the possibility of carrying out procedure in the language of the country instead of in English. He did not absolutely turn down our scheme as it stands now, but he was in favour preferably of standing committees and an elected majority. He is a fine-looking fellow, and I rather liked him. His suggestion is for a promise of complete responsible government in thirty years, " Not in our time, O Lord."

Next came a long interview with Mr. Patel of Willingdon's Legislative Council. I must say he gave the most startling incident to show the limitations of discussion which had goaded these people into their present extreme case. A resolution in favour of support being given to the indigenous School of Medicine had not been allowed by the Bombay Government as being contrary to the public interests. On the Finance Committee he had moved fifty resolutions for the reduction of expenditure ; they were all disallowed by the Finance member on the ground that they dealt with existing services ; it was only the unallotted expenditure that they could discuss. He asked for the minutes, as he was a member of the Finance Committee. He was refused them on the ground that they might get into unauthorised hands. He attempted to move a resolution asking that discussion of the allotted expenditure might be allowed on the Finance Committee ; it was disallowed because it was not in the public interest. He brought in a Bill to allow for optional adoption of compulsory education ; it was disallowed, and so on. He is obviously the most talkative member of the Council.

Next we had Fazulbhoy Currimbhoy, a Mohammedan member of Chelmsford's Council—loquacious, a disciple of the Aga Khan's and rather like him, believing in a Second Chamber and a Royal Viceroy, and binding resolutions. He would not look at departmental work distinction, and got sulky about it. He is on the Industrial Commission.

After spending some time in dictating stuff for the mail, I had in the evening an interview with Mr. Chitale, who had very little to say ; and he was followed by old Chaubal, who was a member of the Islington Commission, and is now a member of Willingdon's Executive Council. He really asked for an interview with me because he has a pension grievance which raises quite a nice point of law. I thought he had come on reforms, and asked Chelmsford to see him with me. I found out afterwards that he was astonished to see Chelmsford, had come armed with Civil Service Regulations, etc., and came out very badly because he had obviously not read the papers on reforms. Really the Home Department has muddled this thing frightfully. The famous Marris letter, over which we quarrelled at Calcutta, is a long document which ought to have been printed plentifully and several copies sent to each local government. They only got one, and have all had to reprint it in order that their members may see it.

In the evening I dined at the Orient Club, which is the oldest Indian and English Club in India. Willingdon and I went, and there was a large gathering, mainly Indians. Chaubal presided, and I sat between him and Fazulbhoy Currimbhoy. My health was proposed in a read speech by

Chaubal, marred by a vehement attack upon the Byculla Club for not admitting Indian guests to its dinner the other night. Chaubal had been asked to entertain Basu, as he could not come. I chaffed English and Indians on their respective views of me; held up the *Bombay Chronicle* to ridicule for stating that the public had been disappointed at my refusal to go to the races; and ended up with a plea for the settlement of this matter by co-operation between all races. I paid a tribute to Chelmsford and a warm one to Willingdon, who received a perfect ovation. It was all most successful, and I was rather flattered to receive a request from the Committee to become an honorary member of the Club. I have also agreed to become a life member of the Willingdon Sports Club.

After dinner I played bridge with Sir Ibrahim Rahimtoolah, Sir Fazulbhoy Currimbhoy, and Sir Jamsetjee Jejeebhoy, hot stuff I can tell you. Old Rahimtoolah plays marvellously well. We ended the evening, after enjoying ourselves very much, three rupees to the good. What a pity it is that this kind of thing cannot be done more often. You could not have wanted a better game of bridge, and they were extremely nice.

Sunday, December 30. On Sunday morning I went with Willingdon and Cadell to the Zoo. I would say that Bombay Zoo ranks among the best of the fifth-rate Zoos. This is not a difficult achievement. You want a nice park or garden, which they certainly have here, and the stock animals—lions, tigers, elephants, bears, hyenas, etc., etc., well caged and decently looked after. The trouble is that here at the Zoo there is nobody with any scientific knowledge, and no effort is made to collect either local or foreign rarer and more interesting specimens of animals.

I went to see Lady Willingdon's home for crippled soldiers, which is extraordinarily good; the men are learning carpentering, chicken rearing, and so forth. She was told that they would not live together because of caste difficulties, and she has found it all nonsense. I think we make of caste more than we need and do not attempt to solve it ; but I am appalled by the small scale upon which these things are being done for the vast number of Indian soldiers. I must return to the charge on this.

I worked hard at the mail, but at 12.15 Charles Roberts came to see me to bring to my attention the annoyance of Willingdon's Executive Council at not having been consulted or sent for by us. I explained to him that I thought neither the local governments nor the Government of India had any *locus standi* formally ; I was consulting as to what the Cabinet should do, and I did not wish them to be bound by anything.

There was a vast luncheon party, and, feeling slack, I got permission to lunch alone in my room. After lunch, Sir Sydney Rowlatt, whom I had asked to come out to consider internees and policy with regard to them after the War, who arrived by yesterday's mail, came to see me. He had been lunching here. He arrived to find it was a holiday ; he had no money ; nobody had met him from the Home Department ; no provision had been made to engage rooms for him or to find him a servant. I was really very, very angry. He tells me that he had not been allowed to join the mail at Marseilles, that he had come all the way from London by sea, and had been forty-one days on the water. But he was in very good spirits, and is a very nice fellow. He looked miles better than when I saw him in London. I explained to him that government by means of internment and police was naturally a delightful method which built up only trouble probably for our successors, and that I hoped he would remember what was parliamentarily defensible in listening to the plan which had been prepared for him by the Government out here.

After lunch we went in the launch "Diamond" to the

Elephanta Caves, a forty minutes sea journey, interesting because we passed one of the new American standard ships, a large four-masted animal which had run on to a reef on its way down from Karachi. We arrived at the island and had to walk about two hundred yards along a narrow stone causeway with intervals between the stones. My head played me very false, and I have never had a much more agonising experience, and I was haunted on the island by the danger of getting back again. The Elephanta Caves are interesting on a small scale, with very nice carvings in the rock of the life of Shiva. I particularly liked that Shiva who cut his wife into fifty-two pieces, only to discover that he had fifty-two wives! This is really what happens to the Government of India when it interns Mrs. Besant.

I came home, did a little more mail, found that Chelmsford had become a fervent believer in the development of my scheme, so has Willingdon, so has Donoughmore, so has Duke. I do not like it as well as my first scheme.

A small dinner party—all men. I sat next to Rowlatt, and discussed people we knew, and the seriousness of the poor lawyers we were getting out here. After dinner, Chelmsford, Donoughmore, Willingdon and I had quite a merry game of bridge, and then to bed.

Monday, December 31. This morning Basu came to breakfast. He is full of a scheme for Second Chambers in the Local Legislative Councils. I am a little afraid this is top heavy and will be found awkward in the future, but he has promised to submit it in writing.

Then we had a deputation from the Chamber of Commerce, which read an extremely good conservative address. The English in Bombay are far more sensible than any other English we have met.

After this deputation we received some of the members of the deputation at an interview, which was very amicable;

and then we saw the European Association Branch, headed by Wardlaw Milne, to whose enterprise in cornering steel plates at the beginning of the War is due the capacity for repairing ships in Bombay. They presented an extraordinarily good address, with most of which I am in thorough agreement. They are anxious to make the civil servants administrators and not politicians, and they would make it necessary for a civil servant who got further than the chief secretaryship to dissociate himself from the Civil Service. They are not opposed to the Curtis scheme. They did not like official majorities. They want all official positions thrown open to everybody in India, and the removal of colour bars. I talked about clubs, and they say there is a movement on foot to allow Indian guests, but it will be very long in becoming successful. They agreed that social discontent was at the bottom of most of this. They do not like the idea of doing away with the statutory disqualification of a man connected with a business becoming a member of an Executive Council. They think it would be possible to get a boxwallah on the eve of going back for a short term. It was a most useful talk, and they promised assistance in the formation of a moderate party.

Afterwards I went to lunch with Chaubal at his house in the centre of the Indian part of the town.

I came back after lunch, and we had three interviews, about which I protested to Willingdon—two men from a district who could hardly speak English and had nothing to say, and a Mohammedan holy man, who spoke through an interpreter, and also had nothing to say.

Then I went with Willingdon to see the Gaekwar of Baroda and the Maharani. They are living in a house belonging to the Nizam, having lent their house as a hospital, which the Maharani much resents. They were suffering from colds and were very snuffy. The Gaekwar quite agrees that the princes must come in very cautiously or they will get left.

Back again to an interview with Shapoorji Broacha, with whom I discussed War Loan. I am quite sure that Meyer is wrong in thinking that you could not raise War Loan if you advertised it and appealed, short term securities. I have suggested the scheme of taking Treasury bills in part payment if cash was produced also. Broacha wants a War profits tax. Chelmsford says it is impossible with the existing machinery in India, and that he has thoroughly thrashed it out. I think it is a pity, as it would give money for the reduction of taxation after the War. Then we had a long interview with Chitnavis, who is a conservative, but has signed progressive schemes. I thought he lacked courage.

In the evening I dined with E. M. Cook, accounting officer, who has been in the U.P. Civil Service. Gubbay[1] and Kisch were staying there. The only other members of the party were Birkett, the commercial man who has been Sheriff of Bombay, and had a great deal to do with the success of the War Loan, and Mrs. Cook. We discussed Cambridge together; currency, finance, War Loan; and Gubbay and I at one period tried to see how much of our Greek and Latin repetition that we had learned at school we could remember. I was rather pleased to find that I had remembered almost the whole of the first piece of the book. Birkett, I knew, was being knighted on New Year's Day. I congratulated him as I left, but he took no notice of my congratulations and did not understand them. I discovered the next day that in India nobody is told of the fate in store for them until it is published in the papers.

Tuesday, January 1. New Year's Day. We start the New Year with the usual uninterrupted sunshine, but in the middle of gloomy War news. I cannot help thinking that everything seems to me to show the likelihood of the War petering out now that Russia has set the example. I hope it may not be so, but once people begin to negotiate

[1] M. M. S. Gubbay, C.I.E. (Controller of Currency).

with anybody the example may be infectious. Shoals of telegrams, presents of fruit, New Year's greetings! The presents of fruit in Bombay are particularly welcome because of the delicious mangoes, a large red plantain, which out here is exquisite, and a peculiar small potato sapodilla looking fruit with a hard brown skin and four black pips, which I believe is called a chiku. Any one of these three when really good is, to my mind, much preferable to the highly-vaunted mangostine which we had at Madras.

We spent the morning with the Central Provinces deputations and representatives of the deputations. The addresses are worthy of note, for they go into detail of constituencies and localities, departments, and all the rest of it, and show very careful thought. One paragraph which appears in many of the addresses, clearly there by accident, is this: "The Provincial Council should possess all powers of legislation and control over matters relating to provincial administration, except the direction of military affairs, or foreign relations, the declaration of War, the making of peace, and the entering into treaties other than commercial treaties." This is a most curious provision, both in its differentiation of treaties from commercial treaties and in the description of these as affairs of provincial administration. There is also in nearly all these addresses a demand for an Indian Judicial Privy Council. This seems to me absurd, as the Privy Council could never be equal to the English one. It is not in the Privy Council that Indian legal delays occur, but in the preparation of the cases for it. A long scheme of dissent by Dr. Pandit, Vice-Chairman of the District Council of Nagpur, is included, also very carefully worked out, with a very complicated constitution.

Perhaps the best of the addresses came from the Central Provinces and Berar Graduates' Association, which went into details of local self-government and the Indianisation of the public services. The position of Berar is very peculiar.

Leased in perpetuity from the Nizam, it is not British territory, and laws made in British territory have to be applied by ordinance to Berar. The Berar people feel this very strongly and want the law altered, a new treaty made, or complete separation from the Central Provinces. Their position is certainly anomalous, and this matter must be subsequently considered.

Note : This dissent of Pandit's and the address to which I have just referred ought to be considered at Delhi. I think somebody ought to go through all the addresses before we start on the final lap to see what is worth re-consideration.

At 12.15 we had an interview with a man called Muhammad Amin, a retired district judge. He has written a very good letter to the Mohammedans of the Central Provinces, but in the interview he was not much good. He had one monstrous phrase, in which he said that local governments should prepare a list of all occasions on which Indians were killed, wounded, or injured by soldiers during the year. He founded this monstrous proposal on one case.

Before breakfast I had dictated a letter to Chelmsford which includes the only extant authoritative draft of the latest scheme. I breakfasted with Roberts, and talked to him about his two-Chamber provincial scheme, which I think makes it top heavy.

After lunch, which I had in my room, and which was the quickest lunch I have ever had, taking only five minutes, I went with Halliday and Laverton to the Bombay Natural History Society's premises over the top of Phipson's, the wine merchants, and was received by Millard and the Committee, including the Maharao of Cutch, very pleased with himself on his New Year's honour. They have done wonderfully well in their mammal survey, and have got a multitude of new species. Their squirrel varieties, showing variations of colouration on different banks of the same river and different distances, sometimes only twenty miles, in Burma, were particularly interesting; also some of their flying squirrels, rats and mice. They have also got some very interesting birds from Mesopotamia, including the large heron, which Maude found, one of them being alive at the Zoo, rather like a giant purple heron. This is the best scientific work now being done in India. They will have to have a good museum built for them, for their collections are getting very large, and they will have to be assisted by the Government after the War, but they must maintain their liberty. The mammal survey is practically at a standstill because of the War. They have got one Indian collector out who is becoming very skilled at skinning and preserving. They have a few interesting live animals, including a most attractive white lory, who woke up and dealt with an enormous beetle which was given him alive, and there was a tremendous tussle for twenty minutes, as he began to eat it from the tail end. The old giant hornbill which I saw five years ago is still alive. He has now been here for twenty-five years in a small cage without a broken feather. He has lost his eyesight, and can no longer catch with his marvellous accuracy from across the room or even close. But he looks most awfully well and has got rather savage. He opens the oil gland on his back every morning and dresses his yellow feathers with the oil from the gland.

I came back at half-past two and talked to the representatives of the Central Provinces and Berar Graduates' Association. They did not mind dyarchy, but did not like it.

At four o'clock I went to the races with Willingdon. It was a very pleasant break, and I saw heaps of people, and enjoyed it.

I came back at six, and we had a talk with Mudholkar, who has an interesting memorandum which ought to be considered at Delhi. He has gone in for dyarchy whole-heartedly, and would approve my scheme—not the new one, which I did not put to him, but the one which held the field till then. He will be a good man for the conference at Delhi.

He was followed by Khaparde, Tilak's right-hand man, pleasant to talk to, but not much use. He has just been returned to the Legislative Council at an election, at which he won by eight votes to six. Could representative institutions ever show a greater mockery!

After that, the last dinner party here. These dinner parties are a severe trial, although they are better at Bombay than anywhere else. I sat next to Lady Willingdon and Lady Petit, the Parsi lady whose daughter is the object of Jinnah's affections. Late at night I read to Willingdon and Donoughmore my letter to Chelmsford, with their general approval. I have here to record that as Khaparde left the room Chelmsford and I shook hands and almost danced for joy. This was the last of the formal interviews; the evidence is at an end. It has been most useful.

Wednesday, January 2. I got up early, in accordance with pre-arrangement, and went down to Willingdon's room, where I explained the latest scheme to Setalwad, Chandarvaka and Rahimtoolah. To my astonishment they all liked it. I cannot see that it is so very different from the old scheme. It gives six years' preparation, and it throws the onus of reserved subjects on the new responsible government who want to reserve instead of on the people who want to obtain control; but these three gentlemen assured me that it would commend itself to 90 per cent. of the people of India.

After they had gone we had Stanley Reed to breakfast. He assured me that the new scheme was a scheme into which he could go heart and soul. In the middle of breakfast Chelmsford sent for me by a letter, in which he complained that I had broken my string, and asked what these secret conclaves were. I looked very sulky and forbidding, and therefore instead of protesting he said he was so glad to think, because I should do so much better with them, that I was seeing these people alone. I told him that I had already explained to him that I was going to see Reed and Setalwad again, and I had not had time to do it until this last day in Bombay, when, unfortunately, he was going away. I went back to Reed, who is really delighted with the scheme. We discussed the necessity of distinguishing in India between administration and politics. He agrees that civil servants must defend themselves, and that if a civil servant becomes more than a chief secretary, he should regard himself not as an official but as a politician.

After breakfast, and after we had seen Chelmsford off in his motor, I was privileged to meet Curtis, Carmichael, Chaubal and Willingdon, in fact the whole Government of Bombay. I threw myself with great keenness into a long harangue, in which I explained the two schemes, the reasons underlying them, and why we wanted to back the local governments against the Government of India. Chaubal, who had damned the old scheme, now preferred it to the new one, and said he had not understood it before. To my surprise Carmichael and Curtis took the same view. This is most interesting, and I was delighted, for I still like the old scheme better. Willingdon is very amused and rather down in the mouth about it. Curtis wants to keep on with local government, but is in frightful difficulty about communal representation on local bodies, which is a very hard nut to crack. We must discuss this at Delhi. I am afraid Carmichael thinks we are going very quickly, but I harangued about the landslide I feared in Europe. Will India stand a chance of moderation if Ukrania and Palestine have it all their own way?

The *Bombay Chronicle* had an article this morning asking me to drive to the station in an open motor car, so I did, but I am afraid I cannot flatter myself that the crowds recognised me. So ends Bombay. I leave with great admiration for the personality and character of Willingdon, and for the thorough energy and success of Lady Willingdon. She has done the thing most awfully well whilst we have been there. She is idolised by the people, and her work, her War work particularly, has been amazing.

Our train is very comfortable. We were properly seen off and guarded at the station. Bombay has been a great success, and is far the happiest and most progressive part of India, in which we ought to be able to go much farther than anywhere else. I feel happier. I am pleased with Chelmsford. It really looks as if only the Government of India is the stumbling block. I am pleased with Meston's contribution to the financial situation, and I am pleased with Bombay. I do not much mind the new scheme. I have been asleep most of the afternoon, and, awaking invigorated, a new idea for the Government of India has occurred to me. Why not abolish the Legislative Council, and have a Legislative Assembly consisting of ten delegates from every provincial council, who can pass such laws as they like and such resolutions as they like, the members of the Government attending their sittings to endeavour to get Bills through and to answer questions and to make speeches? Let us, then, have an Indian Privy Council nominated for life, the Privy Council to consist of the Viceroy's Executive Council and worthies and representative Indians, the Governor to have the power to pass Ordinances through the Privy Council, and no legislation shall have the force of law until ratified by the Privy Council. Princes might easily be members of the Privy Council and summoned to it. This is fluid, and has not the formality of a Second Chamber. I must cogitate upon this at Gwalior.

VI

GWALIOR

Thursday, January 3. I must jot down a few notes in order to keep my record complete. As I have said, we left Bombay at quarter-past one on January 2, after the exciting morning I have described. We lunched immediately. Sleep most of the afternoon, then some work. I read Vincent and Charles Roberts' memos over again; finished my diary of Bombay; revised the letter to Chelmsford, and had a long talk with Willingdon and Donoughmore; then dinner. The dining saloon, of course, was not so comfortable as Chelmsford's, and the food not so good, but it was a very decent meal, after which Donoughmore, Crerar, Willingdon and I played bridge in my saloon. At 11 o'clock I went to bed, leaving them stranded through the impracticability of getting back home owing to Lady Willingdon's bedroom and that of her maid intervening. I heard afterwards that they had to wait till after 12. I slept soundly. This morning I lay in bed, read a novel, thought, and did no work. After lunch I signed the Chelmsford letter and dictated comments on Roberts and Vincent. We arrived at Gwalior at four o'clock, and were met at the station by certain notabilities, headed by Gwalior. We drove through his glorious gardens to his enormous palace, an Indian-Italian structure built by his father and furnished amazingly. The staircase has glass banisters, with a wooden balustrade, glass pendants hanging underneath the staircase. The drawing-room is of enormous size, with a vaulted roof and two of the biggest glass chandeliers I ever saw, each with 380 lamps. Photographs and pictures of tigers, etc., Kings, Viceroys, Gwaliors, decorate the rooms. My own apartment consists of an enormous drawing-room, a dark and comfortable bedroom, and a bright, cheerful dressing-room, with bath-room, hall, and so forth. The bedroom has the softest carpet I have ever seen—white and padded ; and the large drawing-room of the palace has the largest carpet I have ever seen, quite pretty, made specially for it. The avenue outside, with its clipped trees, if it was not for the palm trees, is very English. Everywhere are cigarette boxes in the form of motor cars or aeroplanes, or a stork to lift the cigarettes out. On the dining-table is an electric pump working a fountain. One has often been inclined to wonder what becomes of this sort of ingenuity when one sees them at jewellers or bazaars, or Maples, or Drews, and so forth, and the answer seems to be that they all go to the Indian princes.

After tea, at which Gwalior was obviously very nervous, we drove to the Fort—rather hair-raising, because old Gwalior insisted upon driving his own car, always missed the gears, and stopped his engine. This happened four or five times up steep hills, and was sufficiently alarming to be exciting. However, we got to the Fort, which well repays a second visit. There is some beautiful stone carving of the 17th century in the old palace at the top ; there are some very interesting large stone idols cut in the rock ; there are some nice Jain temples ; there is a well-developed Sirdar school ; there are curious relics, such as a fives court of the British occupation, and the Sirdar school is really the old barracks. Lastly, there is the most glorious view almost in the world, right across the plains of Gwalior, from this great rock, with its Fort three miles in circumference. The palace looked most impressive, surrounded by green trees, and so did the new town. Gwalior is building an industrial city on the site of the old town, so that the old town will fill up again. He has got an oil mill, a cotton factory ; he is going to have a big power station, and one of the things he particularly wishes to do is to make machinery for all the mills in India. He is a very progressive and enthusiastic man, and I think must have made a lot of money during the War, as he is a large shareholder in Tata's and a number of other companies. He has a brick kiln in Bombay, which he says is paying him 12 per cent. He pointed out one part of his town, which he is going to lay out on garden city principles. The new town, which we drove through on the way back, is very imposing, with some very fine buildings, but some of the suburbs are regrettably squalid. I do not think one realises or can ever possibly get at life in a Native State whilst one stays with the prince. There seems to me to be a great deal more servility here than in any State I have been in. Everybody spends all his time in our presence bent to the ground.

In the evening there was a quiet dinner party, followed by bridge. Donoughmore talked, Scindia played Slippery Jane, and his crowing laugh rang out at frequent intervals through the drawing-room. Then bed, but not sleep, for I had to read a paper by Carmichael that Willingdon had given me, which is really a Brunyate scheme, except that the lump sum contribution is taken in the shape of a fixed half of the present land revenue, or a fixed proportion of the present land revenue, leaving all the expansion to the Provinces. I do not see much point in this, and it is not so good as Meston's, but still it is another financial scheme by an expert.

Then I read some papers of Scindia's. He has gone for a Prince's Chamber.

Friday, January 4. Breakfast at nine, and the start for the scene of slaughter at quarter to eleven. Twenty miles drive through typical Gwalior country, along dusty roads, with sparse bushes in the sandy and rocky desert. No wonder that it is a good country for tigers, because a tiger, wandering round this detestable and appalling country, finds a beautiful ravine, with water in it, luxuriant, with trees and thick jungle, and remains there ; so you know where to look for him. We got to our meeting place, where there were horses and three

GWALIOR
Passage leading to tower from which the tiger shoot took place

[*To face page* 168

elephants with howdahs to ride, a dandy in which anybody could be carried who wished it, a whole group of coolies, and a regiment of 400 soldiers to beat. I got on to an elephant and was hurtled over the rocks for about one and a half miles —a very uncomfortable elephant to sit on. Then we got down and walked on tiptoe into the ravine. Right across this ravine stretches a high wall, or rather two high walls, with a passage down in the ravine between them. In the very bottom of this ravine on the wall is a three-storied tower, at the top of which, sheltered partly by a stone awning, sit the guns. The middle story is occupied by a luncheon-room, and the lower story by a sort of cellar. Beyond the tower comes an interruption, and then a smaller wall going up the other side. We got into the tower very quietly and stood whilst the beat came up to us from the shorter side of the ravine. It came quietly, making no noise, and there was no tiger. Nothing appeared, save one peacock and some squirrels. Then we turned round and faced the other way. This time a longer drive took place, accompanied by what the Indians call—a name which we have borrowed—a hullabaloo. Tomtoms beat ; there were great shouts and dreadful noises, so that the tiger should start a long way off and come quietly. Nothing had apparently been expected from the first drive ; from the second drive great things were hoped for, because a buffalo had been killed on the top and dragged by the tiger down to the valley. It was not long after the beat started before, right in the middle of the ravine, and by some water, I saw the tiger coming out, walking very slowly, about 60 yards away from me—walking towards me, showing his left side at an angle of 45 degrees. I aimed as carefully as my excitement would let me, and had the satisfaction of seeing the tiger sit down on his hind legs, put his head right up, and then roll right over. Before I could get in another shot, however, he was off, crawling lop-sidedly, and leaving behind much blood. The beat was then stopped ; the elephants were obtained, but nobody was allowed to go on them because they were notoriously unsteady, and there were reported to be bees in the jungle. They soon sighted the tiger going back towards the beaters. These were then removed, and Gwalior went round to join the beaters. What happened afterwards took almost till dark, but I gather that the tiger was seen crossing a ride towards us, turned by a shot by one of Gwalior's staff, which missed it. He is not popular for this. He then charged an elephant which was sent for in the middle of the beat. The elephant bolted, and has not been seen since, but a man on the elephant, who was much hurt in the flight, succeeded in getting two shots at it, one of which hit it. It then, now severely wounded, charged a man, and I fear hurt him, but not badly, and was finally despatched lying in some water. It is a fine male tiger, 9 ft. 5 in. long, with a short tail. I do not know how one ought to have dealt with the matter ; certainly things were much bungled after the tiger was wounded, I think because of the extraordinary, almost impenetrable, nature of the jungle and the fact that we had no tracker. However, I looked at its body. No shot could have been better than mine ; it hit the tiger in exactly the right place. I cannot think why it did not kill it. I am not at all sure that I am happy about Laverton's split bullets. However, the day was successful. I cannot help thinking about the man, about whom I am sure everything is all right.

We came home thoroughly tired with excitement ; could hardly keep awake for dinner, and went to bed immediately afterwards, where I slept from ten to six without moving, a great deal for me.

When they came after the tiger, throwing at it hand grenades, firing blank cartridges, and so forth, in order to move it and prevent it charging back, flying foxes were disturbed from the trees, peacocks moved backwards and forwards, parrots flew about ; four sambhur passed before my first shot at the tiger, but I am afraid I did not see them. It is a very artificial form of sport, but it gave me sufficient thrill to last me a lifetime.

Saturday, January 5. Apparently the shot which I fired had hit him exactly in the right place and would certainly have killed him eventually, but the bullet, being split, broke up into small pieces, and had not penetrated the heart.

We motored off this morning about twelve miles to a place called Kulaith. Here we found the same paraphernalia of beaters and coolies, luncheon and refreshments, elephants and horses. I walked to the place, a distance of about one and a half miles ; saw nothing but a few partridges. We first put Willingdon, Studd[1] and Crerar into a machan built of bamboo poles with a charpoy at the top, and then went on a little farther, not much more than 100 yards from them, where we had a slightly more solid erection with an awning over it built of old railway lines. Here we stayed for three hours during a very long beat of about seven miles. The nullah was better wooded and wider than yesterday's, and although some of the guns saw some sambhur, one apparently a good stag, and some hares, I saw no living thing. The tiger apparently had got out of the beat, and we came home early, after a very enjoyable blank day.

We drove then to the prison, where we saw the interesting operation of weaving carpets, one man singing out the pattern and the colour to two looms. The carpets are quite nice and the colours very good ; design also good. Every man with a sentence of more than two years is taught to make carpets, and they wove in the jail here the wonderful carpet for the big Durbar Hall of the palace.

Then on to the State Pottery Works, where things are done very well, but, as usual in these things, there is no sign of artistic taste at all, and everything but domestic ware is hideously ugly.

[1] A.D.C. to Lord Willingdon.

Then to the machinery shops, where they are building railway wagons and carriages, and so forth ; on to the Club, quite a nice building, built by Scindia for his subjects ; then to his little suburban house on the river. The garden here is superb, the luxury great, the situation along the river bank adorable. If only one had this climate, this money, these situations and opportunities, with labour and materials plentiful, what beautiful things people could make, but here, as usual, toys are rampant. The Maharaja has made the windows of his bungalow out of his old discarded photographic negatives.

After this we went home. The better news from Russia is very inspiring, and I had a telegram from home saying that the King had sanctioned Rahintoolah. Then followed a banquet. I sat between Lady Willingdon and Lady Ahmed Khan, who is an Englishwoman.

Ahmed Khan was a brother of Aftab Khan on my Council, and married two sisters, one after the other. There were about fifty people to dinner in the dungeon-like dining-room. We entered dinner to a harmonium played mechanically ; the band played outside ; fife and drum bands, first of small boys, the children's band, and then the men's band marched round the table ; the railway train, worked electrically, went round the table. It was a curious mixture. Scindia proposed my health very suddenly, and read a few well-chosen words. I had to respond, and although I did nothing wrong, I cannot consider it a great success. Then bridge, and bed. I played bridge with Willingdon, Donoughmore and a doctor at the Hospital, an Indian, who played quite well.

The man who was mauled by the tiger is still very feverish and the wound is septic, but he is making a fight for it, and I think will be all right.

Sunday, January 6. I saw Dr. Rigby, who had been in consultation with the doctor about the man who was mauled.

He tells me that everything is going well, and that there is very little anxiety. I hope he is right, for these are the horrible parts of this game. I am bound to say that I think they were rather careless, after they knew the tiger was wounded, in the way they pushed the beaters on, although they did the proper thing in stopping them for a moment. It was mainly due to the fact that none of the elephants were steady.

Willingdon went to church in the morning to the intercession service, and the Maharaja came to see me. I am full of sympathy for poor Scindia, who comes back from Delhi crying bitterly. He has lost his friend Hardinge. No one can get much sympathy from Chelmsford, and Bosanquet[1] seems to treat him very badly indeed.

After breakfast we motored off a few miles to Rampur, a long, very narrow gully with steep cliffs on either side. We sat on the top of these cliffs at a fork in the valley, amid the most beautiful scenery imaginable—a flat, dry plain, and then this deep cleft full of trees, with open spaces in it. Scindia had gone on ahead, and had made sure, he said, that the tiger was in the beat. Donoughmore and Willingdon were placed in the positions of advantage. It was a long beat, as many side valleys had to be explored. The kill was only about 200 yards from us. At one time a pig appeared on the opposite bank and ran along the top; partridges moved about. It was great fun not sitting on a tower. The temperature was beautiful. A thoroughly happy three hours. The tiger was very loath to come forward. We heard him give tongue two or three times, which is very rare. The beaters began to yell; he moved 100 yards and then stopped. He appeared in front of Donoughmore at quite a slow trot, but the poor fellow missed him twice. I felt very sorry for him. I am sure I should have done the same. Willingdon jumped to his feet and made a most excellent shot, almost straight below him. The tiger moved forward into some bushes, and was lost. We threw stones at him; heaps of people

[1] O. V. Bosanquet, C.S.I., C.I.E. (A.G.G. Central India).

said they could see him, and finally the elephants were made to come along. They were most reluctant to approach, but the tiger was soon found dead. Everybody was very happy except Donoughmore. It was an enormous tiger, 10 ft. 1½ in. long, and was probably an old beast.

We came home, and as I was rather tired I went to sleep. Just before dinner I received a present from the Maharani in the shape of some Gwalior-made fabric to take to my wife, and Willingdon and I were permitted to go and see the Maharani. It was a new part of the palace, luxuriantly and hideously furnished. We were taken up to a blind, on the other side of which were seated Lady Willingdon, the Maharaja, Gwalior's mother and his two wives. We could see nothing, they could see everything, and I must say it was a most embarrassing situation. We said some perfunctory things, got a laugh or two, and went away.

A small dinner party and a last rubber of bridge, and I left with genuine regret. Scindia is one of the best fellows I know, and none of the treatment he has received makes any difference to his loyalty, but it is astonishing that wherever one traces the hand of the Government of India one sees these absurd personal questions. Scindia told me this morning that once when he was in Delhi he was severely reprimanded for taking his pugaree off after the Viceroy had left. He is not allowed to appear at dinner without his head cover. This, he says, is quite right, because in the presence of his superiors an Indian ought to have his head covered, but why does this not apply to British Indians like Sankaran Nair and only to Indian princes? He says that now whenever somebody like Chelmsford, or a Governor, or myself, comes to shoot with him he has to wear a pugaree to shoot in, although he risks sunstroke by doing so. We live and learn.

Scindia's knowledge of tigers must be unique. He has seen about 700 killed, and really he works it extraordinarily well. It is no easy matter to mark down a tiger in the cold weather. As a rule, when people come early he begins to feed for them about the beginning of December, first one kill a month, then one a fortnight, then six a month. You must not overfeed your tiger, or he won't play straight. Sometimes the tiger, for instance the one that we got this morning, has to be driven into a convenient nullah by disturbing him with sticks and stones a few nights previously in another nullah. He tells me that on a watch tower he saw the eight tigers which Hardinge got in one day killing their buffaloes, the first at twenty minutes past four. Four tigers appeared in Gwalior City last year. One he killed actually in the palace grounds.

I return to Delhi much better for my holiday, with my brain much clearer ; and a new idea has struck me for the Government of India. You might abolish the Legislative Council altogether. Keep it as it is for five years, but when the responsible Governments begin to come in the Provinces cause the Legislative Council of the Government of India to disappear, and have instead a sort of Bundesrath containing delegates appointed by each Government and the Native States. Scindia's own plan for the princes is merely an arbitration court consisting of six princes, a judge, and a political officer. I do not care for this myself ; you want something more than that.

VII

DELHI III—BHARATPUR I—DELHI IV

Thursday, *January* 10. I have not been able to put down anything of the events of the past three days, for they yield to none in their harassing nature, in the perplexities which they have produced, and the profound depression which they have caused. I recorded that before I left Bombay I had thought of a new expedient which had been put to Rahimtoolah, Satalwad, Chandarvarka, and Stanley Reed, and had gained their enthusiasm ; that I had put it to them after putting it quite casually that morning to Chelmsford, who accepted it, and to Willingdon, who delighted in it ; and Donoughmore and Duke were, in my opinion, not adverse. It was, to my mind, so like the old scheme that I could not conceive why men who had condemned the old scheme as useless were willing to accept this scheme, and I often pointed this out to Chelmsford, the sole difference being that at the end of the six years probationary period in the new scheme the presumption was, and was stated to be, in favour of responsible government. The Statutory Commission would have power to reserve subjects if the local government proved it was necessary to reserve them, the onus of proof lying on the local government. That was the difference, and I admitted that it was a substantial difference, but it was of the essence of my scheme. When on Monday morning I arrived at Delhi, to be met at the station by the faithful Hailey, I received a very welcome letter from Chelmsford in answer to the one I sent him from Gwalior station. It was a very satisfactory letter, full of friendship, and contained the welcome news that he had put our new plan to every member of his Council and that they had all accepted it without demur, and were prepared to suggest amendments on detail. As regards the Upper Chamber of the Government of India, he said that his Government were prepared to meet me because they saw the force of my argument, and I should not find them intransigent. This was extraordinarily good news, and I read it to Donoughmore on the way up, who remarked characteristically: "There must be something wrong with the scheme."

In the morning we had a long conference together, because my colleagues as a body had not heard the new scheme. We discussed it rather preliminarily, and agreed that it must be put in writing before coming to any decision. Accordingly, I promised to circulate to them an abstract from my letter to the Viceroy, together with a paper by Roberts in favour of a Second Chamber in the Legislative Councils; one by Basu, and one by Sir William Vincent. We were all united, I think, against Sir William Vincent in his views, particularly in his belief that the Government of India will still be able to keep a directing hand over the Provinces.

In the early morning, before our conference, I saw Chelmsford, who said that Meyer wished us to meet as individuals when we first met the Government of India, so that everybody was free to talk as they liked. To this I gladly assented, and we decided to meet the Government of India as individuals at half-past ten on Wednesday morning.

In the afternoon I saw Ramaswami Aiyar, who happened to be in Delhi. He told me that he had become Secretary of the Congress, and so wielded considerable influence. I put before him my new scheme, which he approved so far as he could understand it, but he explained that it was absolutely essential to get on my side Sankaran Nair, who wielded more influence than any other Indian.

After a game of tennis I saw Sir George Barnes, and we discussed together industrial expansion in India, and the difficult question of Colonial immigration to replace indentured labour in the Crown Colonies. The Indians absolutely refuse to look at Islington's conference scheme, because, I think, they are impressed by a belief that to import Indians as coolies stigmatises as inferior the whole of their race. However, a conference is to be arranged at which Seton is to be interviewed by the Indians who object to the scheme. Barnes was most friendly, and said what a pleasure it was to all of them that the Viceroy and I were so thoroughly in agreement.

The next morning we had another conference, and then it was found that there was a great difference of opinion among us. Roberts is very keen on a Second Chamber in the Provinces ; Duke wants it also ; so do Vincent, Seton and Kisch. Donoughmore and I are hotly opposed to it. Splendid fellow, Donoughmore ; he backs me all the way through, and is becoming a fine Radical. We are going to have some amusement out of this matter, I think, because they are all anxious for Second Chambers, but some of them want it with an official majority, or a very heavy official vote, and others do not, so it is not the same thing really that they want, although they think it is. Apart from this, we are all more or less in agreement, and nothing was disclosed, either in the morning or the afternoon—for we sat both—to vary this.

In the evening, however, the whole glorious atmosphere was suddenly dissipated. Chelmsford has put before his colleagues my new scheme without disclosing to them at all the fact that the onus was admitted and the presumption was in favour of responsible government ; in other words, he presented it to them as though it were a mere question of postponing the evil day for six years. No wonder they accepted it ! I cannot understand it. It is not as though he only had it verbally, because my letter sent to him at Gwalior clearly states it. He cannot have supposed that a scheme which did not command the enthusiasm of anybody pleased

Ramaswami Aiyar, Stanley Reed, and the three Bombay men simply because the evil day is postponed six years. Not to have mentioned this vital fact is absolutely inexplicable. He hinted it to me at the tennis court, and told me about it again in the evening. I had a talk with Maffey, who himself could not understand it, and I felt very, very depressed. Another foolish thing he has done—he has talked about the scheme to all his colleagues except Nair. He did not commit himself because he had not seen it in writing, but so far as I could gather he was not opposed to the scheme, although he wished that the power of Ordinance should be reserved only to things necessary for the maintenance of peace.

I went to bed feeling very depressed, and in the morning went and confronted the Government of India. They were all round a table, and we sat from half-past ten till twenty-five minutes to two. I made my case, and answered some very crucial questions by Meyer, who was very clever and not at all intractable. It went all round the table. There looked to be a considerable Second Chamber feeling, although we were not really discussing that, but they were all opposed to the change of the onus of proof. What strikes me as so curious is that they object to the statement that their powers shall be transferred unless the Statutory Commission has it proved that they should not be transferred. That they object to, and yet they admit in argument that it is quite true that those who object to transferring ought to be the plaintiffs before the Commission. Well, I am perfectly certain that there is not much difference except in wording, if they are genuine in this latter admission. For instance, I do not mind saying that the Committee may reserve such as they are satisfied ought to be reserved instead of saying shall transfer unless they are satisfied, because they cannot reserve if they are not satisfied under either wording, and if they cannot reserve they have got to transfer. But what a terrible tragedy it is that men are so timid as to refuse to commit themselves to such wording as will make the scheme acceptable ! Indeed, if I am going to be beaten on this subject, I am going back to the other scheme. There is no public for it, but it is sound ; there is no argument in favour of it on the ground of tickling public opinion, but it is sound, and I am not going to be tricked, as I have been tricked, into accepting something which merely means six years delay.

In the afternoon we tried to reach a compromise, but I do not think we succeeded. We had some more talk of a Second Chamber.

It was interesting at the morning meeting to see the difference between the men. Claude Hill was easily bullied ; the Commander-in-Chief said nothing, of course ; Lowndes was very vigorous and lawyer-like, and very strong in his opposition to the statement of the onus ; Sankaran Nair was frightfully quarrelsome, vilely mannered, and obviously out to wreck ; Basu, in short, was unintelligible. Lowndes, in particular, does not want to alarm public opinion by what is " eyewash," because he says that you do not intend them to get to responsible government in six years. My answer is : " I certainly do so far as Bombay is concerned." Lowndes only wants Ordinances to last for the period of the new Council, and he and Meyer both suggest that it should be passed in a sort of Privy Council. I think we have agreed to that. Meyer would not state too rigidly that the people are bound to get on to responsible government. Basu stated that agitation would certainly cease if the policy we contemplated were carried out. Lowndes wants a Second Chamber, and objects to anything which, put into lawyer's language, will transfer subjects until cause has been shown why they shall not be handed over. He wants an Ordinance to be only for the period of the new Council. Vincent asked that residuary powers should be " A," and thought that local governments should be consulted upon Second Chambers. Nair stated his preference for the first of the two schemes, but he travestied the second scheme. He said that Meyer's proposals were a farce ; he would not allow any Ordinance to be passed by the Governor which interfered with the civil rights or liberty of the individual ; he would not allow more to a Government than the old Budget if the conference objected to the " A " budget.

In the afternoon we considered various wordings, both for Ordinances and for transference after the six years. The wording for the Ordinance that seems most popular is : " The Governor may pass an Ordinance, which shall hold good for the life of the Government, in a Special Ordinance Committee, which shall consist of his Executive Council, such nominated members as he thinks fit, and the Standing Committee associated with the department concerned, provided that the Ordinance shall not be passed except in matters which, in the opinion of the Governor, are necessary for the preservation of the public peace or the security and preservation of life." The wording which seems most popular on the question of the transfer of powers is : " (1) Thereafter there shall be appointed in each Province governed by a Governor or Lieutenant-Governor Ministers who shall act with the advice and consent of the Legislative Council of the Province, whether in regard to all the subjects of provincial legislation or to some of them as may be determined by the Statutory Commission. (2) The Statutory Commission shall (reserve from) the control of the Ministry any or all of the powers included in Schedule A which they are satisfied cannot be for the time being transferred with due regard to the public interest. Or alternative to (2) There shall be transferred to the control of the Ministry all the powers included in Schedules A and B, provided that the Statutory Commission may reserve from the control of the Ministry in any Province such of the powers included in Schedule A as they are satisfied that it is not in the public interest for the time being so to transfer." Basu still sticks to a Second

Chamber, and wants Ordinances actually to pass a Port Trust Bill. He is getting wildly conservative, I think out of fear, but strangely enough, although he is conservative in the actual working of the constitution, he is very anxious to keep the onus on those who wish to reserve, and even would prefer a definite time without any Commission at all. We discussed as a possible compromise that there should be no Statutory Commission at the end of six years, that then B subjects should be automatically transferred, together with such A subjects as the Government of India, on appeal, wished to transfer, but at the end of nine years or eleven years all A subjects should be transferred unless cause was shown, etc. I do not know whether they would accept this.

In the evening I saw Meyer, who came to talk about his Budget, and in order to try and get him on my side I sent a very strong telegram home in order to help him. He wants gold, and it is frightfully difficult, on the information that the Treasury will give him, to show why he cannot have it. It is inconceivable that India should go on with inconvertibility because America refuses to help us or her, particularly when her difficulties are caused by financing the British Government. Afterwards I talked to him a bit about the schemes, but to show what miles apart we are he gave me a wording of the terms of reference to the Royal Commission which were something like these: To consider what further steps towards the progressive realisation of responsible government can be taken, with special reference to the control of the Executive by the Legislative Council. That is, of course, a roving commission, and it is putting on to a Commission six years hence what we are too cowardly to do now. Just as if this was not complete tragedy enough, Roberts reports to me that he had a long interview with Nair this evening, who refused to look at any scheme, and seems to think he can create a revolution. Perhaps he can. Certainly he will if the Government of India has it its own way. I do not know what to do; I do not know where to turn for help. The whole thing, just as it looked most promising, has tumbled about my ears. Duke is in the depths of depression, because he says that the scheme at its best is only the third best, and is harking back to sub-division of Provinces and a Curtis scheme. Oh! my God, I do not know whether I should not go home at once, frankly confess I have failed, and turn my attention to smashing the whole concern.

Lowndes is coming here to breakfast with me in a few minutes, and I must see what can be done with him, but I call the three days that have just passed the blackest I have ever known.

Friday, January 11. I sent a letter to Sir William Duke, apologising for the shortness of my temper, due to over-anxiety. He wrote me a very good reply, and has been much more tractable. On Thursday morning we had a conference again, when we arrived at three alternative wordings of the reference to the Statutory Committee; discussed at some length Ordinances, and ratified the wording for the Ordinance Committee. We had infinite discussion once again on the all-important topic of how to avoid friction between A and B subjects. Basu keeps his extraordinary optimism. I asked him whether he really meant what he said at the Council yesterday, that agitation would certainly die if our proposals went through. He repeated it; but, strangely enough, he is very conservative in all our talk. He is insisting upon a Second Chamber in the Provinces, over which we had some discussion.

Roberts produced his first valuable contribution. He had prepared a list of provincial functions from the Statutes, and on this we were able to form an A and B list, which shows that if we wait for six years for the preliminary stage, the A list need not be very large. But Vincent, who is also playing up nobly these days, wants to go through it, and spoke very well and forcibly upon the necessity of protecting vested interests.

Duke lunched with me. We went through the Second Chamber business again, and talked about lubricants. He was very sweet and extraordinarily helpful. I have forgotten to record that in the morning I had Lowndes to breakfast. I do not know whether I mentioned that Lowndes was due to see me and Meyer last night (Wednesday) at seven. He had accepted the invitation and had only stipulated that he should be allowed to go at a quarter to eight. Meyer and I waited till twenty to eight, and then Meyer went home. When Lowndes turned up to breakfast, I asked him about this, and I found that he had turned up punctually at seven, had been told by the chaprassi that I was engaged, and had walked up and down outside in the cold evening weather—for it is very cold when the sun sets now—not liking to come in, and had gone home at twenty-five minutes to eight.

At breakfast on Thursday morning we found ourselves very close together. All he wants is three stages, and he is then willing to take our formulæ. We discussed lubricants, such as I had written about to Chelmsford, and I found that he saw eye to eye with me in all subjects. I put to him the danger of being stampeded by those at home who are intoxicated with the liberating influences of the War, and pointed out to him Lloyd George's speeches about self-determination, etc., the right of the East African Hottentots to decide whether they would come under German or British control, and he was much impressed. Meyer had cynically answered this argument last night by saying that the Collectors should then hold a manhood poll of the whole of India, and they would vote against Home Rule, but of course Lowndes does not take this view.

When I returned I saw Woollacott, the *Times* correspondent in Delhi and the representative of the *Pioneer*. He is pretty helpless and hopeless, very garrulous. He was Liberal candidate for Coventry and has edited the *Statesman*. He is wholly against Indian aspirations. One thing in our conversation amused me. He complained of the intolerance of a woman who had told him in Calcutta that Miss Sorabji appeared to be very well educated for a native, and in the next phrase said he did not like Bombay because it was so overrun by Indians.

In the evening there was a dinner party. Two things I have to record : one is that I sat next to Cleveland, cheerful as ever, full of talk of the C.I.D., a Department which I am going to discuss with him on Monday. The other is that Mrs. Barstow, sister-in-law of Barstow of the Treasury and wife of the General out here who has done great work and who had been decorated on January 1, was here. In going through the list of honours at Bombay I had told Alan to telegraph my congratulations to her. It shows how a little thing like that repays ; she was full of gratitude, bubbling over with thanks for what I had done.

On Friday morning I got up after a sleepless night, because everything really hinged upon how far my appeals to Lowndes had been spread among his friends as to what happened this morning at the second conference with the Government of India. In bed I read the telegrams containing Wilson's speech. I am a little surprised to find freedom of the seas in it, but this and Lloyd George's great speech together bring peace, it seems to me, appreciably nearer, and certainly tend to unite the allied forces. Wilson has corrected the possibly unfortunate results of Lloyd George's references to Russia, which I am bound to say were, however, in my opinion, thoroughly deserved.

In my bath a new inspiration reached me. Why not limit the power of the Government of a Province to restore its A desiderata in the Budget to the same things in which a Governor could override the opinion of his Executive Council under section 50 of the Act of 1915 : " Whenever the safety, tranquillity, or interests of his Presidency or any part thereof are essentially affected in the opinion of the Governor."

Vincent came to breakfast. He accepted this idea. He is really a good fellow at heart, thoroughly disturbed, but very loyal. He modified his gloomy prognostications that the Services will be deprived of all English elements as they are transferred by saying that he thought that that would happen for a time, but afterwards they would come back, or at any rate a new set of people would come back, and this I believe is true. He was thoroughly with me on lubricants, and had even suggested some of them himself.

I had a word with Chelmsford and then went to the scaffold, and I must say I come away thoroughly satisfied. My scheme is through. I think I have recorded the results of Roberts' interview with Nair, and his belief that Nair was out to wreck all and any plan ; that Nair had even told him that two or three years of repressive action would give India all that it wanted. I did not record that at yesterday morning's conference we suggested that Donoughmore, who is not known either as a friend or an opponent of Indian aspirations, should see what he could do with Nair ; but at the meeting Nair accepted my new suggestion about A and B finance ; accepted my Ordinance proposals ; and the Government of India, with the possible exception of Du Boulay, accepted the last and preferable reference to the Statutory Committee. This is all absolutely satisfactory, but the plan as it emerges is : Transitional period, six years ; B powers plus any A powers Government of India thinks fit in any Province transferred to responsible government at end of six years ; at the end of twelve years all remaining powers transferred, unless Statutory Committee is satisfied some ought to be reserved, etc. This, of course, puts off the situation I had visualised in six years to twelve years. I explained that six years is not much in the life of a nation, but still that delay might dissipate the reception of the plan, and I agreed that on the whole, despite the advantages of a training period to get such things as re-arrangement of areas and local government determined, it might be better to revert to the first plan when we have started with the B subjects at once and have the Statutory Committee at the end of six years. Sir William Vincent, Sankaran Nair, and Lowndes all preferred this ; Chelmsford does not ; but it was decided to leave it to see if we could not ascertain what public opinion would prefer and what the local governments thought. It will be difficult to ascertain public opinion, but it is worth trying. It was admitted that if we start with B subjects at once the B list will be smaller. This has to be set against the argument that it is better to start at once. We had some discussion on Second Chambers, in which I stuck to my preference for Single Chambers, but we agreed this might vary in different Provinces as it does in Canada, and should be left to the opinion of local governments. We all agreed that it might be necessary to have either in the Upper or the Lower Chamber some nominated members, but all seemed to agree with me that you ought not to use officials to weight or override the opinion of elected members. Nair is, I think, opposed to a Second Chamber. There was, however, nothing about Nair which was intransigent ; on the contrary, he accepted every compromise. I think this must be largely due to the Government of India's acceptance of the third formula. There is now nothing left but the question whether we shall or shall not have a six years probationary period, and there remains over for discussion next week the Government of India and lubricants. The crisis is over for the moment, but it was very near a split, and there are such a large number of other things to think of that one can never be very hopeful, and it looks as if an awful lot of time will be taken up.

The trouble about this exciting week has been that there is absolutely no time left for mail work.

I have nothing further to record on Friday. I spent the day on my mail.

Duke and I had a talk with Chelmsford about the procedure for next week, and we have arranged that we shall have on Tuesday a discussion with the Government of India on communal representation and a Second Chamber in the Provinces; on Wednesday on the Government of India itself; and on Thursday on lubricants. Chelmsford still shies at the Government of India, but we had to bring him to the scratch. He described the Government of India to me as willing to consider the matter, and I hope he is not going back on this. Before we went he got out the letter to the local governments embodying the decisions we have come to, and Marris brought it to me. Marris is a very good fellow, and we have decided to bring him home with us to write our report, so that I shall see much of him. He does not like the six years probation, and I explained to him that he need not worry; I thought that the local governments would bring it back again.

We left at 10.30 for Bharatpur.

Saturday, *January* 12. I sat for some time after breakfast in the train discussing with J. B. Wood, who had returned from Patiala, the princes proposals. An astonishing thing appears to have happened. The princes invited to discuss the matter with them Chintamani and some Congress leaders. It appears that the Congress leaders told them that they regarded the Native States as anachronisms, and did not wish to have anything to do with them. This has set them all babbling again.

We got to Bharatpur, and were greeted by all the notables, including the Maharaja himself. Manners-Smith, the Agent for Rajputana, drove me to the bund on which my butt was. Nothing could have been more lovely than this narrow causeway, stretching across the vast jheel, covered with green rushes and bright patches of water with brown duck weed, and surrounded by luscious green trees. I made myself comfortable, and watched a few duck wheeling about, disturbed by the boats. At ten o'clock the bugle sounded, and at the sound of the bugle the shooting began. Except for when I shot at Bharatpur before, I never have had so much shooting. There was nothing like the usual number of duck, and the birds were very high. I shot with considerable success at first, and killed 74 duck in twenty minutes. Then the strain began to tell upon me. I badly blistered the palm of my hand, and one of my guns began to shake me to pieces by going off suddenly two barrels at a time. The result was that when the bugle sounded at one o'clock it found me dog tired, having a bag of 120 birds exactly. I do not think I have ever enjoyed a morning's shooting so much ; and I am never so happy as when shooting. It is impossible to describe the wonderful scene as the elephants come into the jheel and stir the birds up. It is impossible to describe the wealth of bird life—various storks and kingfishers, cormorants, snake birds, geese and duck. The rarest duck was the common English mallard, but with the exception of a big goose called the comb duck, or nuckla, a big, ugly black-and-white fellow, and the spot-bill, which is a big mallard, all the duck are to be found on my own Norfolk Broads. In number the biggest quantity killed were garganey, gadwall, shoveller, pochard, crested pochard, tufted duck, common teal, white-eyed pochard, widgeon and pintail. When I returned to the luncheon tent with my duck I found that Bikaner had beaten me with 122 duck, and the Maharaja of Dholpur had got 170. I came third. The Viceroy, in a butt next to mine, had killed 56 ; his cheeks were swollen out with pain by his gun ; he said the birds were too high for him, and he was tired out. The Maharaja of Bharatpur had gone home to bed with malaria—alleged, but the real fact of the matter was that this day of all days he was expecting his second child, and we had been waiting anxiously to hear the booming of cannons above the noise of the guns ; but, alas, it had turned out to be a daughter, and his disappointment was extreme. He is a nice fellow, a Rajput, who has been educated at Wellington for a short time.

After lunch I went to see the old Maharani, who had come down into her tent and is sufficiently catholic in her purdah system to permit of interviews with Englishmen. She is only about forty-five ; is a woman of great character, and has done wonderful War work. She has just been given a C.I. ; and she is bitterly disappointed at the birth of a grand-daughter. Bharatpur troops, under her orders, had been in East Africa, and have just come home from there. She was full of loyalty to the King and hatred of political reform. She looks very ill, and is very anxious for her son to have an heir before she departs. Her husband, poor man, is a political *detenu* at Ajmere. He was turned off the Ghadi by the British for his habit of murdering his subjects when he did not like them. She does not seem to be in the least resentful. The bugle sounded at 3.30 again, and we shot till about half-past five. I killed another 33 duck, and finished with the respectable total of 153, Raja Singh beating me by a few. I enjoyed the afternoon's shooting even more than the morning's. The birds were higher, there was less shooting, but it was great, great fun.

Sunday, January 13. The Viceroy went back to Delhi. I, as nobody will work on Sundays, pursued steadfastly my principle to blow the cobwebs out of my head by a long day in the country with hard exercise on Sundays, otherwise I am sure I should die, for I am getting very, very stale, and unless I get a good holiday soon, at least a week, I am afraid of a collapse. It is the constant strain of wheedling, negotiating, threatening. No sooner do you conciliate one set of people than a new one turns up. Accordingly, I got out of

Bharatpur Shoot, January 12th, 1918.

Butt No.	Names.	A. M.	P. M.	Total.	Butt No.	Names.	A. M.	P. M.	Total.
1	Colonel Manners Smith	25	2	27	26	Mr. C. C. Watson	39	18	57
2	Rao Raja Raghonath Singh	115	58	173	27	K. B. Ashfaq Hasan Khan	27	18	45
3	H. E. Lord Chelmsford	56	8	64	28	Mr. Sladen	26	2	28
4	Rt. Hon'ble Mr. E. Montagu	120	33	153	29	*(Vacant)*	...	...	...
5	Captain Holland-Hibbert	42	24	66	30	Maharaja of Bharatpur	1	4	5
6	Sir Charles Miles	29	15	44	31	Major Neale	45	18	63
7	Major J. Mackenzie	31	39	70	32	Major The Hon'ble R. Graham Murray	56	27	83
8	Captain Lord Carnegie	30	12	42	33	Mr. Rowan	38	10	48
9	Maharaj Kumar of Pertabgarh	19	1	20	33A	Lieut.-Colonel Elliot	47	32	79
10	Lieut.-Colonel Verney	33	11	44	34	Faridkot Sardar	4	...	4
11	Earl of Donoughmore	16	10	26	35	Kishangarh Sardar	4	1	5
12	Sir John Wood	9	15	24	36	Major Cole	45	9	54
13	Major H. Hill	16	10	26	37	Colonel Codrington	48	20	68
14	Mr. L. W. Reynolds	37	10	47	38	Maharaj Kumar of Bikaner	90	20	110
15	Sardar Tara Charn	11	9	20	39	Mr. Cruickshank	126	34	160
16	Colonel MacWatt	14	3	17	40	Mr. Maffey	56	12	68
17	Mr. Richardson	17	9	26	41	Maharaj Rana of Dholpur	170	83	253
18	*(Vacant)*	...	...	...	42	Maharaja of Bikaner	122	62	184
19	Captain Wickham	25	10	35	43	Maharaja of Kishengarh	37	55	92
20	Colonel Austen Smith	12	4	16	44	Major Dickinson	21	...	21
21	Mr. A. L. Parsons	26	9	35	45	Major Brown	56	24	80
22	General Sir H. Keary	24	13	37	46	Mr. R. A. Mant	23	21	44
23	Colonel Waddington	26	4	30	47	Captain Bennet	5	...	5
24	Colonel Haig	13	...	13	48	Captain Hammick	19	7	26
25	Maharaja of Faridkot	14	2	16	49	Mr. Gibson	7	2	9
					50	Mr. Evans	3	2	5

[*To face page 190*

the train at seven with the young men—Maffey (Chelmsford's private secretary), Verney (Military Secretary), John Mackenzie (Controller), Baring and Holland Hibbert (A.D.C.s). Baring, splendid fellow, had motored out from Delhi, leaving at five o'clock in the morning.

We breakfasted on the platform ; motored about five miles, split into two parties, and then started walking all day long with guns. The country was under cultivation, mainly cotton and red pepper, but interspersed among the fields were stretches of low jungle, with sparse rocky soil, sometimes breaking into sand. In these jungles live the grey partridges, going out to feed in the crops in the early morning. They are cunning birds, and run all day in front of one, and then get up when least expected. We had great fun, although we were all shooting badly, our sore shoulders from the day before and our fatigue telling on our shooting capacity. We got 12 hares, six quail, 22 brace grey partridges, two black partridges, a Norfolk plover ; and I shot a chincara, which ran within a few yards of me, and which I was yelled at to shoot because it was good eating. We also saw jackals, foxes, hyenas, a flock of sand grouse, many, many parrots, monkeys, eagles and hawks, and the everlasting little brown doves, which are innumerable, and peacocks. The soil was rather difficult to walk on because it was slippery sand, and our party of three staggered back to the motor cars at quarter-past four more dead than alive. Verney, poor fellow, was ready to drop. We found the other party had gone off an hour beforehand, too tired to go on. We motored back and got in at half-past six. A glorious bath, and then I read the English mail till dinner time, eagerly devouring my letters. Lord Morley's reminiscences have arrived : what fun ! I really am developing a social conscience. I should love to have had dinner in my tent and gone straight to bed, but I recognised that I was not dining in a single night this next week, so I decided to be brave and go to dinner. Chelmsford was awfully good, and we all went to bed immediately after dinner. I dropped off straight to sleep, and slept the beautiful sleep that hard physical exercise produces, and awoke in the morning with fresh vigour.

Monday, *January* 14. It was as well, for I had an appalling day. Claude Hill came to breakfast. We talked over many things. I found him generally in sympathy.

At half-past ten we had a long conference, which lasted till lunch time, on the subject of Second Chambers and communal representation. I do not think I have anything to say on the subject.

Then Cleveland came to lunch in my tent, and he convinced me, on the whole, that the C.I.D. is not a subject that one can deal with as a lubricant. I think he promised better things in the future than in the past. I suggested to him that when C.I.D. reports prove nothing criminal against a man, they should not be used for any other purpose, such as the convenience of governing. I think he will ponder this. But I am still obsessed with my new bother, that even when they agree with you they do nothing.

We began again at half-past two, and finished the discussion of the Government of India fairly successfully, Vincent, I fear, dissenting. I have now the material to make the big speech on Wednesday, to which I attach so much importance. If they will not touch themselves, then I shall be free to suggest my Royal Viceroy, whom otherwise I shall bury. A promise is a promise, but if one does not reach it, one is free to go one's own gait.

Then tennis, and in the evening another conference, which lasted till eight, on lubricants. Roberts objects to lubricants altogether. How strange he is! He objects to everything always.

Cleveland told us after dinner that he was a great friend of Mohamed Ali in the old days; that Mohamed Ali had come to see him just before the Turks came in ; that it was the last day of Ramadan, and Mohamed Ali was very hungry. Cleveland gave him a roaring meal, at the end of which Mohamed Ali wished success to the British arms, and agreed to send a telegram to Talaat Bey begging the Turks not to come in against us. He has frequently said since that he wished he had never sent the telegram, but he did send it, Cleveland sending it for him, after keeping it overnight and getting his approval in the morning. What a pity it is that he has gone wrong !

Tuesday, January 15. By the by, Basu tells me he has a friend who is an amateur soothsayer. Basu consulted him once as to whether he was going into the Legislative Council, and he said : "I think so, but it does not much matter, because on June 5, 1917, you will hear news which will be of great importance to you, and of great good to your country." On June 9 he was appointed to my Council. When he was leaving in September he went to his young friend and said good-bye. His young friend said : "You are not going ; you will be stopped in Bombay, and you will return to Calcutta." "But," said Basu, "am I never going at all ?" "Yes," said the man, "in March." "Shall I ever get there ?" said Basu. "Yes." This is highly comforting to me, but it is curious that I intended to go in February, and it now looks like March.

I had a long talk with Marris this afternoon, and aired upon him my Government of India oration for to-morrow. I think he admits its force ; I am sure it is very strong. I am very excited about it, and I wish I had more time to take a lot of trouble. I want to convince them, because if I do not disagreement is certain.

We have just had a violent note in from O'Dwyer, damning our scheme all the way up hill and down dale ; a note from Robertson, saying he does not like it ; and a note from

Pentland, saying he has no time to express any opinions at all. Certainly O'Dwyer's note is very strange, when one considers that he promised to support, and said he did support, Chelmsford's policy and the pronouncement of August 20. This is the difficulty we are always in. There is always somebody new to persuade and to conjole and to placate, but I am full of hope, because I am determined not to lose courage.

Poor Chelmsford was very depressed. He came to see me in my tent to-night about the O'Dwyer note. He said it was so characteristic of people in India to make these high-sounding pronouncements and then do nothing, indeed dissipate them by Executive action. This gave me courage to explain how more and more angry I got at the delays in getting things done. Chelmsford said he agreed, but the trouble about him is that although he agrees, he cannot get things done. Oh ! for six months as Viceroy !

In the evening I dined with Vincent, Muddiman,[1] Edwards (the new director of the I.M.S.), Stewart, of the Munitions Board, Meyer, Marris, and a few other people—a pleasant men's dinner. Vincent is really very good company and a very nice fellow, and it was a pleasant evening.

Wednesday, January 16. I spent my time before breakfast in elaborating my speech to the Council, and we had our conference, fateful as it was, at half-past ten. I urged upon them that it was impossible to have two Chambers in any Province if we had only one in the Government of India ; that it was impossible to consider 27 elected members of the Legislative Council as sufficient to represent India ; and that we must have something that could develop hereafter into a Parliament. Second Chambers might be impossible later on. I was quite willing to keep, and insisted upon keeping, the authority of the Government of India over the Legislative Council, until we had seen how the other process

[1] A. P. Muddiman, C.I.E. (Secretary to Government of India Legislative Department).

worked in the Provinces. I suggested an Upper House consisting of 50 members, of whom 28 should be nominated, preferring to leave officials to the discretion of the Viceroy ; but if they did not like that composition, any House which made it certain that the Government should prevail would be sufficient. Meyer and Claude Hill accepted my proposals ; Chelmsford passed me a note to "Cheer up" ; everything seemed to be going well. Lowndes leapt on them with fury and objected to them *in toto*. It was obvious that the paper which we had prepared at Madras on the Government of India had never been circulated to his colleagues. It is a fatal mistake, as it took them completely by surprise, and may cost us much, because although my Mission, with the exception of Vincent, loyally supported me to a man, Lowndes' attack received the assent of Du Boulay and the Commander-in-Chief, whom I had foolishly antagonised by suggesting a Standing Committee on Army affairs. Barnes was not there, and Chelmsford, I thought, agreed with Lowndes. It was a little depressing, but I am not losing heart, and I am taking other methods.

Afterwards I drove to lunch with Mahmudabad.[1] Mahmudabad offered me his house the day he heard that Donoughmore's tent was burned down. We lunched alone. He said he approved of the Curtis scheme, but he feared the officials. He also wants to be consulted at a conference, and said he was prepared to come to England for six months. He speaks bad English, and is, I think, thoroughly hostile.

After lunch I came back to my tent and had an interview with Kapurthala, who asked me to go and stay with him ; explained to me the beauties of his estate and the splendours of his French renaissance palace, which had been built by a French architect. He is a wide traveller, and has been all over the world.

After him came Alwar, passing through Delhi on the way home from Patiala—delightful, intelligent, pleasant, friendly.

[1] The Raja of Mahmudabad.

I tackled him on the question of the grievance always raised against his not wearing his Orders on State occasions. He assured me that he was not guilty of any eccentricity; that he was not well versed in the niceties of official procedure; that he would never think of doing such a thing, because he honoured the Orders that the King had given him; that he always wore them on State occasions; sometimes he did not wear all his medals because they were obscured by his jewels. He left me a copy of the princes proposals. They seem to me to be very good ones, but I am sure the Government of India will never take them.

Then I had a talk with my old friend Alma Latifi, who tied with me for the Secretaryship of the Union. He is now a district officer quite close here. He seemed young-looking, happy, vigorous. He had not got on well in Hyderabad, but he says he got on too well to please his superiors; he was glad to have left. I had heard he was very distressed, but he did not seem to show it at all. I promised to see him again, and then went to play tennis.

In the evening we had a conference. Duke made a happy suggestion, that the old Legislative Council of the Government of India should be the Upper Chamber, and that you should have a new Lower Chamber. I am not sure that this will not meet some of the difficulties.

I had a talk with Chelmsford, who seems on the whole much more friendly to my proposals for the Government of India. I think he thinks himself under an obligation to me for my not having said something about the Viceroyalty. I shall write to him on this subject before I leave India.

In the evening I dined with the Commander-in-Chief, a very pleasant dinner. I talked to the Commander-in-Chief, and got him to admit that his ambitions were to get rid of local armies. I said this involved an army for Indian defence. He is coming to lunch on Friday for a business talk.

Thursday, January 17. This morning Lowndes came to breakfast, and we had a very, very pleasant talk. He said that already last night he came to understand my proposals better and to see the force of them, and I think I have got him. I am going to see Maffey later on. He thoroughly agrees with me about lubricants, which, he agrees with me, have got an unfortunate name, and about the Viceroyalty. He said if I made my proposals they would be unanimously rejected by the Government of India out of loyalty to the Viceroy, but they would all agree with them.

Maffey came to my tent and we had a long talk. He sees the difficulties which cause the opposition to my Government of India proposals, but at the same time he was very sympathetic. I have talked him completely round, but he told me that my talk on lubricants had frightened the Viceroy. I said the Viceroy had never suggested this to me ; lubricants was a bad name ; it was really the remedying of real grievances that I wanted. Really his attitude is coloured by his hatred of the separation of Judicial and Executive. I again urged him to look into the question of the Indianisation of the Services, which I regard as his special subject. I asked him if he would ask me to dinner one day, and we parted very good friends.

Then Chelmsford came to my tent in a particularly affectionate mood, and asked me if I would revise the speech with which he proposed to open the Legislative Council. We talked over many subjects. I told him Lowndes' attitude had improved, and he left, saying : " I should like you to stay here for ever ; you cannot tell how we shall miss you." We are getting on !

Then I went to lunch with Nair. It was a curious experience. There was Lady Nair, as I prefer to call her, although that is not her right name, for descent among the Nairs is in the female line, and they take their mother's name. Her three daughters were present, too—demure, quiet little things, who were very much troubled by their *saris* over their heads, which were continually falling off. There was a long English lunch, with Indian musicians playing in the passage outside. Butter would not melt in Nair's mouth. He expressed himself, in conversation after lunch, as very satisfied with the way things were moving. He wants to come to England to help me. They all seem to want that! He told me how he had refused to pass orders on a proposed prayer by the Bishop of Calcutta for the victory of the English; he said that he did not approve of such things as these, and he could pass no orders; it was ridiculous to appeal to Jesus Christ, who was the God of Peace, for the victory of either side. Chelmsford was much shocked, he says, and suggested the transference of the ecclesiastical department to himself. Nair gladly assented to this, and then got a wigging from the Roman Catholic Archbishop, who said he would rather have a well-educated Hindu than a Protestant. "So you see," Nair said, "there is an advantage in being a pagan." Chelmsford told me afterwards that the whole of this story is a complete fabrication; there was no such order and no such incident; that Chelmsford, as soon as he came out, suggested to Nair that he took an interest in the Church and would like to take over ecclesiastical matters, and Nair assented. Nair also told me that he did not wish to be egotistical, but anything he commended to the Indians the Indians would accept, but if this was not done, nobody else could make them accept it. As I have heard this from all other sources, I quite agree. Nair told me that it was with great regret that he found his relations were not good with the Viceroy; that Hardinge had told him when he was appointed as Education member he should tell Hardinge what Indians thought. Hardinge used to send him all his proposed speeches, and told him that if he passed anything which afterwards got Hardinge into trouble with the Indians, Hardinge would hold him responsible; whereas, if Hardinge disregarded his advice, the responsibility would be Hardinge's own. Chelmsford has done nothing of this sort, " because," Nair says, " I have lost his confidence." He also told me that Malaviya was very unhappy at having lost the confidence of the Government ; that Bikaner had suggested his going and having a talk with Chelmsford, as he once did with Hardinge, with the result that the relations were afterwards satisfactory. Malaviya came to Nair and asked him whether he should go ; he said he would only go if Nair would give him a satisfactory assurance that the result would be the same. Nair said : " How can I do this when I have no relations with Chelmsford myself ? " I told him that I thought he had made himself a little difficult to his colleagues before I came out, but I would see what I could do. He then told me that he would naturally go on fighting his own cause, that he thought two Indians could always do anything with the Government of India, and that if I told him that the proposals were all I could get, he would accept them.

I left him and came home, being very satisfied with his attitude, and went for a short drive with Alan to Humayun's Tomb ; then a game of tennis and a talk with Chelmsford, who said he was only too willing to meet Nair and Malaviya half-way.

Following this, I went to dinner with Sir William Meyer—nothing but financial people, and we had a very interesting general discussion. Meyer is quite pleasant company, with a pretty wit.

Friday, January 18. I was taking no risks about the fateful meeting of Chelmsford's Council to-day. Barnes, who had not been at the preceding meeting, returned from Calcutta, and I sent for him to see me at half-past nine. I went over all the ground with him and found him very friendly. He tells me that Ronaldshay had read into our document—how touchy these people are !—that we had agreed on our provincial scheme without waiting for them. Of course I am only too much afraid that they will upset the whole apple cart. Ronaldshay said : "What is the use of people conferring and then asking us to come ?" Ronaldshay does not want the liberty of private members to tax ; he also thinks the Governor has too much power, and would like to begin at once rather than take six years. So would Barnes. I told Barnes that Nair reported to me that Chintamani had come to him in great anger and said that he had heard that I had said to a member of the Executive Council : "The moderates are cowards ; the extremists are hopeless ; therefore there is no Indian public opinion."

Then I had a very long talk with the new Director-General of the Indian Medical Service, Edwards, Cleveland, the surgeon, and Austen-Smith, the surgeon to the Viceroy. We all agreed that this was a pivotal service, because without good doctors you could not have any other good service. They want to amalgamate the I.M.S. and the R.A.M.C. One must, of course, swallow the other ; they naturally wanted to swallow the R.A.M.C. I feel that any proposal which awakes the antagonism of the War Office would be so hard fought as not likely to succeed. You must have Indians in the Service, and you must try and avoid separation between civil and military, for neither would give sufficient scope to doctors. We discussed station hospitals, the discontent of the lower ranks of the Service, and so forth. They are going to prepare a scheme. I suggested to them that they should form an Imperial Medical Corps for the whole Empire, with an Indian section, which should have Home Rule under a director of the Imperial section, appointed on the recommendation of the Viceroy, who should have charge of promotions and appointments. I think this scheme seems the most hopeful. Of course they had financial grievances. I urged them to put these as conservatively as possible ; I assured them that I recognised the seething discontent in the Service, and the absolute necessity of avoiding wholesale resignations at the end of the War.

The Council lasted a frightfully long time. The Commander-in-Chief, who came to lunch with me in my tent, did not arrive till two o'clock. We had much talk about Indian munitions.

He is not at all illiberal in his views. He thoroughly agrees with me about Boy Scouts, which he promises to take up. He thoroughly agrees with me about the necessity of proceeding with the Indian Defence Force, in which he proposes to have Indian officers as soon as he can. He is going to make proposals for the giving of commissions to Indians who are acceptable to the officers and who have won distinction on the field. He is very indignant at the idea that Englishmen will not be led by Indians ; he said it is not in the least true ; that Naoroji, who has been wounded as a private in France, ought to be given a commission, and ought then to be given his choice as to whether he wants a commission in an English or Indian regiment : if you do not want him to be in an English regiment, you ought not to have had him as a private. Every private ought to have a field-marshal's baton in his knapsack. He very strongly objects to trying to bring English people out to an Indian Sandhurst. He says Islington[1] does not want Indians to come home because of the dangers to which they will be exposed ; why should he ask Englishmen to come out to the same dangers in India at a tender age ? He tells me that an Indian Service Club here has passed a resolution to the effect that Indian officers shall not be admitted as members. He told the Club at once that he could not control the resolutions passed by their Committee but he hoped they would not press him to take a course which he might have to take if necessary, namely, to forbid English officers to become or remain members of the Club. That is the spirit in which to tackle this question. I was much impressed by his vigour and the way he was handling matters.

[1] Lord Islington was acting as Secretary of State for India in E.S.M.'s absence.

Of course he wants to make the Indian Army part of the Home Army. That depends, to my mind, on the size and well-being of the Indian Defence Force and the scope it offers to Indians. He is a warm admirer of Robertson's.

After lunch I went up to see Chelmsford in hot haste ; it was half-past three. On the way up Alan brought me very gratifying news—that Chelmsford had written to Islington in high praise of me. Maffey had shown him the letter. That's all right ! Chelmsford reports that the Council this morning swallowed my proposals for the Government of India—bless them ! Details are to be worked out between Basu, Duke, Lowndes and Meyer.

Then tennis, and quite a harmonious meeting with my colleagues for two hours this evening. After dinner I go off to Patiala for two days rest, but we shall there have the question of the Chiefs and their reforms, so that I do not suppose it will be much rest. God, how tired I am getting !

G. E. F. F. C. T. H. R. Verney D. A. P. H.H. of Bikaner

J. L. Maffey H.H. of Dholpur E. S. M. H.H. of Patiala Lord Chelmsford

BREAKFAST AT PINJORE, PATALIA

[To face page 202

VIII
PATIALA—DELHI V—THE CROCODILE SHOOT—DELHI VI—DHOLPUR—DELHI VII

We left Delhi at 10.30. The faithful Hailey and the red carpet were on the platform at Delhi station. Before I went to bed the Viceroy gave me the East India Railway Company despatch which had been sent home some time ago. When they telegraphed for an answer to it the India Office had asked them to discuss it with me. It seems that they favour State management, but have suggested a Company in India out of deference to the local governments. I must study this well.

Saturday, January 19. We arrived at Kalka station at 8 o'clock this morning, and were met by the Maharaja of Patiala and Prince Hitti, of Cooch Behar, who is acting as his A.D.C. We motored a few miles to Pinjore, an old Patiala palace without much accommodation, situated in a beautiful Mogul garden, with its rectangular gardens and fountains and seven terraces—gorgeously situated in the foothills of the Himalayas. We breakfasted out of doors in our overcoats—blue sky, cold, fresh morning. It was quite glorious. Then a few more miles in the motor to meet the elephants, on which we rode to the jungle we were going to beat. I shall not describe the beats in detail. Suffice it to say that the jungle was low and thick, and that we were in large circular stone butts along the dry beds of rivers. My armoury consisted of two guns, one loaded with shot and one with lethal bullets, and a rifle which I had borrowed from Mackenzie. Hitti was in my butt with me to protect me in case I bungled a leopard coming out. It was exciting work, and we were constantly on the look out for leopards, or even tigers. We had no protection against them at all except our weapons ; but nothing happened. A dead leopard cub was picked up in the beat, gored by a pig. No big game of any sort was shot. During one beat some very good cheetal stag came out. I was very anxious to get one, and had been specially given permission to shoot one, although they are endeavouring to protect them, but owing to the mismanagement of two beats at a time nobody got shots at them. A hyena was seen, and Baring shot a fox. There were two species of game which are very good shooting—pigeons, which were plentiful, but which are sacred to everybody, and pea-fowl, which flew high and fast across the narrow river beds, but are sacred to the villagers. All we shot were hares and jungle fowl of the red variety, which are to all intents and purposes exactly like bantams. We got some 100 of these. Some of them flew extraordinarily well and high, but they were all difficult, because they were nearly all falling shots. I have forgotten to record that Bikaner and Dholpur were fellow guests. Dholpur is a very nice little fellow, very shy and young. The son of a famous sporting father, he has become an excellent shot with a gun. There were three beats we had not time for, although everything was done to save time ; and after an almost endless ride on an elephant home, we reached the train so late that all thought of Patiala that night was abandoned, and we slept on the train, dining on it as well. Bikaner and Dholpur came to dinner, and afterwards we played bridge with Bikaner. Patiala motored back to his home, taking an hour and twenty minutes to go 70 miles. This is the man who drives a Rolls Royce across country after black buck. When you come to think of it, there were 3,500 beaters, horsemen, etc., out to kill 100 farmyard chickens, and yet I cannot deny that the day was extraordinarily amusing, with just a spice of excitement about it, and very delightful after hard work at Delhi.

In the evening the Viceroy showed me a telegram from Ronaldshay, saying that Sinha would come later in the week.

Sunday, *January* 20. We got out of bed early and drove to Patiala's palace, which is situated in a nice garden. It is new ; was planned by himself and an engineer, and has one enormously long facade with no depth at all, but is curious for its marvellous library. It has almost every known book, including Hansard, and a great supply of light novels.

Donoughmore tells me that the Viceroy has asked him to warn the Lieutenant-Governors as a conservative of the danger of dissenting from us, and the possibility of a landslide in England. He is obviously very nervous, and keeps on referring to it. I am afraid, desperately afraid, that he may say : "Well, you see I was ready to agree with all you proposed, but the local governments will not have it." However, the next fortnight will see success or failure. I cannot get the thing out of my head, and I am racking my brains for improvements all day. I suggested to Chelmsford alterations in his speech, which he took very well.

After breakfast we started off, motored a few miles, and then started on a great shoot—42 elephants, a regiment of infantry, lancers, etc., etc., etc. We rode across the grassy jungle in a line on howdahs, with rifles and shot guns, and shot partridges, black and grey, quail, black buck, and pig, and Thesiger, the Viceroy's brother, shot a wild cat. I saw another one, but could not get a shot at it. Shooting from an elephant is frightfully difficult. Most people find it easiest to stand up, with their knees bent, not touching the sides of the howdah. I find that the danger is of falling out if you do that. I tried a compromise, and broke my howdah ! The pig run very fast through the long grass, and only give one rare chances. They would never be shot if pig-sticking was possible, but the grass is too thick. Yesterday and to-day we shot a few Norfolk plover. I think my net bag for the day was about ten partridges, five hares, two black buck, and four pigs. All would have been better if the elephants had kept in line. Poor Clutterbuck would have had a fit if he had seen the way they were constantly all over the place. It was a long line, but it suffered from the fact that Bikaner and Patiala both tried to manage it by shouting contradictory orders. The confusion was awful, and why nobody was shot I cannot for the life of me understand. Rifles were cracking all round the place, and lethal pullets were being pumped into pigs and black buck. The total bag was about 50 pigs, 12 black buck, 100 hares. We arrived back at Patiala thoroughly tired from the sea-sick-like motion of the elephants, and after dinner are going back to Delhi to meet the wild Lieutenant-Governors.

We had a large dinner at Patiala. I sat in my usual place, between Patiala and Dholpur. Then we drove to the station, and went off to the fateful week at Delhi, Chelmsford genuinely apprehensive.

Monday, January 21. Willingdon came to breakfast with me in excellent spirits, and then we went to the scaffold. The morning was spent in discussing finance, with a view to getting a committee appointed. I had agreed to say nothing. Now there are three finance schemes before us—Duke's, or rather Brunyate's, Meston's, and Meyer's. At a conference on finance any sensible person would have said : "Let us hear these three people on their own schemes first, and then discuss them" ; but, incredible though it may sound, the discussion of this sort of thing in India has got to go by seniority.

Chelmsford, therefore, asked that the three subjects—divided heads of revenue, power of taxation, and borrowing power—should be discussed separately, and called upon Lord Pentland, as the senior man present, to open the discussion. On each question he began an illuminating discussion by

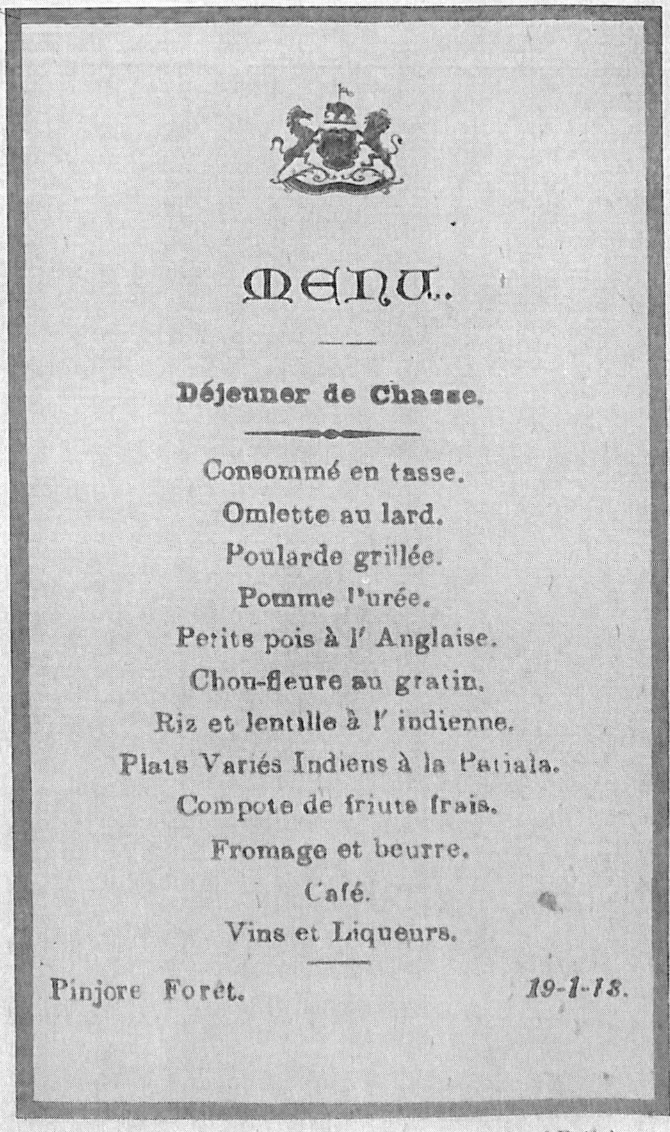

MENU.

Déjeuner de Chasse.

Consommé en tasse.
Omlette au lard.
Poularde grillée.
Pomme Purée.
Petits pois à l' Anglaise.
Chou-fleure au gratin.
Riz et lentille à l' indienne.
Plats Variés Indiens à la Patiala.
Compote de friute frais.
Fromage et beurre.
Café.
Vins et Liqueurs.

Pinjore Forêt. 19-1-18.

Luncheon menu—many miles out in the jungle of Patiala

[*To face page* 206

saying : " I have nothing to say on this subject; it is all in the memorandum." Unfortunately, the memorandum, which was prepared by the Government of Madras, has not yet arrived ; therefore his contribution was not illuminating or helpful, and it made him appear absolutely ridiculous. The discussion was hopeful. O'Dwyer frankly wants divided heads kept in order that the Government of India may protect him against the inhabitants of the Punjab, but he was alone ; everybody else wanted to get rid of them. Meyer, in reply and in interjections, was excellent. Although faced with opposition to his proposals, he was extraordinarily gentle. He remembers everything against everybody.

I made quite a short speech, in which I pointed out that finance should not guide policy, but was the handmaiden of policy, and financial difficulties must be got over. It was no use pretending you were getting rid of divided heads if you keep land revenue divided ; and a committee of Meston, Duke, and Meyer was appointed, with instructions to get rid of divided heads. So that is all to the good.

I lunched in my tent with Meston, who won't have the preliminary period, but is prepared to go back to my original scheme.

Then I saw O'Dwyer, who is still opposed to everything. As his memoranda show, he is determined to maintain his position as the idol of the reactionary forces, and to try and govern by the iron hand.

Benjamin Robertson, so very like Robertson of the General Staff, was extraordinarily blunt and honest and worried, and anxious to help. Ronaldshay was also very anxious to help.

Tuesday, January 22. I had breakfast with Sir Benjamin Robertson, and then arrived the very critical period, really the worst of all mornings, the one obstacle to success.

I started the ball. I had to lay before the conference the various variants of the schemes that seemed acceptable to us.

I spoke for an hour, and put everything I knew into it. I endeavoured to be as clear as possible, as conciliatory as possible, and endeavoured to carry the day. I cannot give myself any credit for success. Clarity I achieved ; I know the subject by now, I hope, thoroughly. My logic I thought unanswerable. Speaker after speaker got up, thanked me for my frankness, my lucidity, my powerful statement, and so forth—the same epithets that are used in the House of Commons by those who do not intend to agree with you.

Pentland, who was called upon to begin, said it was a most interesting speech, and that the only way of showing their thanks was to be as frank as I had been. But he would say nothing ; it was all in the memorandum, which he told us had arrived that minute and would be circulated in the afternoon.

He was followed by Willingdon, who objected to everything, to my dismay, and proposed a scheme of his own, which was very like the transitional six years stage of January 12 scheme, but refused afterwards to consider any dyarchy or beginning of responsibility. I cannot understand this. Willingdon had enthusiastically endorsed the scheme of January 12, and why he had rounded on it I cannot for the life of me conceive.

Ronaldshay followed—very good, saying that he was a paragraph 35 die-hard. He trounced the six years period, but when it was pointed out to him that it was not intended that resolutions should be binding in that time he agreed to it, and said that it was all along what the Bengal Government wanted. So far, so good.

I do not understand this talk about binding resolutions. There is no sanction ; the Government does not go out if it refuses ; and if it refuses and stays in, a resolution cannot be enforceable in a court of law unless you give it statutory powers.

Then followed Meston, who would not have a probationary period at any price.

Then lunch with Donoughmore and Willingdon. Willingdon agreed at lunch to take January 12 as a compromise between his views and mine. So far, so good.

After lunch, O'Dwyer—long, pugnacious, narrow. He would not have anything, particularly no elected majority. Then Gait, in agreement with him; then Earle, then Robertson, a Willingdonian.

So ended the Lieutenant-Governors, all at sixes and sevens.

Then the most extraordinary event of the day—Sir William Vincent—a violent speech warning us of disorder, objecting, and saying he could never sign his name to any of the proposals, refusing to make promises for the future, saying that our scheme would be taken to mean a promise of responsible government in twelve years.

Then Pentland asked to be allowed to speak, having read, I presume, the memorandum. He suggested elected majorities, purely advisory, and said that the Madras Council went very smoothly. Of course it does, because he refuses permission to deal with disagreeable subjects.

Then a short and very admirable speech from Chelmsford, and a reply from me—vigorous, excited, bad-tempered. I trounced Vincent, congratulated him on having made a speech which might come from a somebody who had never made a speech before on this subject ; told him that I insisted upon a promise, which I would see would be carried out because it should be statutory. I tried to bring Meston into accepting the six years period by saying that it really amounted to an appointed day for bringing into force an Act of Parliament, and then laying down certain things that should be done before the appointed day.

We adjourned at quarter-past six, thoroughly tired, having sat ever since half-past ten continuously. It was pouring with rain by that time and icy cold. Everybody was depressed and excited. I came back to my tent tired and worried, but with a strange feeling that it will all come right.

Meston asked to see me, and we hammered out a compromise, viz. that the Councils should remain as they are during the transitory period, which should be fixed as five years from the date of the report. Meanwhile, Standing Committees would be set up, electoral arrangements made, and so forth. I said if he could get his people to agree to this I would accept it, but it would not give us the opportunity of training the new electorates in the interval.

I dined alone in my tent and thought hard.

Wednesday, January 23. In the morning Chelmsford came to see me to suggest the Meston compromise. I agreed ; and then I suggested a new scheme, viz. to have an Executive Committee instead of Standing Committees after the five years. This Executive Committee should, on B subjects, be binding upon the departments, two members of the Executive Committee being attached to each department. At the end of ten years sub-committees of the Executive Committee should take over the portfolios from the members of the Executive Council, unless cause was shown why certain Executive Councillors should remain. This is going to responsibility by partial responsibility, for the members of the Executive Committee could be turned out for the departmental decisions in which they were involved. I rather like it. I put it to Willingdon at breakfast, and he promised to consider it. What he wants is a complete elected majority for ten years, and then a Statutory Commission which should give responsible government, reserving any departments which the Government thinks ought to be reserved. He does not think the electorate will be ready before ten years, but he is willing to compromise, as he was yesterday.

We had our meeting, and I put to them Chelmsford's

ideas that we should start dyarchy as a compromise five years from the publication of the report, but to keep the existing method of electing Councils until then. Those Provinces that would like to have an elected majority could get it in the existing Councils by not nominating their official members. Nobody liked it, because they said that it was with the new electorates that you wanted the period of training. I then suggested to them that we should keep to the six years of the January 12 proposals, but during that time associate with the Executive Council an Executive Committee of elected members of the Legislative Council. These men would share the responsibility with the Executive Council when specially consulted. They would be consulted on all B subjects, and, at the pleasure of the Council, on A subjects. In that they would not hold their seats on the Executive Committee unless they were supported by the Legislative Council, and unless they retained their seats in the Legislative Council they had some responsibility to the electorate. Everybody liked this and thought it was better than Parliamentary Under-Secretaries and better than Standing Committees. We asked Chelmsford to come and see us, and we put it to him. He liked it. Vincent then objected to B subjects coming automatically at the end of the six years, and I suggested that the Government of India should have power at the end of six years to withhold certain B subjects pending the arrival of the Statutory Committee in the tenth year, and also to have the power on petition to add A subjects on appeal, the reasons for refusing A subjects and granting B subjects to be laid on the table of the House. Basu promised to consider this, but obviously did not like it.

When we went to lunch we heard that the meeting of the heads of Provinces had been a failure ; they were all at sixes and sevens ; they had hoped to come to an agreement, but they found it quite impossible ; that they were going to present us with a report, and they were going to meet that afternoon to see if they could come nearer. It looked as if they would compromise on a suggestion of Ronaldshay's, that you should have a three-year period instead of a six-year period, with an elected majority, which Meston agreed to take.

I saw Meston after lunch, and he said he thought it looked all right. I suggested to him my new plan ; and finally I went to the meeting in the afternoon and described it to them with a view to helping them. When they broke up in the afternoon they had apparently not taken the new plan, or liked it, and the compromise which Meston had expected had broken down. He and Willingdon were ready to take it, but Robertson and O'Dwyer refused. Meston was very depressed when I saw him in the evening, because he said he thought they had disgraced themselves by not being able to help me more. He told me that he had agreed, after all, to become finance member.

A very good paper has come in from Craddock, who damns dyarchy, and then suggests our paragraph 35 scheme by another name. He has got a very inadequate B list, and he has a terminology of his own, but it is practically that scheme.

I have telegraphed to the King about Meston ; we had better get that announced.

The afternoon was broken at four by a State visit from the Nizam, who has come up here with all his wives and, by a strange irony of fate, installed himself in the Baptist Mission House. He arrived at my tent in a motor car with two A.D.C.s and Sir Stewart Fraser. The Nizam is, of course, enormously important to us, because he has kept the Mohammedans of India straight, and we have used him, by means of his wily old Ministers and our Resident, for this purpose. But we have made all the princes very sick by segregating him as "His Exalted Highness." At 7 o'clock I had to return his visit, and went to his house, all newly furnished, and there found almost everybody from his State—old

Farrideeonje, old Bilgrami, Colonel Egerton, etc., etc., and several small children. I am bound to confess that the size of the family compared to the number of wives was rather like our bag of jungle cock compared to the number of beaters. We sat and talked for about ten minutes, and then I left and went to call on Willingdon, whom I found in the depths of depression. I commended to him Craddock's letter, and left him much more cheerful.

I had sent a note to Chelmsford saying that the heads of Provinces ought to meet again ; it was ridiculous leaving them in this condition, and we ought to postpone our talk on agitation. Chelmsford came to Willingdon's tent, and after a talk thought we had better have agitation in the morning, as arranged, and let them meet in the afternoon.

On the way home I met Pentland. Pentland said : " I want to tell you, after presiding over the meeting of heads of Provinces, that however long we sit together it will be no use. We are all at sixes and sevens. I have done my best to help. I have not said anything about my views because I regard myself as outside of this. I think everything you suggest is wrong. I am prepared to put my views forward, but I am afraid they are no use, so I said nothing. We shall never get on, and it is no use our sitting again. I am only telling you because I should like to help. You see, none of us know what we are here for." (This was nice, after pretty nearly a week's work !) " Are we to accept the policy that you lay down, or tell you what we think you ought to do ? " I said : " You are there to suggest the best policy that you can possibly devise. If you do not like my policy and can suggest a better one, tear my schemes up." " Oh," he said, " if that is what you want from us you will never get it." This was consoling !

I went to a large dinner party, not feeling any too happy. The dinner party was not as bad as most, as I had the pleasure of meeting Sir Thomas Holland, who is a live man, and we talked munitions.

After dinner Chelmsford sent for me into his room, and I found him sitting domestically with his wife. They were both most awfully sweet and mellow, and said that they insisted upon me going out to dinner on the following night; that Cleveland was the best man for me to dine with; that Cleveland was dining with them, but they had written to him to tell him that they could not entertain him and that he must entertain me. It was very kind of them, because they realised how tired I was of their enormous functions. Then we cracked a few jokes. I told them a story, which I do not believe, but which I had just heard, that Curtis had developed a desire to become a Hindu; that he had summoned some men from the Central Provinces and told them this; that they said: "No man not born a Hindu can become a Hindu." He said, quite characteristically: "Oh, nonsense; any man can change his religion." So they promised eventually to consult the Pandits at Benares, and the reply came back: "Mr. Curtis must feed a thousand Brahmans every day for a year. At the end of the year he must commit suicide, and then possibly in his next incarnation he may become a sweeper."

Chelmsford told me that Robertson had told him that they were all within an ace of coming to an agreement, but that Pentland was an impossible chairman, who kept on interrupting to say: "Well, we seem to have agreed on nothing, but I take it that——" and then summarising everything completely wrongly; so Chelmsford had suggested that he and I should take charge of the meeting on the next afternoon. I agreed to this; told him that Willingdon said he was happier, and so on; and went to bed feeling that light was coming out of the darkness.

Thursday, January 24. A great day! In the morning I

had a divine letter from Willingdon saying that I had cheered him up by coming to see him ; that he had exchanged notes with Meston ; that everything was coming right.

Then Willingdon and Meston came to see me, and said that they had all practically agreed to a compromise, under which, after the appointed day, any Province could start its dyarchy as soon as they liked, but not later than six years, so that you will have the January 12 programme in some Provinces and paragraph 35 in others. So that is all right.

Then we went to the meeting on agitation. It was a gloomy proceeding. Chelmsford threw out suggestions, such as my suggestion for power to sue for criminal libel ; my suggestion of making a paper insert a contradiction of a lie ; my suggestion that officials should have freedom to answer attacks upon them. Then the Governors and Lieutenant-Governors began and went on talking. I will not record what they said, because the best account I can give of the meeting is by saying what I said when they had finished, after two hours. I was then asked to give my views. I told them that I was more depressed than I could say by what they had said ; that I did not seem to talk the same language as they did ; that I daresay they were right, but if they were right, then our policy was wrong ; we need not discuss political reform any further. The announcement of August 20 was wrong ; the Morley-Minto reform scheme was wrong, and India ought not to have any political institutions. It was monstrous to say that a man could not make the same speech outside the Council that he could inside ; it was monstrous to say that an official must be a politician inside a Council, using his vote and influence in political matters, sitting on Executive Councils which were really Cabinets, and then must take no part in politics outside. Their scheme dated from a day before Parliamentary institutions dawned in India. I heard them say, to my amazement, that it was a most disquieting sign that agitation was spreading to the villages. What was the unfortunate politician in India to do? He was told he could not have self-government because there were no electorate, because only the educated wanted it, because the villagers had no political instincts; and then when he went out into the villages to try and make an electorate, to try and create a political desire, he was told that he was agitating, and that the agitation must be put a stop to. The right answer to agitation was to remove all justifiable causes for it, and then we had a good answer to everything that the agitator said. Agitation should be answered by agitation. We should try and educate the villagers; we should put our case; but to sit quite quiet whilst an agitator was agitating and then intern him showed that we had no answer. I differed from Lord Chelmsford that we could not intern before the pronouncement, because we had made no effort to deal with the situation, and that we had a better case for interning now. I told them that now we had no case to intern because we had an answer. If our policy was adequate, and if we thoroughly believed it, the only right way to answer agitation was by advocating it; that if the Government defended itself, the moderates would soon rally to the Government. It was only because we left the moderates without any backing or stiffening or assistance from the real leaders of the Government political party, the officials, that they were so doubtful of themselves. I said law and order was not my business; I could not keep law and order from England, and those who governed the Provinces were responsible for it. But I could not defend them if they did things that I did not agree with; then I would resign and they must get somebody else to do it. The idea that they could get a reporter into a private house when more than 20 people were assembled seemed to me to be a thing that the House of Commons would never stand. They must learn to be politicians; they must learn to defend themselves, and not to think of suppressing agitation. I told them that I had met no extremists, except Tilak and Mrs. Besant, and even Mrs. Besant was not an extremist ; she was a suffragette. In just the same way I had met no reactionaries, or only one or two, looking hard at certain people. It was really only a matter of terms. Disaffection was an excellent thing if it meant that you were teaching a man that he must hope for better things. Our whole policy was to make India a political country, and it was absolutely impossible to associate that with repression.

Willingdon quite agreed with me ; the others looked very gloomy.

Then the Commander-in-Chief read us a lecture, at the invitation of Lord Chelmsford, on the War, and we separated for lunch.

Sinha and Basu lunched with me. I put to them the possibility that I should be asked to assent to power being given to the Government of India to modify the B list after the six years. They did not like it because they wanted certainty, and I promised to try and resist it. I also put to them that I should be asked to assent to a power of recall of powers, and I thought this might lead to trouble. They did not like that ; they said you could never recall once it was given, but it would give the extremists something to hit the moderates with. They were very nice, although I fear that Basu was a little sobered and not so certain of the future as he said he was. We talked about the formation of a moderate party ; they were very enthusiastic ; and talked about editing newspapers, and so forth. I think they mean business.

Then to the meeting of heads of Provinces. Meston produced his compromise. It differs from the January 12 plan in two essential points. One is, as I have said, that we shall start dyarchy in some Provinces sooner than in others ; the other is that they want power of recall of B subjects to the Committee. They did not put it that way, but I put it to them that these were the only two points, and they agreed. It is very essential, because I cannot take their wording. I told them that I would not wrangle about wording, because that must be left to me in drafting the Bill. All I understood was that they wanted a safeguarded power of recall, which I could try and get for them.

I think it is all over. We meet to consider the compromise of the local governments with the Government of India to-morrow, and then we have to sit down to details, the scheme being agreed and the chances of friction practically over. My trouble is that we may whittle away a good scheme by finicky safeguards, such as this recall of powers, power to modify the B list, and so forth, so as to make it unacceptable to the Indians, but I am still going to put it to the Indians. If we can get the details properly worked out and the princes fitted in, I shall feel fairly satisfied with my mission, but always with the horror before me that the scheme will be acceptable to no one when it is published, and I am bound to say I am very apprehensive of this, because I do not think they like dyarchy. All depends on the A and B lists, which are now going to be remitted to a committee consisting of Vincent, Roberts, Willingdon, Nair, O'Dwyer, Lowndes.

I had a game of tennis. The Nizam came and watched with his whole family and staff. He is dining here on Monday, and I have been asked to dine out because they do not want him to feel that my precedence of him is embarrassing to him. Really, this is ridiculous, and they are going to have trouble with this man by exalting him into a position of kingship.

We were all disturbed and very shocked by the manner of death of poor Duff. I am constantly haunted in talking to all men who have committed the indiscretion of assuming public office and in thinking of my own position by the knowledge of the small dividing line which exists between considerable success and catastrophic failure. If Duff had been sent out when Creagh was sent out, he must have done better than Creagh, and I believe would have gone down to history as a very successful Commander-in-Chief. He found himself, a man of essentially civilian mind, plunged into a great position in a war. He suffered, like all of us, from domestic casualties, and finally an overdose of veronal after the Mesopotamian Commission Report, after a controversy in which no one has had anything to say for him. India is full of stories as to how he disregarded advice, but then how many of us disregard advice which is showered upon us all day. It is a sad business, and I cannot help remembering how I insisted, to the best of my power, on his appointment in preference to that of Ian Hamilton. Would the latter have been better?

I had my little dinner at Curzon House with Cleveland, and a merry evening it was. The other guests were Keeling, the engineer of New Delhi, and Mant, of the Revenue Department. We laughed and told stories all through dinner, and afterwards played bridge.

Friday, January 25. Slocock,[1] of the Central Provinces, came to breakfast with me, and I think we got closer together than we have done in the past, but he is very talkative and pugnacious. I have got to have another talk with him to-morrow morning at breakfast.

We had a meeting this morning with the Government of India. Real difficulties are arising which will have to be met. The transitional period that we have got to have to oblige Willingdon, Robertson and Gait will give to the Legislative Assembly powers over A subjects which, after this transitional period, will go to the A Council. The 11th, 12th, or 13th commandment is: "Thou shalt not take butter out of a dog's mouth." We have got to get over these difficulties without whittling away our scheme. I told the people that I had thought of a way of drafting, which

[1] F. S. A. Slocock, C.I.E. (Chief Secretary to Chief Commissioner, Central Provinces).

Meyer described as camouflage, which has the advantage of getting rid of the separation between A and B subjects, dividing subjects as to whether they shall be dealt with in the Council or the Assembly :—Not later than six years after the passing of this Act there shall be a Legislative Assembly, whose prime functions are in schedule 1 of this Act, and a Legislative Council, whose prime functions are not in schedule 1, each being able to advise the other as to their prime functions. The Ministry shall consist of members of the Legislative Assembly, who shall have charge of the portfolios in schedule 1, and members of the Legislative Council, half of whom shall be Indians, who shall have charge of the portfolios not mentioned in schedule 1. I think this will make the thing look better and get rid of dyarchy, which stinks in people's nostrils as a word.

It was quite amicable, and in order to make quite sure everything was going right I lunched with Nair. I hear the heads of Provinces are rather alarmed about my speech yesterday on agitation.

I had some talk with Chelmsford about princes. It is quite clear that he will go all the way with me, and that the last point of difference is now disappearing.

To-night the Commander-in-Chief is entertaining us to dinner—the members of the Executive Council and the heads of Provinces. Chelmsford and I have got to make speeches. The trouble is I have no time to think of what to say, and I am terribly stale—more stale than I can possibly describe. I now begin to say Standing Committee when I mean Government of India, and Legislative Council when I mean motor car.

So I close my mail, on the whole very pleased when I think what we have got : complete provincial decentralisation ; at least half Indians on every Executive Council ; at least two Indians on the Governor's Council ; a Second Chamber in the Government of India ; disappearance of official blocs, responsible government coming as quickly as possible in the Provinces ; abolition of divided heads of revenue ; and, I hope, proper treatment of the princes. It all seems to me to be splendid, but "There's many a slip 'twixt the cup and the lip."

The dinner to-night was a great success. Some 75 people sat down to dinner, people in the Indian world who, I suppose, were unique in the history of the country. I thought it was simply a dinner of the members of the Council and their wives to the members of my delegation and the heads of Provinces, but all sorts of people were there—secretaries, Sir Thomas Holland, and so forth. The room had been built originally as the post office for the Durbar, and was as full as it would hold.

As regards the speeches, I do not remember having heard three better speeches than those delivered by my fellow guests after dinner—none too long or too short, and all extraordinarily good. My only regret was that my speech was, I must confess, fourth best. The toast was proposed by the Commander-in-Chief, whose manner, rather than his words, was extraordinarily successful ; and the way in which he laughed at his own jokes and beamed round the room made whatever he said a success. But he had many witty touches. Perhaps the one that was most appreciated was his attack on his colleagues for making him do it, coupled with a sudden remark, blurted out : "No one knows their own abilities better than my colleagues do." Chelmsford followed, leading off with the most undisguised split infinitive that ever dropped with a thud upon a dinner table. But apart from this, his speech was very good ; his banter of the heads of Government extraordinarily successful, coupled with compliments to Pentland—"A perfect English gentleman." Also his little quotation about the way in which Mrs. Besant's name was not mentioned at Madras : "Oh ! no, we never mention her. Her name is never heard," etc. But it was a curious speech for Chelmsford, and it contained things which I was surprised to hear from his lips. He had obviously been reading the Athanasian Creed as blasphemously paraphased to represent the commands in Egypt, and as he was responding to a toast to three people he played with the Trinity at considerable length and elaboration. It was appreciated, and I have no reason to complain, but it was strange for him in such an audience. He later on told a story about a friend of his, a bishop, who forbade his servants to use his bathroom, and who came back from what is properly called a "visitation" in the case of bishops to discover a long black hair in his bath. Discovering it was the cook's, he reprimanded her for doing behind his back what she would never dare to do in front of his face! Could this have been the real Chelmsford? It must have been written by Maffey or somebody.

Pentland's speech, which came last, was beautifully worded, extraordinarily well delivered, reserved, serious, in contrast with all the others, and contained a very much applauded and peculiarly appropriate tribute to the district officer.

I have little to say about my own, except that it was distinguished by some quite apt quotations that I was fortunate enough to find. Alan provided two good lines, I think from *Ulysses* :

> "Much have I seen and known, cities and men,
> 'And manners, climates, councils, governments."

The third line, which I stated I would not quote in the hope that some of the audience would at least remember it, ran :

> "Myself not least, but honoured of them all."

The next in the serious line I got from Morley, and comes from Burke : "Reflect seriously on the possible consequences of keeping in the hearts of your community a bank of discontent, every hour accumulating, upon which every company of seditious men may draw at pleasure."

But perhaps the most successful were three quotations, which had to be used with niceness, from Pepys : " In the afternoon, my lord and lady being at cards in his room, in comes Mr. Edward Montagu. He did rip up all that could be said to be unworthy and in the basest terms they could be spoken in. To which my lord answered with great good temper and did allay him so that he fell to weeping." (I liked the last lines particularly myself, for Chelmsford's great good temper does make one weep sometimes, but perhaps not in the sense that Pepys meant of my famous namesake.) " My lord so much contemns Mr. Edward Montagu, as my lord knows himself very secure against anything the fool can do ; and notwithstanding this, so noble is his nature that he professes himself ready to show kindness and pity to Mr. Montagu on any occasion." " Mr. Edward Montagu is turned out of the court never to return again. So he is gone, nobody pitying, but laughing at him."

I came home and spent three-quarters of an hour in walking up and down the garden outside my tent, cold though it was, because I am not happy. The Lieutenant-Governors and heads of Provinces have been rather poor creatures. They have put their names to a compromise which none of them believe in, and they are going away very sore at heart.

Saturday, January 26. This morning Slocock came to breakfast, and our conversation gave me a new idea, certainly an idea which he liked better than any yet proposed. I had in my mind Sastri's reported comment upon our schemes : " For God's sake do not separate us into an A house and a B house. We want to work with the officials, and not to be penned off from them." We began with the intention of an A Government and a B Government, which has been modified into an A committee and a B committee of the same Government. Why do we, then, want two houses ? Let us go on the principle of keeping them together for deliberation, and separating them for decision. During the first six years we have an Ordinance Committee for A subjects—call it a Grand Committee, in composition much like the present Council, either binding, in which case it must be an official majority, or advisory, in which case it does not matter. Then in a second period, when your B Ministers come into existence, you have a Council, with the Governor as President and an elected member as Vice-President. After discussion on the B subjects, a Bill goes to a B Select Committee, and is finally ratified by the B members, the A members not voting. An A Bill, after joint discussion, goes to the Grand Committee, whose decision is final.

We had a short meeting to say good-bye to the heads of Provinces ; heard of the very satisfactory financial solution, which Meyer accepts with reluctance, and then said good-bye.

I then proceeded to lobby on behalf of my new scheme. Meston thinks it has great advantages, but prefers his own for his own Province. I told him that my scheme seemed to me to be an essential result of the six years trial period, because you could not take butter out of a dog's mouth, but that if he started at once there was no harm in his having two houses, and that my scheme could develop into two houses even in the other Provinces. It looks to me as if we ought to state that responsible government is our goal, and that the Provinces can march to it by either of two methods. All the other Provinces enthusiastically welcomed it.

I lunched with Sly,[1] vigorous in his hatred of the old scheme, but liking the new one. He takes A and B subjects reluctantly, but he has to admit that even he does not call them by this name ; he has got to recognise there are A and B subjects.

Robertson, Gait, and Earle went away delighted ; so did O'Dwyer ; so did Sinha and Basu. Willingdon says his committee on A and B subjects has done quite good work, and he is quite satisfied. He is leaving happier, and Chelms-

[1] Sir F. G. Sly, K.C.S.I. (Commissioner, Central Provinces).

ford promised them that the conference of heads of Governments should be annual. That is a great achievement in itself.

Most of the day was spent very fatiguingly in airing my new scheme to each of them separately, and finally at eight o'clock I sat down to dinner in my tent, feeling much happier, with Cleveland. At nine o'clock we started off to motor 50 miles to a Dak bungalow in the United Provinces at a place called Garhmuktesar, where we slept the night. I was awfully cold when I arrived, but Cleveland, the perfect host, had provided a cup of hot soup and a whisky and soda. We got to bed about twelve, and I slept like a log till six, when I was called.

Sunday, January 27. A beautiful, cold morning, sun shining brightly. Then a motor drive of some eight miles along a canal bank, the level top of which is always kept for the canal officer to go along, the public not being allowed to go along it. Then two miles on a very fast elephant, and we reached the bank of the Ganges. By this time the wind was high and strong, and it was obvious we were not going to have a successful morning. Crocodiles come out of the water in the heat, and the sand of the banks was blowing in such clouds that sometimes you could not see the banks at all. Why should a crocodile lie on them? However, we got into Cleveland's boat, a little, flat-bottomed punt of great stability, with an oil engine fixed to the stern to help us when we had to go across the current, and behind us came a large barge to carry the crocodiles. Long distances, past sandbanks, which in better weather would have been perfect places for crocodiles, yielded nothing. Finally, on a small strip of sand in the water, near a high bank, we saw a very large crocodile. We determined to land and stalk from the bank. At that moment a boy came running along shouting at the top of his voice: "There's a big mugger, there's a big mugger," and, of course, the mugger disappeared into the water. They are strangely quick in their movements and extraordinarily quick of hearing. They just gently subside until they disappear, and they always seem to lie very close to deep water, so that unless the animal is killed stone dead without a movement, although you have the satisfaction of knowing that you have taken one of these beastly things out of the river, you do not recover the body or the prized leather. We were about to give it up when suddenly we saw two heads come out of the water at the same place. We sat down and ate our breakfast, which was to do as lunch, it being then eleven, and which consisted mainly of the cold hump of an ox, which was quite excellent, like the best pressed beef, and by that time the large mugger was back again on the strip of sand.

Then I did a very cautious stalk and got to the top of the cliff, some 90 yards from the mugger. Drawing a very careful bead, I fired. The bullet hit him a tremendous whack ; he lay lashing with his tail for about four seconds, and then disappeared into the water. The betting is a thousand to one against you in this game.

Then another very long and cold journey down stream. Finally, a huge garial, which is supposed to live entirely on fish, has a long thin nose, and always grows to a much bigger size than the crocodile, was seen in the middle of the water. There was no way to approach him. We simply travelled down as near as we could to him, and when he showed signs of movement I fired at about 200 yards. The bullet went just over his back.

The next incident was a large crocodile, who saw us before we saw him. Boat going hard, engines at work up and down, crocodile moving ; a wild shot from me and another from Cleveland left him unscathed.

To cut a long story short, the only other two shots I got were these. We saw the biggest crocodile I have ever seen in my life lying on a spit of sand, separated by a narrow channel of water, below one of these sand cliffs. If we could have got above him, the shot would have been simple at about 40 yards, but although he could not see us, he heard the grass moving on the top, knew that it was not cattle, and when we looked out he had disappeared. Beyond him were two much smaller crocodiles. I stalked to them, fired as one left the land for the water, the other just beginning to move. I got him ; I hit him in the right place, and shot again before he could get away. So we bagged him, but he was only about 7 ft. long and had not much leather on him. It was a great disappointment that the grass was so thick so that we did not get the big one.

Late in the evening I got another shot at a big garial, also from a bank after a stalk. It was a desperate shot, 500 yards away, but I hit him in the right place, because he lashed his tail and appeared unable to move ; but the trouble about crocodile shooting is that nearly always you want two shots, and if you do a gallery shot with the first barrel, you cannot repeat it with the second. I had time to have three more shots at him, and Cleveland two ; but the light was failing, the distance was great, and accuracy was impossible. Alas ! he got away, only to die at once ; but they are irrecoverable.

It is very pleasant work and requires very good marksmanship, and at the same time is doing extraordinarily good work. But it is very difficult and disheartening if one wants leather, as Cleveland does, because he makes it a business. He told me that on a clear day we should have at least 25 shots at crocodiles, and we ought to have bagged about eight. As it was, I missed two, and should have had three with any luck. It was very pleasant. Cleveland is the best and kindest of hosts. There was no flurry and organisation ; it was like a rough day in England. I like him more and more. He is very simple, and so keen, and such a charming host. It is difficult to believe him as head of the C.I.D., and a successful head. During the last year the revolutionary movement has practically been scotched. Fifty absconders were giving them great trouble. They have got all of them now except 15, and in order to catch each one, he is starting a new organisation. If we can catch these 15 before they do any new harm, things are promising, but it looks very much like a race between the police and their organising ability. It is curious how we use Indians for this work and how reliable they are. Cleveland told me that a man who was doing the work in Europe with him years ago, when he came back from England in 1913 had obviously become unreliable, and is now a leading anarchist, so we sometimes fail. When he was in Europe I remember him as always being suspected of being recognised as one of the three leading anarchists in Europe, but he was not an anarchist at all, but a spy. Now he appears not to have become a spy, but an anarchist. He threatens to publish his experiences of the C.I.D., but Cleveland says he can do no harm ; he never knew any work but his own. It is true he can say we have spies in the anarchist camp, but then as the Indian anarchist suspects every other anarchist of being a spy, I do not think this much matters.

I got a most awful cold and am feeling very rheumaticky this (Monday) morning.

For the rest, we saw many darters, many eagles, great quantities of ruddy sheldrakes or Brahmany ducks, as they are called here, a few mallard, some black storks, some goggle-eyed plovers, a few sandpipers, and some godwits. The big muggers always seem to have birds in attendance, who often, Cleveland tells me, warn them.

We motored back 30 miles and had dinner on a canal bank, round a large fire—very pleasant and quite a good dinner. The terrible cough that had been bothering me all day long seems to have left as suddenly as it came, and to have left rheumatism. It has been a strenuous day. We had 40 miles to motor after dinner, which went very slowly.

Cleveland slept all the time; I cannot sleep in a car, particularly an open one. We had a special pass to allow us to get over the big Jumma Bridge after dark, but, unfortunately, all the sentries were asleep, and it took half an hour before we could get somebody to climb over and wake them up. We got into Delhi at last, and I went to bed.

Monday, January 28. I woke up quite early and turned over the political situation as it struck me after a rest, and I think I have got a suggestion which may possibly get rid of A subjects. The more one examines the A list, it looks as if it ought to consist of nothing except those things in which the Government of India is interested. Law and order it is interested in, and this definition applied to everything except land revenue. If we could get over land revenue, it would look as if the B men with the new governments would have control of everything which was really essentially provincial.

We have got a meeting this morning at eleven, to which I propose to put this suggestion.

I have very little to record. The visit of the heads of Provinces and its great strenuousness has left me absolutely limp.

We had a very successful meeting of our delegation, and we went through the whole of the topics now outstanding. The new scheme, under which an A house and a B house in the Provinces is avoided, was received by all with enthusiasm as a great improvement, and it was agreed to go ahead with this. We received the satisfactory results of the Committee on A and B subjects, and we came to three determinations: (1) to push again the Administrative Committee idea in the first six years as being a great improvement on Standing Committees; (2) that Vincent and Basu together should write a note on Indianisation; (3) that Duke, Kisch, and Seton should confer as to the future of the India Office, (*a*) its constitution; (*b*) its relations to the House of Commons; (*c*) its relations to the Government of India. I am bound to say I am much struck by Hirtzel's suggestion that previous sanction ought to be abolished, the right of veto being retained. If the Home Government then interfered, it would be only after public opinion in India had been expressed. If the Viceroy and his Government were going to do something of which his Legislative Council would disapprove, knowing the risk of veto, he would informally obtain the approval of the Secretary of State first. If the Secretary of State were going to veto, he would do it only with reluctance if he knew that public opinion was behind the Government of India.

After lunch I saw the Viceroy—a very cordial meeting, and we discussed the situation generally. He seemed very pleased with the way things were going. He also is very tired, and apparently spent most of Sunday in bed. We discussed various matters that ought to be in the report, and felt that we must say something about social difficulties between Indians and Europeans, caste and caste, Mohammedans and Hindus. We are not going to have any further discussion on lubricants, but the Viceroy is going to give me his assurance of what he is going to do.

In the evening I dined with Maffey, to avoid meeting the Nizam.

Tuesday, January 29. Lowndes, Hill, Donoughmore and I had a long talk about the new scheme. They were all in agreement. Lowndes wants to extend it to the Government of India instead of an Upper House. I do not much like this idea. Our scheme for the Government of India is not comparable at all to our scheme for the local governments, and the more we accentuate the difference the better. Besides, if we do not get a Second Chamber now, we shall never get one.

Then I had a letter from Alwar urging that the deputation of princes should be postponed for three weeks, and I went up to see the Viceroy. Before that Maffey came to see me and told me that the Viceroy was considering going to Mesopotamia : had I any views ? I determined that if the Viceroy really wanted to go to Mesopotamia we could go together on my way home, and that I would telegraph to the Prime Minister for his views. It would, to my mind, be enormously useful to go, but, on the other hand, no human being can realise how anxious I am now to get home, and anything that prolongs my absence causes me infinite regret. It will be heartrending to find how small India, which is absorbing the whole of my mind and activities, will loom when I get home.

The Viceroy and I agreed at our interview that Alwar should be told that the deputation of princes could not be postponed, and that although the princes had not obtained the ratification of all their number to their proposals a preliminary talk would be useful, but it was impossible to contemplate any conference of all the princes at Delhi. I told Chelmsford about Mesopotamia and Maffey's conversation, and he promised to let me know to-day.

I then had some talk with Donoughmore ; some talk with Duke about the Government of India ; told him that the Viceroy agreed with me that a Second Chamber was necessary, and then went up to lunch.

Then, tired out, I went to sleep. Afterwards I met the Viceroy at tennis, and he told me that he had contemplated feeding the British Army in India on beef from Australia, but had to give it up when he discovered that you could buy beef for 1½d. per pound in parts of India. He told me that a motor car had dashed a few days ago through the Kyber Pass, the two occupants of which had been detained on the railway between Peshawar and Lahore, and it was suspected that one of them was the fourth son of the Amir, who had apparently run away from his father. Enquiries are pending.

After tennis I had a long talk with Curtis ; interesting, as usual. He began by telling me that he had come here to stay with the Viceroy because the Viceroy thought he would be of use, but he could not accept Chelmsford's hospitality without telling Chelmsford that he was not going any longer to take action at the end of the War about Chelmsford's prohibition of Indian civilians joining round table groups ; he came as a disarmed man, but he did hope that civil servants would get more political liberty. I told him what had been occurring in this connection, and he was quite satisfied. We discussed the possibility of Gourlay editing a magazine for Indian civil servants, to keep them informed of political developments, and of running a propagandist department, and he liked it enormously. He tells me that unless something of this sort is done Gourlay proposes to go to England at the end of the War and devote himself to educating Indians in London. This is splendid work, of course, but is very fruitless, and I think Gourlay is too good for it.

I dined in ; had one rubber of bridge, and then a very long talk with Chelmsford. He approved of everything that Curtis had suggested, and told me of Lowndes' difficulties, of two houses in the Government of India and the segregation of officials. He suggests a compromise of a Grand Committee scheme such as in the Provinces, together with an Upper House of Notables. All my radical instincts jib at an Upper House of Notables. I think the committee must go a little further, Meyer and Lowndes on the one hand, and Basu and Duke on the other, and if they cannot arrive at a compromise, Chelmsford and I must take charge.

Wednesday, January 30. This morning I had a talk in this direction with Duke, who agrees.

I spent the morning dictating notes, as material for our report. This is going to be my main work for the next few days. In the afternoon I had a long sitting with Chelmsford and Wood about the princes. It was not at all satisfactory. They want to leave everything in a very woolly condition, and I am not at all sure that it is not true that we shall have to be very indefinite in our recommendations. The great thing is to show the way. Wood is particularly of the school which wants to keep the princes in cold storage. Zealously criticising every word of their address, always looking for an encroachment upon Government of India privileges, I can understand the irritation that is caused.

In the evening I had a very long talk with Curtis, which was very satisfactory. I think he is in whole-hearted agreement with us, and thinks we have done well.

Then dinner at the Commander-in-Chief's. I was told that these informal dinners that the Commander-in-Chief is so fond of giving were most delightful. I like the old man enormously, and I like his wife, too. On my other side sat Sir Charles Cleveland, who, I understand, is now being invited to meet me wherever I dine, and held out as a bait for me when I am given dinner invitations, much as a young and beautiful woman is sometimes associated with a particular man in England. I like him, although I think he has overdone the C.I.D., but he has certainly a great success to his name.

I must record a story which strikes me as worth remembering.

After Hardinge's bomb, it occurred to the C.I.D. that they would like to know the whereabouts of a man who had previously been associated with bombing. They got hold of an old spy and informer, and promised him a thousand rupees reward for the detection of the man. He found the man living in a village in Indore and qualifying for his matriculation examination. As the man in his former incarnation was a B.A. of Edinburgh University, this struck Cleveland as very amusing. He said he was doing no harm, and they did not interfere with him. He introduced him to his wife, whom he had deserted to go to Edinburgh and France to be associated with the anarchist group there. The informer got his thousand rupees, and was so pleased with it that he said he would get for Cleveland any other man he wanted in India. Cleveland said he wanted nobody else at present. The old man then said that if he was given a lakh he would introduce Cleveland to Nana Sahib! He persisted in assuring Cleveland that he need not pay a penny until he was convinced that it was Nana Sahib. Cleveland came to the conclusion that to find Nana Sahib in 1913 might be embarrassing, and was not worth a lakh, and the informer is now dead; but I am bound to confess that this story that Nana Sahib was alive—I presume he must be over 90—four or five years ago is very thrilling to me. I wonder if we shall ever hear his whole story of the last 50 years! If I had a lakh I should pay it gladly to have a talk with him about the Mutiny, and I should have liked to see him hanged.

Thursday, January 31. A heavy cold; very slack. Spent morning on the mail. Very satisfactory in many ways. Uneasy about omissions from air-raid news. I discovered that a bomb fell in Queen Anne's Gate, six doors from my own house—a "dud." Nothing mentioned in correspondence, but my valet has it from his brother. Thought at first it was not true, but fear that raid was not mentioned in my letters at all so as to avoid mention of this. Of course, a "dud" bomb may be a shrapnel shell which does not burst on reaching ground. India Office letters contained a reference to the fact that the Reforms Committee has decided on a scheme of financial devolution closely in agreement with the results of last week's work. This is very satisfactory.

In the afternoon I had an interview with Prosanto K. Sen, who tells me that the Congress was a great failure and the feeling against Mrs. Besant is running high.

Then rather a nice little interview with old Jaipur, who

apparently agrees with all the recommendations of the Ruling Chiefs Committee. I expected him to be very conservative. To hear him talking about chambers of princes and arbitration boards, and so forth, and to see him driving up in a two-horse carriage, because he objects to motor cars as modern inventions, was rather remarkable. Progress with these Chiefs is a very thin veneer, and usually comes from a trusted Diwan.

Then a glorious drive with Lady Chelmsford in the country. We had a very interesting afternoon. We went first to the Mosque and Tomb of Nizam-ud-din. It is a very pretty place, full of interesting old tombs, with glorious marble doors, of rather late in the 18th century; the tomb of one of Shah Jahan's daughters, interesting because, alone of all the tombs, she objected to a marble top, and insisted upon grass growing out of the top of hers, which it does; and in the centre a very deep green tank, into which, from startling heights, boys jump head first. But the interesting part of it was that we had fixed upon a day upon which a great pilgrimage was going on. The whole place was swarming with holy Mohammedans of all ages and all sexes—women closely veiled, prostrate in prayer; unkempt men; crowds rushing about shouting their prayers; holy men nearly naked and unkempt, shouting on the name of Allah; the Mosque crowded with people praying; the tombs covered with offerings of vegetables and covered with rose leaves; everywhere wild Mohammedan eyes, and we the only two Europeans, welcomed, people endeavouring to explain everything to us in languages we could not understand, although Lady Chelmsford talks Hindustani. How on earth we ever escaped the C.I.D. and the police I do not know. Then on to one of Delhi's oldest cities, Tughlakabad, right out in the country, with a glorious view over the plains of Delhi and the Kutb three miles off; great ruddy walls in ruin; a nice tomb; fine rocks all set in among the young corn.

In the evening I had a talk with Marris, who is rather upset about the Civil Service, who fears that everything is crumbling under them. They approve schemes one by one, and find that nothing is being left. I tried to soothe him. Bridge at Government House, and so to bed.

Friday, February 1. Duke and Basu have got a good scheme for the Government of India. I do not know whether Meyer and Lowndes will accept it.

I had another talk with Curtis in the afternoon, the main upshot of which was that he wants me to express my own opinion even when it differed from Chelmsford's, because he thought it was a duty to the Cabinet. I find I see eye to eye with him on every question, but I have since had a letter from him in which he says this is due to suppression, and he wants another interview.

At three o'clock Chelmsford and I had an interview with Sastri, which lasted till half-past four. Chelmsford professed himself very pleased with it. I told him the scheme, and I must say I was rather depressed. He would not commit himself to anything ; he thought there would be no objection to what we proposed among the minority, which would become the majority. This does not look, from the so-called leader of the moderates of India, like any enthusiasm for the scheme. It increased my certainty that although I have had a great success with the Government of India, the local governments, and a personal success with deputations, I think our remedies will fall far short of the circumstances of the country. Sastri reverted to the idea of discussing the matter with chosen Indians, and he and Basu promised to prepare a list again.

In the evening Bikaner came to see me. He told me that Alwar had reverted to the idea that he did not like to refer to their alliance with the King as a privilege ; he even, according to Bikaner, objected to the use of the term " Government of India," and wanted to call it " the Crown's Government of India." He also, according to Bikaner, objected to the use of the word "Chamber," just as he objected to the use of the word "Council," and now wants "Assemblage." I told Bikaner that Alwar was wrong in thinking Councils were always summoned by a superior body; what about the Council of Public Schools, the London County Council, and so forth. A Chamber was not an ambiguous term, although it might refer to lavatory accommodation; so might a "Cabinet." "Assemblage" only meant, to my knowledge, a journalistic word to signify a meeting of crows. I told Bikaner that although we would always defend the States against interference by British Indians, yet British Indians would be bound to criticise more and more if Indian Native States did not come into line with modern developments. He said he quite agreed, and expected bombs in Native States. I asked how many Native States had separate civil lists, and he said: "Very few." He himself has. He takes five per cent. of the revenues, but they give him some motor cars, some electric light, some furniture for his palaces, and so forth, but taking it as an inclusive sum he thinks it will work out at under 10 per cent. He says that when he came to the throne he only got under the arrangement one lakh a year; now he gets three lakhs, and he has only succeeded in saving 30 lakhs in 20 years, which is his whole personal property, although 21 lakhs of this was a debt recovered, through the Government of India, from the State, of money which had been wrongfully taken by the State from his mother. This confirms my impression that India is a cheap country for a rich man, although a dear country for a poor one.

Then dinner, after which we left for my much-needed week-end. Before leaving I pressed into Chelmsford's hand the various notes for the report, explaining to him that they were only as the basis for discussion.

Saturday, February 2. At Dholpur we had a royal time. Nothing could have been nicer than our greeting, our welcome, and our host. He is a gentleman, if ever there was one—well-educated, shy, with a gentle demeanour and a reserved manner which is most attractive. No one would think he was of the same age as Patiala. He looks a mere boy, although he is over 27.

Quite a gifted musician on the Indian national instrument, which looks like a big guitar; he plays it very well in his own gentle way. An excellent shot, he is a real sportsman.

After breakfast at a very nice and modest red-stone palace, tiled all over with Doulton sanitary tiles, we motored some 13 miles to Sat Kezari, and then on to our first beat. Comfortably ensconced on the edge of a cliff, we had a delightful view across the jungle and fine plains to the Gwalior Hills. The beat was managed by a curious Frenchman, Honret, a descendant of a French prisoner of war in 1815, whose father had been in the service of Gwalior. He quarrelled with Gwalior, where he had been his tiger hunter for 20 years, and last year came to Dholpur. The beat was extraordinarily interesting, full of sambhur, black buck, chincara, pigs, but no stags came forward. There was a tiger in it, although the beat had missed it. It appeared suddenly on a rock high up away to the right of the landscape when we were all concentrated on the left, and it dashed off over the hill, followed by two shots from Verney and his company away to our right. It was a big tiger, and poor little Dholpur was very much disappointed. It was just one of the unfortunate circumstances of war. Afterwards a bear came ambling down the hill towards us, the first I had seen. I fired at it too soon and missed it, and then again, when I think I hit it. Donoughmore sent it rolling down the hill; it got up again and I finished it off. Whose it was will always remain a mystery. There were four bullet wounds

D. H.H. of Dholpur A. P. E. S. M.

MOTORING AT DHOLPUR

[To face page 238

in it, but many people shot at it when it was wounded. It was a big bear, over 6 ft. in length.

Then lunch at Tal Tabli and another beat. We were on a small tower in one of those indescribable ravines with views all round. There were several fine sambhur stags. I killed a blue bull first; then I gave Donoughmore a chance at a sambhur, which he killed—a very fine one with 37 in. horns. Parsons did a marvellous shot right across our front and killed another sambhur, but a smaller one; then another bear, which I wounded, but which disappeared after scratching three men, not very severely. One of them, I found out afterwards, who said he was scratched by the bear sat down on a thorn bush!

Then home to dinner, after a most delightful day. On the way home I was presented with a poem, a copy of which I append. The poor man who presented it was greeted with roars of laughter from everybody who read it. We behaved very badly, led by Dholpur, but it could not be helped, as anybody who reads may see.

Tal Tabli's Jungle Echo on February 2, 1918.

At the time of the

SECRETARY OF THE STATES SHOOTING VISIT.

1 Tal Tabli's lovely tank and sacred place,
How pure 'tis looking in its natural grace.

2 The more so as the SECRETARY OF THE STATE
Has given it honour with his good mate.

3 How do the beautiful JUNGLE branches bow,
How good the beasts of prey do jump in row.

4 As if saluting all THE SECRETARY OF THE STATE,
Coming to sacrifice themselves at any rate.

5 Where lamb and Lion on this lovely tank
Safely drink their water on the only bank.

6 Reminding old-day justice how good thing
Of our H.H. Secretary, Emperor King. . . .

7 Where lovely lotus grows as pure as much
Standing in water but without its touch.

8 Reminding of the Piety, Purity Indian thing
Of our H.H. Secretary, Emperor King.

By JIWA RAM, B.A.,
Tehsildar Gird,
Dholpur Station
Dated the 2nd February, 1918. (Camp Tal Tabli).

In the evening we saw the gold scabbarded sword dresented by Akbar to Dholpur's ancestors, and also the diamond he presented; Dholpur's new potato-like pearls; and we had some music.

Dholpur told me at dinner that his family originally came from Nepal ; occupied Gwalior for 1,300 years ; and was finally driven out to their present territory, given to them by the East India Company, with a promise of enlargement that has never been fulfilled. Originally Sikh, they are connected with the Patiala's, and have recently become Rajputs. Dholpur's ancestors had in command of their army a curious Italian family of Filoses, the last remnant of which is the old man at Gwalior who built Gwalior's palace. Dholpur told me that his ancestor was warned that he ought not to employ Italians, who would betray them. During the first six months of the war between his ancestors and the Scindia of the time no impression was made upon Dholpur's forces, and then the Filoses were bought. The prophecy came true, and they were vanquished. The population now is only about 300,000 souls, but he knows everything about them all, and when the land settlement was made he went round every village with the settlement officer, and knows the whole thing intimately. The State produces the most lovely red-stone, and he has the contract for supplying all the stone for New Delhi.

We went to bed at ten.

Sunday, February 3. We started at half-past seven by train, and went to a place called Bari, and then had a motor drive of six miles to a lovely old palace of Shah Jehan's at Teysildar, on the edge of a tank too lovely for words. After breakfast we drove back towards the station and motored along another road until we came to another enormous tank made by bunding, and journeyed on it in motor launches for six miles. It reminded me of nothing so much as a Northern Scottish loch, with its blue water right to the edge of the rocks, which are covered with short jungle that might for all the world be birch scrub. There were a few duck, snake birds, egrets, kingfishers, harriers, eagles, ospreys, and the place swarms with fish-eating muggers, although we did not see any. Then a short drive of four miles along a primitive road to a tiger beat. Here was great excitement—three tigers for certain in one beat! They would all come out together! Then news came that a fourth had been seen that morning that might or might not be in the beat. More excitement! We sat in a very comfortable brick tower on the edge of a cliff, with the jungle before us and an open space below in the jungle, so that it would have been nice easy shooting. The "kill" was quite close to us, and the vultures were all over the place. They had been sitting on our tower, and were quarrelling over the kill. The beat was a short one. One incident disturbed it, a large tame buffalo crashing through the jungle. The beat came closer and closer. No sign of tigers. So incredible was it that they spent a full hour sending in dogs and throwing bombs into a cave in the rocks, thinking that the tigers must be lurking there, but it was all of no avail. The whole thing was a great disappointment, and poor Dholpur was on the verge of tears, and could not be got to smile all through lunch. Afterwards, when we assured him that Donoughmore would come back again, and begged him to come with us to Kheri for our holiday, he picked up.

In the afternoon Franey and Verney went off a mile and a half to look for a bear. Three bears came out a quarter of a mile away : no result. A panther was also seen in the beat. We went to try a chance beat at a tiger which had been seen in another nullah. It was an enormous nullah, nearly half a mile wide where we were, and thickly jungled. The beat saw the tiger ; we did not, and it all ended with nothing.

We went back in the evening, as it was getting dark, and Donoughmore did a marvellous shot at a mugger, which, as usual, got into the water. It was a most pleasant day, but it was difficult to persuade our host how pleasant it was. News came that my bear of yesterday had been found in a cave ; so far, so good.

After dinner and a very friendly leave-taking we came back to Delhi.

Monday, February 4. It is very cold. I found my notes for the report returned.

The morning opened with alarms and excursions. I had a letter from Curtis telling me that his agreement with me in all my propositions was not so real as it sounded, and asking if he could see me to talk about it. Then I had a visit from Basu, who told me that Nair had given away our schemes freely to the members of the Legislative Council. He was gently chidden by Sastri, and said that they had a right to know it, and he was not going to keep it secret. Without a moment's hesitation I came to the conclusion that I must not know this, so I told Basu to tell Nair not to play the fool, and I decided that if I told Chelmsford anything about it Nair would get into serious trouble, rightly, which would react on our schemes, because Nair would then oppose them. The exposition seems to have been on the whole successful.

At eleven o'clock we started with the Native States, and gave them their chamber of princes, their advisory committee, and agreed to redraft their paragraphs asking for a Commission of Enquiry and a Hague Tribunal. I rather staggered them by asking them what their allegations of broken treaties were due to. They had all been to me with their stories of the scandalous interference by Residents, and I wanted them to make a clean breast of it. They tried to hedge, and said they were afraid of the future, so I asked them very pointedly whether they had anything to complain of in the past. Again they tried to hedge. They said : " Not since Lord Minto's time." Again I asked them : Could I take it that all grievances had been righted ? I told them that they were our allies, of whom the King-Emperor was proud, and we wanted them to be happy, and they they ought to state their case. They said then that they would prepare lists of statements and send them in later on.

We adjoined for lunch, which I had with Nair. He was very friendly, but he complains of not beginning till 1922. I assured him that I was going to take no fixed period ; they would have to begin as soon after the Act was ready as was possible. He then also said that he would never support the scheme at all if I gave way on the right of the Governor to restore the Budget figures on any other subjects but peace and order. He would far rather take butter out of a dog's mouth than give way on this ; the Budget was everything ; he would never accept a division of subjects without this. I argued with him a lot, but he was stubborn. I do not think he meant much. However, I wrote to Basu and Donoughmore to tackle him. He said he had heard that Vincent was preparing a note, and that he hoped no members of the Council would be asked to record any opinion at the present stage ; that even though one accepted the conclusions, one would have to take objection to some of the arguments put forward ; that Sir Michael O'Dwyer's memorandum had bitten into his mind, and he would have to answer it some day. He told me that we could never again rely upon Mohammedans, and that therefore he would like three Indian members of the Viceroy's Council, one not a Hindu or Mohammedan—an Indian Christian or Parsi ; otherwise, in a crisis you could not rely on the Mohammedan, and the Hindu might side with him for his support on other things. This was an interesting argument from Nair. Nair also reiterated his desire that I should not tackle lubricants, because he was afraid it would arouse opposition so as to endanger reforms.

Back to the princes in the afternoon. We gave them direct access to the Government of India, and I got from them an admission that they would prefer the Resident abolished and the Agent to the Governor-General kept, than the other way round. We also agreed that they should have some system of joint discussion on matters affecting both Native States and British India in the reform scheme ; they were highly delighted, and we adjourned at four.

The Jam Saheb came to tea with me—very nice, very pleasant.

After he had left I did a little writing, and then the Viceroy came to see me, and we talked till nearly dinner time.

Tuesday, *February* 5. In the afternoon we finished the Chief's conference with votes of thanks, and they all went away.

Then I had to see the youngest son of the Begum, whom she has made her Chief Secretary at the age of 23—a very nice little fellow who has been instrumental in writing the articles in the *Pioneer* which come from Bhopal on the Indian States. I think I have referred to them before as being excellent articles. He was educated at the Mayo College at Ajmer, and seems to be getting into the saddle well.

In the evening I discussed with the Viceroy my notes. Curtis's objections to dealing with anything more than the mere reform schemes, I am afraid, will defeat every effort I have tried to make to get trial by jury, judicial and executive, etc., solved. Well, I cannot help it ; I must give it up for the present ; the reform schemes are the most important.

In the evening I dined with Sir George Barnes—quite a pleasant little party. After dinner I had some talk with Lady Grant : she is one of the few well-dressed women here.

Wednesday, February 6. This morning I am momentarily expecting Alwar to breakfast.

I forget whether I have recorded a story which shows, if true, that the Indian coolie is not such a fool politically as people say he is, but I doubt whether it is true. It came to me again yesterday. Two men who were discussing how much a coolie knew, asked a coolie if he knew who and what the Secretary of State was, and he replied : "Yes. The Secretariat Saheb is he who tells the King-Emperor to sack the Lord Saheb."

Alwar came to breakfast, and we had an entrancing one and a quarter hours. I am afraid I burden these pages with tributes to this man's intelligence. The burden of his song was this—that our position *vis-a-vis* the Native States was unintelligible. He only wanted to know ; he was a searcher and an enquirer after truth ; and he was quite willing to accept anything which he was convinced was true, but that, unfortunately, when he proceeded to argue on these matters he was called treacherous and traitorous. He is the only Chief who has taken the trouble to read the treaties—Aitchison's collection. As he explained to me pathetically, the Viceroy has not read them. There are only 15 volumes; it would only take a month!

I came home to a late and hurried lunch to find Curtis. He began a dismal complaint. He appears to have been thoroughly frightened by something or other, and begs me to drop most of my proposals. At this eleventh hour he beseeches me: "We are standing on the edge of the most frightful calamity." Have you ever been talked to in this strain by the Round Table? I like Curtis very much; I thought he was so closely in accord with me, and I am deeply disappointed at this new turn of affairs. He appears to have had a letter from Chirol expressing alarm. He appears to be afraid that Curzon and Milner will say to Lloyd George: "We cannot support this." He is afraid I shall be driven to resignation, in which case he says there is nothing but martial law possible in India; that there must be no delay in completing my proposals; that the larger they are the less chance there is of getting them through, therefore they must be small. Indian public opinion does not matter; those whom I think will support me are going to turn and rend me; no scheme has a chance, and so on.

I went back to the Council in a fit of deep depression, and listened to the debate on re-arrangement of provincial boundaries. Sarma read his long speech as badly as possible. He was followed by Hamilton Grant. Fagan of the Punjab strung together a series of proverbs and made a curiously poor contribution—"more haste less speed," "the higher the fewer," and so forth; Bannerjea again imploring, with all the thunder of the platform, Sarma not to complicate the issue by bringing in this resolution. There was a good speech from Kincade of the Bombay Government, saying that Sarma's and Shafi's reasons for attaching Sind to the Punjab were for much the same reasons as the Germans wanted to attach Holland. I think the really good speech of the day was from Sastri—well delivered, well phrased, and very impressive, urging the rejection of the motion. It had no supporters ; it was rather unfairly treated, and was finally negatived without a division.

I came back and had a little interview with Jaipur, who came to take his leave ; the Maharao of Cutch, who talked to me about the interminable and difficult dispute between Cutch and Morvi, which does not seem to me to have been well handled ; the Diwan of Jhind, who came to complain that everything that the princes asked for ought to be resisted, but that His Highness of Jhind was neutral.

Then I went to see Curtis, to whom I had given to read my notes for my report—more gloomy than ever, more certain of disaster than ever. It is the most depressing circumstance, which has nearly driven me to the verge of suicide, because up till to-day Curtis has seemed to be a supporter of everything we proposed.

A pleasant little dinner in my tent—Donoughmore, Halliday, and Parsons, with a bottle of wine that we had been dying for for a long time. Then a big party at Government House, with 23 investitures of various Orders. Basu celebrated the occasion by telling me that Nair had said he would never accept anything proposed at present for the restoration of Budget items ; he could not have the words " Interests of good Government or interests of the Government." Vincent tells me he wants to get back into the Government of India in order to express his opinion against our proposals. Really it is black Wednesday, if ever there was one.

Thursday, February 7. So I write this morning, probably not being able to add anything more before I leave to-night for my holiday. This is practically the end. Our proposals in principle are complete. We are engaged on the writing of the report, which will be complete by the end of this month. But I leave, as I say, in the depths of gloom—no chance of public acceptance ; no possibility of getting any trimmings which the Government of India are shying at ; Curtis, Nair, and Vincent, all hostile—Curtis with his power of working Milner and Curzon. Well, things may look brighter, but I must say that they have never looked worse. I have come to an agreement with the Government of India which nobody accepts, and that is what I have always feared might be the outcome. You see, there has been nobody who has constructed ; they have only acquiesced ; and where I fear that my own proposals may have been spoiled is in my desperate endeavour to find compromises at every stage.

I end up with a story which is new to me, told to me last night by Donoughmore, who says he had it from Major Alexander, as an illustration of the red tape of the Indian Army. A baby was born in the married quarters, and after it was born an indent was made for rations for it. The Babu in charge of the accounts queried this item, and asked what time the child was born. When he got the answer : " Two o'clock in the afternoon," he made the comment : " Rations disallowed ; see section blank of the Army Regulations." When the Army Regulations were turned up the section was found to run something as follows : " Troops disembarking after mid-day will receive their rations on board ship."

I started work with the grim determination that I must go through with this thing, and that, after all, most of the fears that people were expressing were the fears of frightened men. Nobody could have gone to the debate at the Legislative Council yesterday without realising what a farce it all was—that these 27 creatures should claim to be a representative institution.

It is absolutely essential to put things on a better basis, and I think that the emendations of our schemes which Meyer, Lowndes, Basu, and Duke have arrived at, under which, in a House of 67 elected members and 33 nominated, unless there is a two-thirds majority the Government have the right to take the Bill to the Upper House, will prove effective.

Basu and Vincent came to tell me about their Indianisation scheme, which works up to 50 per cent. in the I.C.S. in 25 years. Basu, Vincent tells me, expressed his approval of his conclusions, if not of his arguments. Vincent approves of the idea of nominating 50 Indians this year, but the difficulty is that speeches were made by Chamberlain that the Emergency Bill passed for the War would not be used for Indianisation. Vincent is of opinion that if you do not go back on the vacancies, (111), which exist at present, but nominate Indians for the new ones, largely on the ground of the new policy of the Government and on the fact that the War is lasting so long and there are no Europeans available, it could be done. I must consult Chamberlain about this. Basu left me, and I begged him, when his Committee met in the afternoon to try and get over the difficulty. I said: "I do not want dissenting minutes in the Viceroy's Council." I said this passionately, because Vincent was there, who I knew was contemplating one. Vincent immediately said that he hoped nobody would write a dissenting minute, because if one was written several would be written.

Then Basu left, and Vincent and I had a heart to heart talk. He is a strange creature. I told him that I wanted to pose as a man who said to the I.C.S.: "My friends, times are changing, and you are in for a bad time. You have got to put up with it. I will do everything to help you, and you will have my support all the way through in the functions that still remain to you." Instead of that, I found that they felt that in assenting to the constitution policy, by discussions about Judicial and Executive, and so forth, the ground was crumbling under their feet. Vincent said this was true. I then said: "Well, I will drop all talk of lubricants; I will defend the indefensible by seeing that the Civil Service are left with certain functions to perform. It regarded these things as essential. When the time came to relieve them of this responsibility, it would be the time to criticise the armoury. Now they must have whatever they wanted." To my astonishment, the old man said at once : " No, say in Parliament that these things did require examination and that you would see that the Government of India examined them." Imagine the horror with which the Viceroy would regard such an announcement. It is the very thing I thought Vincent wanted to avoid, although, of course, very, very difficult to defend. Then Vincent began a prayer for an Act this year. I told him that I was convinced it would be a good thing to get an Act as soon as possible, and that I would tell the Cabinet that, although what we were sent out to do was to discuss a policy to put into force at the end of the War. I said to him that a statute this year was impossible. He replied : " A statute is no good unless it is this year," that he feared something akin to martial law if there is any delay.

When he left me I went to talk to Duke. To my horror, I found him infected with the Curtis bacillus and inclined to go back on everything. So far as I could I kept my temper. I was interrupted by a visit from Tony Grant, just back from Mesopotamia. He tells me that Cox has come round to the belief that the Arabs would welcome Indian colonisation, that the potentialities by irrigation of Mesopotamia are enormous, and that even with what they are doing by flood irrigation the wheat area this year will be four times what it was last, and will probably support all the troops there. He says it is marvellous what we have done. Of course, irrigation will destroy the waterway for anything but native craft, but the railways will form our communications.

Then I wrote my mail letters, which I am afraid were rather gloomy ; went to lunch, and after lunch had a talk with Basu. Basu had had a talk with Curtis. He says that Curtis's desire to be in a hurry is based on an apprehension that unless the statute comes forward at once there will be agitation. It is quite certain that it is not so ; people are not so much in a hurry as all that. I put one or two of Curtis's suggestions to him, and he scouted them. I am perfectly convinced that if I water down my proposals there will be no sort of acceptance for any of them, and a politician who does not think of his public is a fool.

Then I had a three hours' session with the Viceroy, and we went through all my notes, Duke being there, and we approved them generally. I was a little horrified to find that the Viceroy had been re-writing the one which embodies the scheme itself, and I do not think improving it. He seemed to think that he was not re-writing it, but that it was a note of his own. So long as we keep to the fixed point in our scheme, responsibility in the Provinces, through dyarchy to responsibility, we shall be all right.

After that I saw Donoughmore, and learned that his Committee had finished its work, keeping for Budget restoration purposes peace, tranquillity, and interests of the Province or any part thereof, provided that if they do not approve the Legislative Council may appeal to the Government, and the Government can register a protest which is to be laid on the table of the House of Commons. I do not know whether Nair will take this.

Dinner in the A.D.C.'s room, and a start at nine ; a comfortable railway journey to Bareilly, which we reached at quarter-past two ; then a rush across the platform in undress, and on to the Rohilkhand-Kumosan narrow gauge railway, where we turned into bed after a hot cup of tea. Bitterly cold.

IX
KHERI

Friday, *February* 8. We reached Palia Kalan at half-past seven this morning, and found Clutterbuck, my dear old friend Bambahadur, and the Deputy Commissioner for the district, Campbell, waiting for us on the platform. We motored four miles to our camp. This is situated on a flat plain on the edge of the jungle, in a mango grove ; very comfortable tents, in two rows, with a dining tent in the centre. Bambahadur has a camp of his own about a quarter of a mile off. There is a telegraph office and a post office, so that we are in close communication with home. When I was in camp here five years ago we shifted camp every day. Now, during the last three weeks roads have been driven through the jungle which just take motor cars. Of course they will all be washed away in the rains ; and these, with our 52 elephants, enable us to see and do everything we want. I was astonished to find that permission to put up a mango grove was given to ryots, and that there was no land revenue on the grove ; they live on the fruit, and the timber reverts to the Zemindar as soon as it ceases to be fruit bearing.

Here is a time, a glorious time, for clear thinking, and the whole day I have been thinking hard. Two new parts of the report have come to me. What could be better for thought ? During the early morning in bed I can read all the papers I have brought with me ; during the long solitary rides, ambling along on an elephant, undisturbed by anything, I can turn over all the incidents of the last two months, and when I leave here my mind will be made up.

After breakfast I had a rare treat and a sight I shall never forget. One of the party here is a man called Jack Hearsey, who owns the land round about outside the State forests. He is a Eurasian, the fourth generation from General Hearsey, of Mutiny fame, who settled in this country and married an Indian woman. He is a very nice fellow, I think—very knowledgeable on natural history and the country generally. His great interest in life is hawking, and I went with him to his camp, where I saw three peregrins, a saker, a lagger, which is the resident falcon of the plains, a red-headed merlin ; and, although this is not part of the hawking outfit, a young sarus crane, two and a half months old, which he has brought up from a fledgling, and is very tame. The birds that they hawk are mainly blue jays, black ibises, grey herons, pond egrets. What struck me as very extraordinary is that the red-headed merlin, which is very little bigger than our merlin, will hawk the pond egret. He has got one fine old hen peregrin, which he told me killed nearly a thousand birds last year. After we had looked at them for some time three black ibises were reported in a field of young wheat close by, and we went for a demonstration. A boy put the ibises up ; the hood was removed from the hawk, and away he dashed for them. Up into the air went the ibises ; round in great circles went the hawk to get above them. They did not move more than 200 yards away from us, but it was all up in the air. When he had finally got over, there came the downward swoop and the crash of the ibis to the ground with the hawk on top. When they landed in some long grass the ibis got away, but the hawk dashed after him and got him down again about 150 yards away from where he originally fell, and killed him. It was a glorious sight.

We had heard news at breakfast of a tiger kill of a most confiding kind, right on the edge of the jungle in a little outlying thicket. We beat for it ; the excitement was very great, for all round were the pug-marks of tigers, at least two, and probably two cubs. But, unfortunately, the tiger had apparently killed and had then gone to join his tigress in the main jungle, which is too big to beat, so that the result was another blank. However, we found a bear in the beat, which Duke afterwards wounded—or so it is alleged—and Clutterbuck killed, a fine female bear, 6 ft. 7 in. long.

Then lunch, and a slow mouch home, when general shooting was supposed to be the order, but there was nothing to shoot. I saw some floricans, which got up very wild, partridges, snipe, and a lot of duck, and a peacock or two, but there was no chance of any shots. We had a drive for swamp deer, and three fine stags came out, but they were too far off, and the afternoon was a blank. But there were three hours of riding, during which I left my guns and went through everything. I came home in the evening, and have been dictating ever since, and I am going to bed tired out. I am purposely not putting down my two new paragraphs to-night, because I want to think to-morrow about them a little bit further, but they are roughly these :

1. We must include in our report, to ease the situation, a statement that although in ten years the statutory commission is to go to responsible government unless good cause is shown, this does not mean that we anticipate that all Provinces, or many Provinces, or any Provinces, will be ready for complete responsible government.

2. The second idea is to get a simple statute and a statutory commission immediately to work out details. These things I shall put down to-morrow afternoon.

Sunday, February 10. Sunday was a glorious day. Donoughmore and Franey had letters to write, as the mail was going out to England. We all went out, therefore, without them, over Hearsey's ground, along the banks of the River Sarda, Donoughmore and Franey going out after lunch to sit for a tiger over two kills. We rode out through the jungle, and saw several blue bull, with which we did not interfere ; but going along the stream to where the howdah elephants were waiting for us, we saw a glorious sight—about 70 stags in the burnt grass. When we reached the howdahs the Maharaja of Dholpur went off alone with Hearsey, to stalk the stags, and shot the best of them, which turned out, on measurement, to be 34 ins. We went along in line, gons dashing before us, till we reached a point where the place was alive with deer, who galloped across the front, and took to the water. It was a beautiful sight. I selected two stags that I thought to be good, and killed them—31¾ ins. and 30 ins. Halliday got one, and so did Parsons, but they were poor ones.

Then a late lunch, and very little after it, save that we saw some more stags, and I and the Maharaja went after them. I did not want to shoot any more ; the Maharaja killed one with an extraordinarily good shot. I then missed a still better one, and he got it ; and we came home in the dark. Donoughmore and Franey saw nothing.

Monday, February 11. I remained all the morning talking to Duke. In the afternoon we went out to join the party. Donoughmore had had a wonderful morning and had killed two jackals, a blue bull and a pig. Clutter had also got a pig, and they had put up a leopard which had sprung on to an elephant and got through the line, when it was wounded, it was said, by Clutter, and also shot at with shot by Taracharan.[1] We saw nothing when we joined them except a family of otters and a large number of hog deer. Donoughmore got one, and Parsons got another. I chased the otters, and must have gone within five yards of where the leopard was sitting. Taracharan shot it afterwards and killed it—a small male, 6 ft. 7½ in. long. A very pleasant afternoon out.

Tuesday, February 12. Before we started, rather late, in order to let the howdahs get off, we had a wonderful exhibition of hawking. The peregrin killed another ibis which gave him a longer flight, although not so high vertically ; and the

[1] A.D.C. to the Maharaja.

red-headed merlin killed a pond egret. It did not get above it and swoop for it, but chased it in among the trees, and eventually killed it within a yard of the block on which it lives.

We went to a place called Gohola, belonging to Hearsey, an enormous tract of 6,000 acres of grass on the edge of the forest, full of stags. Sir William Duke killed a stag which was 38 ins. long in horn and very massive, but with very few points. It is the biggest that has been seen here for a long time, but I did not envy the head, as it had very few points. I came to lunch thoroughly miserable. I had had the best of the shooting ; had had three shots at one quite good stag and two shots at another, galloping, and had missed them both. Shooting from an elephant which may move is extraordinarily difficult, particularly with strange rifles, but this incompetence distressed me. The place is so lovely ; the opportunities for thought on the elephant are so marvellous ; the glory of seeing the beasts move makes me quite happy even if I do not get a shot all day. But what does annoy me is when I prove myself to be bad at the job. Just before lunch I had a shot at a third one, missed it with both barrels, and it was killed by Parsons—a very nice stag, 32 ins. I am glad he is doing so well. The only thing that worries me is that so many of my friends are new to the job, and although, therefore, they have been very steady, I cannot reconcile it to my conscience that Clutterbuck has told them so little about it. Poor Franey is alone on the howdah, and is never told what to shoot at and what not to shoot at. Elephants are all over the place, and are very difficult to see in the long grass. It is not merely that one ought not to shoot at an elephant, but water and clay ricochet tremendously, and one ought therefore never to shoot in the direction of an elephant unless the beast is straight down at one's feet, like in a leopard ring. But, as I have said, these are only the anxieties of the nervous, for there have been no *contretemps* or anything approaching to a *contretemps*. Sir William Duke's rifle

KHERI
Starting for the day's shoot

[To face page 256

sometimes sweeps the howdahs, but we all hope that it is at safety. Halliday shot a very nice hog deer with horns 15 ins. long. Lunch was late, because a leopard had been seen by Franey, but unfortunately it was not rounded up. It was a good one, and it says much for Franey's alertness that he was the only one who saw it. Pug-marks were discovered showing the direction in which he had gone.

We lunched on the edge of the Government forests. It was hot and glorious, the range of the Nepal Hills showing clearly. The huge fir trees, the yellow grass, the smell of wild thyme, the song of the oriole—all were quite lovely.

After lunch, Donoughmore, Taracharan and I rode forward whilst the line beat through some hugh grass in which the elephants were completely enveloped, and which is a sanctuary for the biggest gons in the place. The water was deep, and they could see nothing but a herd of rushing stags all round them. As we rode to our places we had to cross an open space in the swamp, and at the crossing, which was deep enough to come up to the elephant's pads, we saw two small crocodiles lying on the bank opposite. I was ahead, but decided not to shoot, because the chances of their getting into the water are so great, and we might disturb the gon. Cormorants and snake birds were darting all over the place. There was a female peregrin and several Montagu's harriers. Gons were calling in the thicket. We got half-way across the water when I saw beyond, and higher up the bank than the other, two crocodiles, the biggest crocodile I have ever seen, facing us. I determined to risk everything to get it, and drawing a careful bead, I fired and hit him in exactly the right place. Like an idiot, I took my small rifle. The crocodile slipped into the river, and we saw him churning up the mud. I think he will be recovered. Then to our places, disturbing as we went scores of purple gallinuls, that flew about like great coots, shining blue in the sun. We were facing an open piece of water, and nothing could have been more beautiful than to see the gons, hinds and small stags swimming across to the other side. Taracharan killed three duck, which were swarming, mainly mallard, and some white-eyed pochards. A good stag came out, and I fired at it, missing it completely with all my armoury, and Taracharan the same. Donoughmore then had five shots at it, and killed it. Another stag came out, which I killed, and that was all. Then just before the line joined us Parsons finished off a wounded stag. This turned out, to my great joy, to be one of those that I thought I had missed before lunch. There was no mistaking its horns, and when the skin was examined a bullet was found in it corresponding to the bore of my rifle. It was a bungled shot, but not a complete miss. Watchers up trees had seen the stags that I had fired at going in this direction, so I think I can claim it without any doubt. My two stags were very good ones, 34½ ins. and 35 ins., beautiful heads. We all went back through the long grass in the swamp. It was getting very dark, but just as we were going out a large number of excellent stags which had never left the grass at all, despite the closely beating line of elephants, broke away across the burnt stuff. Donoughmore fired, and so did Taracharan, without result. Clutterbuck went along to head them off, and intercepted a stag moving very slowly in the dark at 250 yards. He fired at it and got it. We were not after stags at all, and it was curious that in that light we succeeded in bagging by these means the best stag ever got in this district, 37½ ins. long, with no less than 21 points. We came home, therefore, with seven stags and a para, all very tired ; but it has been a most wonderful day for its sheer beauty and enjoyment, added to which I had been thinking hard on the elephant, and I think at last I have got a scheme which gets over all our difficulties for the transitional period.

Wednesday, February 13. Duke is going off to-day, and so is Dholpur, who has really been a most delightful person in camp—a thorough sportsman and extraordinarily amiable. He is thoroughly happy, and, I think, has enjoyed himself, and he has got three of these very rare stags, all of them fine heads. We are all so happy, and we have been fed awfully well by Clutterbuck, who, in addition, is continually receiving presents of highly tasty curries from Bambahadur and from Kukra, the jolly little Mohammedan who does not speak a word of English, but who spends his whole time praying. He carried with him a prayer carpet, which he stretches out on the ground, and prays morning, noon and night.

This morning I have spent in working, discussing my scheme and elaborating it, and I am now prepared to put it in writing.

In the afternoon, the Maharaja of Dholpur and Duke having left, Franey remained in camp working, and Donoughmore and I went off for a shoot, while Parsons and Halliday went off to sit for tigers. Our shoot did not yield much. We started a leopard and two cubs in the long grass and tried to surround them. It was beautifully conceived, but, as usual in this shooting, in the case of Bambahadur nobody was told what they were to do, and they got away. The total bag for the day was a nilghai to me; a fairly poor gon, 30 ins., with broken horns, to Donoughmore, and I finished off a wounded para, a male, that I found, which had dropped its horns. We also got a few partridges.

Thursday, February 14. We had a very pleasant day on Thursday. The morning was spent chasing a leopard, which was eventually bagged by Campbell, after Donoughmore, Parsons, and I had all missed it. It took the whole morning to get; the consequence was that we were rather late in starting off in the afternoon. However, we shot several peacocks and partridges; I got a nilghai; Donoughmore got another small gon and a hyena, and Franey got a smallish sambur: a pleasant, miscellaneous day. Marris arrived in the afternoon. He brought a message from the Viceroy that the Viceroy hoped that the report would be ready as a finished document before I left, and that he hoped we would work this week-end. I think this is pretty cool, considering that not one single suggestion has come from him, or even a criticism ; in fact, I am getting so terribly worried by the fact that I have not only got to propound my own schemes because nobody else does, but criticise them myself because nobody else does. Chelmsford, during the whole of this week, has done nothing that I can discover.

Marris also brought with him the report of the Meyer, Duke, Lowndes, Basu committee on the Government of India ; and of the Lowndes, Donoughmore, Hill, Basu Committee on A and B finance. This adds to the horror of my position, because neither report seems to me to be acceptable. The Meyer one contains a perfectly idiotic Electoral College, some of the members of which are to be nominated, and others people who have lost their seats for the local Legislative Councils. The other committee recommends an appeal to the Government of India on almost every sort of conceivable subject, particularly on A and B finance, so that if the local government wanted four new inspecting engineers, the Legislative Council might appeal to the Government of India against it. That is quite impossible. Marris says the report cannot be ready by the time I want to go home.

Friday, February 15. The two days have now dawned when we are to see miracles on Bambahadur's own shoot at Darkiwa and Hathibojh. We left at nine o'clock, the elephants having gone on overnight. The whole of the first day was taken up, on the borders of Nepal, separated from it only by a river, by a drive for a tiger which had killed ever since January 1 in a small jungle consisting of trees and enormously long grass, sometimes as much as 30 ft. high. The tiger was to be driven to Donoughmore and Halliday. They discovered it early in the first beat and lost it by turning the whole beat round and trying to drive it to me. It made me perfectly furious, as, of course, I could not see it in the long grass, nor did it come anywhere near me. Then they finished the beat out in the original direction, and brought out to Donoughmore a small tiger cub about four feet long. It was furiously fired at in a circle of elephants, to the risk of everybody's life, and finally dispatched. Lunch ; and then more chasing the tiger, but we never got it, although we saw two, if not three, more cubs. We ought never to have driven for a tiger which had cubs, and it says badly for the shikari that he never twigged this. The line was wonderful ; the elephants marvellously disciplined; but Bambahadur's idea of ringing tigers round with elephants so that nobody can shoot, so that every second must lead to the jumping of the tiger on to one of the elephants, so that the elephants are in a perpetual state of nervous fear because they think their riders are in fear because of the slowness with which we approach—all this is wrong. If he had tried to drive the tiger straight and quickly out to six stops, Clutterbuck thinks we could have got it in half an hour. So that the first wonderful day ended in nothing but a tiger cub !

Saturday, *February* 16. We spent Saturday in driving to the home of all the gons at Miria Tal. Once again the whole *banderbast* was wrong. Two stops were sent forward, and did not know where they were to go to ; they began to move and crashed about the water in the middle of the drive. The line could have shot several gons, but were told they must not shoot, and we who were the stops got the gons crashing past us in hundreds—just forests of horns. It was a marvellous sight. Dillipat kept on urging me to shoot, and finally I shot three, but selection was quite impossible. Donoughmore shot three, too, but again selection was impossible. Galloping stags in a crowd cannot be measured, and therefore our average in this home of the gons, where big ones abound, is lower than anywhere else. My best was 33½ ins., and the smallest I dare not mention. Clutterbuck got one in the line, which he killed for his mahouts to eat ; Franey got one in the line, which we picked up on the way back after lunch ; and at the last moment Halliday got one just as we were getting off the elephants. We also got two or three partridges. We saw a wonderful sight of stags, but the thing as a shoot was a failure.

We got home early, and I found waiting for me a letter from Curtis. This extraordinary man, who is much to be dreaded because of his influence with Geoffrey Robinson of the *Times*, Phillip Kerr, Chirol, etc., seems now to have been persuaded by somebody or other into a state of blue funk. I carried him with me in all my proposals at the earlier stage of these proceedings, but now he is not only criticising my schemes, but actually going back on suggestions of which he himself was the father, and I am afraid, cost what it may, I must break off relations. His suggestions are impossible. They amount to this, that we should leave absolutely everything that we are asked to decide this winter to a series of committees, doing nothing now but jerry-building the existing Councils. If he thinks that by this means you can get a manageable India, I am quite certain he is wrong.

Sunday, *February* 17. In the morning we went to examine the heads. Although the biggest was my head of 33½ ins., that head is one I am glad to have got, for it has a very wide spread of 38½ ins., and is very handsome. The other two heads of mine turned out to be 33 ins. and 29 ins. Donoughmore's were 30 ins., 24 ins., and 30 ins., I think.

We were then promised a partridge fight, but one partridge was so aggressive, so truculent in his challenge, that none of the other birds would stand up to him, and it had to be abandoned.

We then went off for our last shoot to Tirhia Tal, along

Typical swamp-deer country

P. H. Clutterbuck D. E. S. M.

KHERI

[*To face page* 262

the banks of the Sohali, and glorious fun it was. Parsons and Franey both killed gons, and Franey killed a sambur. The other big game consisted of three pigs, of which I killed one, Donoughmore one, and Clutterbuck one ; but we had a very jolly day with the birds, and killed several partridges and innumerable peacocks. I had great fun with my elephant, trying to persuade it to pick up a dead peacock. I managed to explain to the mahout what I wanted the elephant to do, and he succeeded in getting him to retrieve one, but when we tried again the peacock was not quite dead, and the most awful battle ensued, the elephant doing its best to kill it by kneeling on it. This was very disconcerting to the person in the howdah, and the peacock suffered a general collapse. The elephant did not pick it up.

We came home solemnly in the evening, and said good-bye to our many very dear friends, and left for Delhi, where we arrived on Monday morning.

X

DELHI VIII—BHARATPUR II—DELHI IX

Monday, *February* 18. Chelmsford asks me to postpone my departure for another month. I really find myself despairing of this man. Here he is faced with the greatest issue of his life—if only it were not merely India, about which nobody knows, I would say the greatest issue of anybody's life. He has had ten days away from me ; I have sent him new suggestion after new suggestion, and I find that the ten days has produced no corresponding thought of any kind whatever from him : he has done nothing, except sit and wait to be fed, and then even does not criticise. Well, it cannot be helped ; I have got to go on alone. It is appalling to have to create one's own schemes, and, not only that, but to create one's criticisms of one's own schemes. However, the rest of my party seem to me to like the new scheme very much which I described in my letter to Chelmsford, and after a morning's talk I decided to stick to the boat of March 19 and to refuse to wait any longer. I have abandoned my projected trip to Kathiawar. This was to celebrate the conclusion of the whole matter. It is now quite clear that I shall not conclude by March 1, and so I have wired to chuck it : very, very disappointed.

Tuesday, *February* 19. We are to meet this morning to discuss the Government of India proposals.

We had a hectic morning on the Government of India proposals, but it ended fairly well. After much worrying about it, we all agreed to accept the suggestion of a Privy Council, with a Council of State as a committee of it. After a long wrangle, it was suggested that the numbers should consist of 22 nominated by the Governor-General, of whom not more than 18 should be officials, and 14 nominated by the Governments of the Provinces on the recommendation of the Legislative Councils, these latter to be over 35 years of age, to have sat for two sessions in the Legislative Council of the local government or of the Government of India, or to have held some public office. We also decided that we would not ask or accept the provision in the committee's recommendation that if the Government were defeated by a three-fifth majority in the Lower House they could not take the Bill to the Upper House. The cardinal principles of our reform in the Government of India are that the will of the Government shall, if it chooses, prevail, and that it would be ridiculous to put into the statute a provision which enacted the possibility that the Government of India would be mad enough to fly in the faces of all the elected members of the new Legislative Council.

Basu was very eloquent, very fiery. He made speeches about Mrs. Besant and the partition of Bengal, which all, as I told him, indicated that the Government ought not to fly in the faces of such a majority, but did not indicate that it was a good thing to put in the Bill. After a time he accepted.

As regards election to the Lower House, we were unable to come to any agreement, and it was finally decided that the method of election, franchises and constituencies for this purpose should also be left to the committee which we are going to set up.

Chelmsford came to see me in the morning, and told me that he had found Meston in a very cheerful mood, and that Meston had liked and approved our new plan.

Meston came to see me at lunch ; said that he was in a state of complete bewilderment ; that he had not understood anything that Chelmsford had said to him last evening ; that he had worried over it all night ; and he now came to me and begged me to elucidate matters. I described the new schemes. He said he now completely understood them, but he had not before, and he was quite sure that Chelmsford did not ; that he would not commit himself, but he thought they were attractive in their simplicity. He was a little afraid of the Government of India proposals, but I was able to explain to him why I thought they were absolutely necessary. He then gave me a peroration of admiration ; an expression of his determination to do everything he could for us in England in the propaganda line, and we left, he in the best of spirits.

At three o'clock there came the holy man, Curtis. He said that Chelmsford had explained the whole scheme to him ; that he was infinitely happier ; that he was quite satisfied, and was going back in a much better mood. Knowing that Meston had told me, I repeated the scheme. He had not understood it, but did not dissent from it, except that what he says I call two halves of the same Government he calls two Governments. I said I did not care a damn what he called it, but that he was wrong. We parted friends ; he thought that the report was going to be a success.

In the evening old man Basu came to see me, and I tried to soothe him after the morning's heated argument. He was very pleasant, thought that everything was going very well, but he had to make a fight, and so forth.

Then I went up to see Chelmsford ; discussed the events of the day with him ; asked him what he was doing about the propaganda department and Gourlay, and he told me that he was discussing it with Du Boulay.

I then went to dinner with Maffey, and found, to my astonishment, that Gourlay was coming here on Wednesday, a fact that Chelmsford, for some reason or other, seems to have suppressed. That ended a very pleasant day of strenuous work, but a satisfactory day.

Wednesday, February 20. When I arose on Wednesday

morning I felt quite certain that, as usual in India, a good day is followed by a black day. Marris came to see me in the morning, and suggested an emendation of the new plan by which there should be no B Ministers until the B Ministers were responsible to the Legislative Assembly, but that there should simply be two, and two members of the Executive Council. I object to this. In the first place it does not show the line upon which we are going so clearly. In the second place it makes it necessary that the Indian members of the Executive Council should be responsible for A and B subjects ; and, in the third place, it makes it necessary that when they become responsible and leave the Executive Council, the Indians chosen for A subjects must, like the other Indians, be chosen from the Legislative Council. This means, therefore, that you are beginning responsibility for A subjects then. I do not like it. We had a long discussion about it, also about the necessity of his getting on with the report, which he promised to do.

Then Duke came in, who liked Marris's variant ; and also sprang a mine of his own—that he must have room for sub-provincial councils.

Then I wrote some letters and went to see old Basu. I discovered him in a great state of mind, because the dinner which the Legislative Council is to give me to-morrow night was to have taken place at Metcalf House, where they are put up ; but they wanted to give me a good dinner, and, knowing their caterer was inadequate, they engaged Peliti's. Then the Government of India came down and said that they could not have the dinner there at all, because the caterer had a contract to supply everything in Metcalf House. This is ludicrous, because the dinner was not to be in the house at all but in a shamiana outside. The Legislative Council then thought of abandoning the dinner, but Basu soothed them down, and they are giving it in the same shamiana that we dined in the other night at Nair's house—a shamiana which, I believe, belongs to the Raja of Mahmadabad. We discussed the two new points. Basu said that he did not like Marris's—although it was nearer the Congress and Moslem League scheme—as much as mine ; and he did not like Duke's proposal, because it might leave it open to a new partition of Bengal, or what would be regarded as such ; but still he was unperturbed and quite happy about the situation.

Then Montagu of Beaulieu came to lunch with me. He talked about the archaic methods of doing everything in this country and insisted upon its great potential development. He tells me that he is going to join the Board of Boulton's and the Alliance Bank of Simla after the War. He wants ropeways everywhere, particularly up to the hill stations, and development of India's enormous water power. He speaks with enthusiasm of the Commander-in-Chief, who he says is very unhappy about Robertson's resignation. He has brought out with him Major Alan Burgoyne, of the House of Commons. He came to see me after lunch, because I thought it was better to get all the House of Commons support that I can. "Well," he began, "how do you like this sleepy old country ?" This was pretty good, after about three days in the country ! He explained to me how he thought that the whole place was civilian-ridden ; he was a man of business ; he was able to see the possibilities that were allowed to slip ; there was no "drive," and so forth. He takes a sound view about commissions for Indians, and so on. I think it was a good thing to have seen him.

Then I had a very long sitting with my friends. We discussed Indianisation and the points raised in the morning by Marris and Duke. As regards Marris's point, the majority were against him. Nobody felt very strongly either way, except Charles Roberts, who felt very strongly against Marris, and Seton, who felt very strongly for him. As regards Duke's point, there was much wrangling, and we finally arrived at the conclusions that there should be power taken to create sub-provincial councils in the case of Berar and the C.P. and Bihar and Orissa. Then we discussed Indianisation, and came to the following conclusions :

1. That the Government of India should be asked at once to consider the removal of all racial bars.

2. That we should adopt as a principle the desire to obtain an avenue to all employment in India.

3. That we should fix the percentage we desired to recruit from India for the Indian Civil Service. Duke suggested 33⅓ per cent. in the first five years ; 40 per cent. in the next five years ; and then leave it to the Statutory Commission.

4. That we should take this opportunity of increasing the pay or pension or leave rules of the Indian Civil Service. They were monstrously underpaid at present : their salaries were fixed by Lord Cornwallis, when they were deprived of the liberty to trade, and if they were a disappearing service, it was essential that those who remained should be treated fairly.

Then I went up to see Chelmsford ; told him what had happened all day. He once more made a prayer for finality. I told him that his desire for finality was ridiculous ; I was not going to say anything was final until I was quite sure it could not be improved. He said Marris could not write his report. I said that also was ridiculous ; Marris could write his report now and alter such paragraphs as were necessary ; almost everything was ready, indeed my notes could be made into a complete report in a short time. He said that Meyer was complaining that we had carried Nair with us all along, and at any moment we might not be able to. I told him that Meyer was wrong ; that Nair was not satisfied with the proposals about the Budget, and these had not been satisfactorily remedied ; that I did not like the settlement which was now suggested, but only did it to try and please Basu, who took Nair's view of the old arrangement, and Marris and

Duke, who did not like the annual wrangle over the Budget. I thought an annual wrangle over the Budget was helpful. Chelmsford suggested a Privy Councillorship for Meston, which I think is rather a good idea. Chelmsford then told me that he had no idea that I was dining with the members of the Legislative Council. This, therefore, explains the refusal of Metcalf House. What idiots they are! He says also that I am not dining with the unofficial members of the Legislative Council, but only with the Indians, and that Muddiman had been to him and asked him not to accept a similar invitation. I told him that if that were so I had been deceived, and I was not to blame. He told me that a paragraph had appeared in the *Hindu* by Mrs. Besant, saying that she had told me that the English had broken their pledges in the past to the Indian, and that I had answered: "Yes, I know; we must see that it does not happen again." Chelmsford asked me what I was going to do about it. I said that I was not going to do anything about it. If he would be good enough to read my notes for the report he would see what I thought about pledges which were alleged to have been broken. That report, signed with my own name, would be my answer to such accusations. Anyhow, matters ended with nearly a breach of the peace, because then Chelmsford got up from his chair, paced the room, and in an excited voice recited to me draft conclusions of a report which he had either written himself or had had written for him. To my astonishment, as he developed them I discovered that he had left everything to the Statutory Commission, just as Curtis wanted to. I stopped him in the middle, and asked him what on earth he was doing. He said that he thought that was the new plan. I explained to him that it was not. He told me that he had quite misunderstood it then; he always thought it was. I told him that he was wrong, and that he could not have done that if he had been good enough to read my notes, or even the notes which I had circulated that day as the basis of the discussion with the Government of India. Now, you know, this is all over again what happened when we were coming back from Bombay, when he talked me into the January 12 scheme because he pretended not to have understood what I had written. My notes are what I want in the report, and I told him so. He then said : "I am so afraid of putting my signature to something which will be criticised and held up to scorn." I said : "That is exactly what I wish to avoid, but we must have courage to sign something." I said that criticisms would afterwards be made, and if they were good criticisms we would adopt them in the Bill. He then began to smile and said that that completely met his view. He became pleasantness itself then, and we had two or three minutes talk on pleasant subjects. Then he asked what I had said to Meston about the Government of India, and said it might be made quite clear in the report that we were prepared to drop this part of the scheme. I said : No, it could not be made clear at all in our report that we were prepared to drop it. It was quite possible that we should have to drop it, but I was going to fight for it for all I could ; and I was perfectly certain that public opinion in India would not let us drop it. He said it was not an essential part of our scheme. I said it was. It was a separate part of our scheme, but that if he had been good enough to read my notes on the Government of India he would see it was an essential part of the scheme.

I then went and had a very pleasant dinner with Mr. and Mrs. Mant, and played bridge afterwards, and went to bed thoroughly weary after a hard and difficult day, much complicated by the new light on Chelmsford's present attitude.

Thursday, February 21. I am dictating the notes for Tuesday's and Wednesday's diary before breakfast, and have in store for me another hard day—Lowndes and Hill to breakfast ; a friend of Basu's, a member of the extremist party in Bengal, after breakfast ; then a meeting with my colleagues ; then lunch with Roos Keppel ; then an interview with Chintamani ; then one with Meyer ; then one with Bannerjea ; then dinner with the Legislative Council ; and it looks as if I shall have to have Nair to breakfast to-morrow before a long meeting with the Government of India, which is to last all day. Then I am going to insist, I think, upon Marris drafting the report in my tent ; I cannot let him out of my sight. If I do not have to have Nair to breakfast to-morrow I will have Marris.

Lowndes and Hill came to breakfast, and things turned out better than I had expected. We had a discussion about their committee and the Government of India committee, and I think we seemed to be in agreement on all points. I think they like the scheme as circulated, save this, that they have grave objection to a financial settlement, and the more I think of it, the more have I. We talked about Indianisation, and they stayed till half-past ten.

Then arrived Mr. Chatterji, Basu's friend, who is a son-in-law of Surendrenath Bannerjea. This man is extraordinarily intelligent, and if Basu had done no other work for India than to convert him, it would have been a great work. He was originally an anarchist, a close friend of Arabindo Ghose's, and his brother Barindra. Now he has joined the moderate party and was a signatory to the Curtis scheme ; very keen on young men going into industry instead of law. He told me that his friends had bought a Swadeshi mill after the partition and had lost many lakhs of rupees, but that his brother had now made it into a commercial success, having been trained at Leeds. They were Brahmans, but had now completely got over their prejudice against working with their hands, which was the result of travel. Then he told me that in the main the so-called anarchists would be far, far easier to get on our side than the extremists in the Congress. The extremists in the Congress were mere windbags who loved agitation and denunciatory speeches. They were also conservative in politics, believing in keeping the Brahman influence intact and the other classes subject to them. Tilak himself would neither receive nor give water to anybody but men of his caste, whilst these seditionists who throw bombs are the real social democrats, the men who want reform on Western lines. It is they who go into a house to carry out and burn the corpse of an "untouchable"; it is they who go about among the depressed classes, nursing them in cases of plague and malaria, when nobody else will touch them. He says that he has been defending and befriending a large humber of extremists who are now interned. He is not now talking of those bought with German gold, but his friends are friends who want, he says, not to destroy the British connection, but to get rid of this Administration—this Administration which orders them about, makes them citizens of a subject race, and so forth. Therefore they want revolution. They murdered policemen in order to discourage the police from interfering with them; they committed dacoities in order to raise funds for their propaganda. That celebrated Indian novel which contains "*Bande mataram*" told stories of brigandage for this purpose, and they have learned, said this man quite simply, that the Italian revolution started with acts of brigandage. But Chatterji himself is convinced that if our policy, whatever it is, has as its keynote partnership and not subordination, these young men will see the error of their ways.

His purpose in coming all the way from Calcutta to see me was this—that when the report comes out he wants permission to go with Sinha as a witness to see these internees, to ask them to swear loyalty to the new order of things, and then, if he guarantees that they will behave, to let them out. I put the matter later on to Chelmsford, who talked about blood guiltiness; but, after all, they are people whom you have interned, and not punished, and therefore the question of blood guiltiness does not seem to me to arise. You cannot think of using interment as a substitute for punishment.

Duke was late for our meeting at eleven o'clock because he had been sent for by the Viceroy, but he came down and raised four points against the new scheme as set out. I boiled with fury because Duke when he came in said that the Viceroy had said that he had come to see me, but found that I was engaged. Nobody approached the door of my tent all the morning, nor is it a likely story on the face of it, because every one of the four points is a point which I urged with Chelmsford last night without, I am afraid, being able to make him understand the situation. It is not likely that he would come and argue the same points again the next morning. However, I think we have got over one difficulty this morning by putting in the words " The Governor shall have power at his discretion to include in the deliberations of his Executive Council both the B members of the Government and/or the Financial Commissioner and the Advocate-General." This gets over the difficulty of the one European confronted with four Indians.

I went up to see Chelmsford and talked to him about this. He again jeered at the Legislative Council dinner, which was to exclude Europeans.

I came back after lunch and saw Ramiswami Aiyar, very friendly, as usual, and liking the new plan.

Then came Sir William Meyer, with whom I had an hour. He was cynical, critical, amused, not very helpful, but also not very obstructive. He obviously feels that he is going very shortly, and that he is not going to be bothered by quarrelling with anybody about it.

Then a short game of tennis ; then a long interview with Surendrenath Bannerjea, who interested me because he obviously knew the whole of our scheme. He described himself as a moderate, and kept on saying that all he wants is power over the Budget. He has got a resolution down asking for an advisory board for the internees. I really must try and see that the Government of India do not smash it.

Then Roos-Keppel came to talk, and we had a very long conversation. I think he is a little anxious to get out of employment. After all, he has been ten years in his present job and thirty-two years on the frontier. He told me how he had very nearly got Egypt when MacMahon did. He certainly would have been much better, because he knows French, and, of course, is fully up on Mohammedan problems. He hopes that our reform schemes will give the Indians some real share. He does not care about Legislative Councils "and all that rot," as he described it, but he wants to give them positions of equality, so that they can feel that they are men. I think what annoys him is that his friend Abdul Quayum, who is now in the marvellous position of political agent in the Khyber, a native, is not permitted to join the Political Service because they will not have Indians there. He told me one interesting yarn—that the blackest year in India that he knew was 1907, when the Rajas all woke up, and when Scindia planned a Hindu kingdom from Bombay to Calcutta because he thought that we were going to clear out, because we were weakening our grip. He also told me that the word "Casement" had come into the vernacular, and anybody who was a traitor was called a "Casement" by the Indians.

Then we went to the dinner of the Legislative Council given in Nair's garden. The story that they had excluded the English non-official members from the dinner turned out to be an absolute fabrication. Malcolm Hogg was there; Sir Hugh Bray was not in Delhi, or he would have been asked. Basu seemed to be nervous because he had been accused of being too compromising. Nair looked most angry and sullen and forbidding all the evening, and I am afraid the explosion will come this (Friday) morning.

Friday, February 22. I shall know in a few minutes, because I have asked him to breakfast. You see, I have to spend my time lobbying the whole of Chelmsford's colleagues, a task he ought to do himself. Yesterday he told me that he had been thinking about interviewing representative Indians to get their support, and had come to the conclusion that I had better do it alone without him.

I forgot to record in Bannerjea's conversation yesterday not only that he knew all about our plans, which shows that Basu and Nair have been talking, but all about them in detail, because he knew of the difficulties about the financial provision for A heads. He also said he wanted an advisory committee to deal with internees, to review those that had already been made, to enquire into their health and treatment, and to advise on future internments, both under the Regulations of 1918 and under the Defence of the Realm Act. He said he was going to move for this in the Viceroy's Legislative Council, and he begged us not to meet him with a direct negative. The moderates wanted it to answer the accusations of the extremists.

This morning I saw Nair ; we had a long breakfast party. He refused to keep the words "peace, tranquillity, or the interests of the Province or any part thereof" as a condition of getting money for A subjects, his reason being because the officials will always insist upon appointing new Europeans. He recognised that you cannot by statute exclude this, but if you could, it would get over all his objections ; or, in the alternative, if the Indian on the Executive Council was a good fighting Indian, and not a tame one, if he was an elected member of the Legislative Council he would accept it. I do not think this can be done, and I am determined to stick to my proposals.

Then followed a meeting with the Government of India, which lasted until half-past four this afternoon, with an interval for lunch. I explained the new scheme conclusively, and argued against my own suggestion for a financial settlement in favour of the annual wrangle. The note I circulated is appended. I have never spoken better, and I was intensely gratified to find that everybody unanimously agreed that this new scheme was much the best that has been produced ; in fact, it all went through very smoothly, including what are called the *adlati*, which are not dealt with in the note circulated, but under which the Governor will on A subjects be able to consult two officials who hold other portfolios, plus his B Ministers, if he wants more advice on a big A subject, the decision being taken by his Executive Council. Basu and Nair refused to accept the words " interests essentially affected." Nair wanted an elected member also for the A subjects. Lowndes made the extraordinary proposal that an elected member should be on the Executive Council and one of the B Ministers should be from outside the Council. This gives no responsibility at all for the B subjects, and was scouted by everybody else. Basu suggested a panel. This I do not think will do, because if there was a row they might put Mohamed Ali and Mrs. Besant on as the only members of the panel. Meyer " ragged " me about what he called the " new dispensation " which I had brought back, like the tables of stone, from the jungle, and hoped it was final. In my reply I got a bit of my own back. I said that all these transitional things were matters of expediency ; that I was trying to get the one that would be most generally accepted ; that I thought we were approaching finality, but as Basu and Nair were not satisfied I should not rest content until I had tried to find some words to meet them ; that, after all, I admired the patience of the Government of India, but was not surprised at it, because I had always understood that they were more renowned for their patient investigation of the subject than for any undue haste. I also said that it would be infinitely preferable for my own convenience to make no suggestions and to criticise other people's, to wait for suggestions to drop into my lap, but I felt that was an impossible attitude for anybody to take.

Since the meeting I have suggested that the Indian member might be chosen from the elected members of the Legislative Council or of the Viceroy's Council, or from the Council of State of the Viceroy. That gives a wider field. I have also suggested in the alternative that the Governor might suggest a panel from which he would be willing to take names, and that the House might strike off any name. This, I think, would not do. I have also suggested that there should be an understanding given that the Governor should take such steps as he was able to before he made a recommendation to see that a name he proposed to recommend was not unacceptable to his Legislative Council. This, I think, would meet the case, and could easily be worked in practice.

At two o'clock, in between the two meetings, Mrs. Besant came to see me. Of course, owing to the leakage, she knows pretty well what is going on, and I think she means to support in principle, although she will suggest all sorts of amendments. I did not tell this to the Viceroy, because he would then object to the proposals. She brought forward two grievances. One was that she hoped action would not be taken against papers for criticising my report. I said: Of course not, provided the criticism was done decently, and you do not fire the public imagination against officials. I told her that I complained bitterly about her having said that I had agreed that the English had broken pledges, but that I was going to say what I thought about pledges in my report. She said that she must have been misreported; she had forgotten the incident. She also complained about the internees. She said that the Viceroy had promised to investigate the cases that she brought up of torture, etc. Finally, she said that the Labour Party were urging her to come to England: would she be of any use to me there, or did I think she could do me any harm? I said: "Of course you can do me no harm."

I do not know whether she saw how ironically I meant this, but it would not do, in loyalty to Chelmsford, to discourage her from leaving India. She asked whether I thought she would ever get back again, because otherwise she would not go. I reminded her of what the Viceroy had said on this subject. "Oh, dear man," she said, "he always jokes about it." I said I would not interfere with a case of that kind ; it must be the Viceroy who decided whether she came back again or not, and there I left the subject with her. I repeated the conversation to the Viceroy, who told me that nothing would ever induce him to let her come back again to India. This is such a foolish thing to say ; it might be that she wanted to come back quite tame and docile. It might be that she would be too feeble to do any harm owing to the sea voyages, whereas keeping her out here might mean that she would at once be re-elected President of the Congress, etc.

We finished the conference this afternoon, but Lowndes, Hill, Basu, and Donoughmore are again to sit to see if they cannot adjust the differences on Monday. I urged Chelmsford to have a conference with the Government of India some time on Monday about the Government of India itself, for it looks gloomier than ever about getting home, and I am impatient about the thing, but I am not dissatisfied with my day.

In the evening Chintamani came to see me, and we had a little gossip, particularly about the appointment of the Indian member of the A council.

Next Gourlay came to see me. Chelmsford had told me that he had talked to him about being the head of the propaganda department, but, as usual, I found Gourlay completely perplexed by what Chelmsford had said and not understanding my scheme, which consists of :

1. Supplying leaflets.
2. Helping the moderates to organise.
3. Editing quarterlies.

4. Answering criticisms on the new reform scheme, and generally being the link between the Government and those who are willing to support it. Gourlay liked the idea very much, and is, I think, willing to work it. I told him I wanted him to settle his own conditions and form his own department ; to treat the proposal just as Lloyd George treated the proposal that he should form a Ministry of Munitions. So ends the week. I have done fairly well, but, oh ! there is such a lot to do before I go home.

Monday, *February* 25. I have to record two days of much-needed absence from Delhi. I went, by the invitation of Watson, the Resident, to Bharatpur, for their second duck shoot. This time I occupied the butt that had been occupied at the first shoot by the Maharaja of Dholpur. There were nothing like the same number of ducks, it being too late and the moon being full, and there were only 25 guns, as opposed to 50 on the last occasion. I discovered, to my amusement, that all the coolies who beat are concentrated at whatever end of the jheel the Indian illustrious guests are ; indeed, before lunch I had very little shooting, because we had no coolies at all at our end. The ducks kept on getting up and flying to a sort of sanctuary behind our butts. After lunch it was better, because Watson sent a protest, and one man in a boat with a tom-tom came down. He worked very hard, but even he could not keep the ducks moving ; it requires about 50 men really to do it properly. I did fairly well ; I got 41 in the morning and 51 in the afternoon, making 92 in all. I was astonished to learn that Dholpur, who was shooting on the Raja's bund behind us, had got 92 in the morning, and I determined, therefore, to try an experiment. When filling in my card in the evening, which contains in staring letters the statement that only duck picked up are to be counted, I put down : " Morning, 41 picked up ; afternoon, 51 picked up ; not picked up : morning, 6 ;

afternoon, 14 ; total picked up, 102 ; not picked up, 20." To my surprise, in the official return in the evening I was credited with a bag of 112, from which I deduce that, despite the printed instructions to their honest guests, they include the birds they knock down.

I had a very good talk in the evening with Watson about the Native States, and am more than ever convinced that the right thing to do would be to scrap all their treaties, provided they were willing to do so, and to form a model treaty for all of them, something on these lines : They are sovereign within their own States ; we have control of their foreign relations ; we have the right to tender them advice on any matters that seem fit to us ; to see that their railway arrangements do not interfere with Indian communications ; and to intervene in cases of gross abuse, otherwise they would be absolutely all right. He tells me that Alwar is under the impression that eventually a full Mrs. Besant programme will be accomplished in India in ten years. Watson does not like the abolition of Agents of the Governor-General, but seems to agree that a Resident has not enough to do. I cannot understand what he finds to do, and he actually has an assistant, a young fellow named Gibson, who is also a sort of tutor to the Maharaja. Raoji, the Maharaja'a uncle and heir apparent, came to dinner. He is a young man of 34, and a very nice fellow ; Watson says he is a very good worker and an excellent member of the Regency Council. Watson tells me he has got to go and see Dholpur about the reinstatement of a Thakor whom he had promised to reinstate, but whom he delays in reinstating because his uncle likes shooting over his country. The uncle is, I think, now dying, so that that difficulty seems to be solved. Plague is very bad in Bharatpur. People are dying in the villages ; inoculation goes very slowly. It is spreading to the towns, and even the Raja found a dead rat in his palace, and has migrated. I was told of two cases of small children who picked up semidead squirrels, were bitten by them, and died within 24 hours. I did not know that plague affected squirrels ; but it is a country in which one must not touch anything without careful consideration of the consequences.

On Sunday I had a perfectly delightful day with Watson alone. We went through the reedy end of the jheel up to our waists all day in water. It was awfully hard work, but we got the wonderful bag of 50 couple of snipe, five teel, a bittern—which the old shikari insisted upon my shooting—and a coot. We worked until we had not a cartridge left and the sun was setting, so anxious were we to get our 100 snipe. We thought we had 102, but when we laid the bag out we found that in the dark we had killed two sandpipers by mistake for snipe. It was one of the hardest and most enjoyable days I have ever spent, and I feel very fit as a consequence.

I have solved, I think, the difficulty of the formula, and have got a way of expediting business, which is all the more important because Kisch tells me this morning that there is no steamer after March 17 till the end of April.

The Maharaja came in after dinner on Sunday night, and we had a talk. He is a nice little man, only 18 years of age, but looks older than Dholpur. He is very fond of animals ; has two baby elephants living in his palace, and, I think, will make a good naturalist. He is not interested in public affairs.

On Monday morning we had a conference in my tent and made some progress with Indianisation. We also considered Duke's suggestions for the amelioration of the pay of the services ; to put the Civil Service on a time scale ; to do away with the maximum pension of half £850 for the subordinate services ; to do away with contributions to pensions in the Civil Service, and to amend the leave rules ; to do away with the theory that it must be on half the average pay of the last three years.

In the afternoon we had a long and very wearisome meeting with the Government of India. We were concerned with the composition of the Council of State and the Government of India. Basu was very, very trying. Every time he got some compromise admitted he wanted to push it further, and I began to despair, and addressed a sharp rebuke to him, warning him that he was going to lose everything. We did not come to a settlement, Meyer and Lowndes strongly objecting to electing the provincial representatives to the Council of State even with the qualifying suggestions I had made, because it would not allow for communal representation, Chelmsford objecting that his power of nomination was not enough on our figures. Finally, Vincent, Basu, and Duke were appointed a committee to work it out. Then I raised my question about Indianisation and the improvement of the services. Chelmsford objected to fixing percentages; Meyer objected to the possibility of doing anything for the services in the way of amelioration of pay. I harangued them very fiercely, and we broke up at half-past five, after sitting for three hours, with nothing definite decided.

Then I had a long interview with Chelmsford. He urged me to be patient. I told him my patience was coming to an end. Then followed from Chelmsford a burning desire that I should agree to abandon the idea of going home on March 17 or 19. I told him that I could not—that I must go home; that I was sick and tired of this. "But," he said, "surely you won't spoil everything by not having finished?" I said: "We must try and finish." He said it was impossible to work against a time limit. I said that if we were not through I would miss the steamer, but I was not going to tell people at home I was not coming home on the date mentioned.

I then went back to my tent; wrote till dinner time; and then up to dinner at Government House. There were no people to dinner.

Tuesday, February 26. In the morning, bearing in mind Chelmsford's words, I wrote letters of apology for hasty temper to Meyer and Basu. Both wrote very kindly replies. Basu assured me that he would not risk everything by being uncompromising. Meyer wrote a vigorous letter, saying that you can fix percentages of recruitment in the police, education, public works, and Civil Service, but do nothing for the pay. He goes further than I wanted to go in the report as regards percentages, but I must insist upon something being done for pay. The objections to increasing pay are due to a belief that Indianisation is going to be postponed thereby. The condition of Indianisation ought to be decent payment of the services that remain.

Then I read the three sections of the report that have come to hand, and made the comments upon them which are shown in the appended letter to Chelmsford. I did not send the letter, because I thought my comments would appear better if I made them verbally, but they save me dictating now what I felt about them.

Then I had a discussion with Duke, Roberts, and Seton, and we got a little further on all matters of importance outstanding. I also had a talk with Marris, and I think we are speeding up the report.

Next I had an interview with Nair, who had demanded one on the telephone. I was very frightened, but he came along cooing like a sucking dove. He pointed out difficulties which had arisen on the affirmative powers of the provincial Governments, and assured me that he wanted to see me rather than to raise difficulties at a conference. He pointed out that we had asked for affirmative powers on A subjects which was not as generous as Lord Hardinge suggested in his red book or as the Government of India had suggested in its despatch of November, 1916. He told me that he thought he could defend the proposals as they stood, but he wanted this question considered. It is an important question, and

I promised it consideration. It really amounts to this—that with our big elective majorities and without the Government of India power of legislating on provincial affairs, this is necessary, but I do not think we ought to keep both the affirmative powers and the overriding powers of legislation of the Government of India. Both are unnecessary, and of the two the affirmative powers is the best. Basu and Duke, to whom I talked about this later on, agreed.

Donoughmore's committee this afternoon on affirmative powers came quickly to agreement. The new formula on the Budget is—" Essential to the maintenance of peace and tranquillity in the Province or any part thereof, or to the discharge of the Government's responsibility for the reserved subjects." Duke, Vincent, and Basu came to complete agreement about the Council of State, which is to consist of 48 members—24 officials, including the Executive Council ; four nominated by the Viceroy, two elected by the Chambers of Commerce, two by the landholders, two by the Mohammedans, and 14 by the provincial Legislative Councils, the Viceroy to allot the Mohammedans to any Province that he likes, or to the landholders or Mohammedans in the Lower Chamber, all such elected men to become members of the Privy Council. Qualifications, 35 years of age, twice elected to some legislative council or high public office.

Then a long talk with Chelmsford, once more urging that I should remain in Delhi, and saying that the tents were becoming insufferably hot. I agreed. Then he said that he had arranged that from March 12 Maffey's house should become an office for us. I told him this was not necessary for four days. He then said that Parliament or the Government at home would not be so unreasonable as to insist on my coming home before my work was finished. I reminded him that they expected me much earlier, and I should not feel justified yet, until I saw the progress made, in telegraphing to them to ask for longer time. He showed me

Gourlay's notes about the proposal for a propagandist department.

Conference in the evening with Donoughmore, Roberts, Duke, and Basu. Parcelling out of pieces of the report ensued. We are getting on!

Wednesday, February 27. Up early this morning, dealing with the report, on which I am spending the whole morning.

I spent the whole morning on the report, with the exception of a talk with the Viceroy on the same subject, and on Persia. The Viceroy still has objections to fixing percentages of recruitment for the services. Meyer still has objections to doing anything for the Civil Service. What they will not see is that now is their opportunity to do both or neither, and if they do neither there is great difficulty about Indianisation, unless we go in for simultaneous examinations. Simultaneous examinations have the objection that they will allow the services to be swamped by the Indians who are clever at examinations. If they were coupled with nomination it would not be so bad, and I always hanker for nomination in England too.

After lunch I had a very long talk with Malivaya, who urged us not to fix percentages, but to let the best man win, and who told me that he wanted to talk to me next week about the Government of India and the powers the Legislative Council was going to get. He was very nice, very conciliatory, fully understanding that if Indians opposed our scheme we should never get it through, because the Anglo-Indian community would say: "We object to it, and the Indians do not want it." I assured him that we would be ready to consider any amendments, but they must not be coupled with abuse of the Civil Service. I like him very much. He is so earnest. It is difficult to believe what everybody here tells you—that he is a snake in the grass and absolutely untrustworthy. I feel that they do not handle him the right way. Do they handle anyone in the right way? I know that my views may be considered prejudiced, but I do not think England knows what the Government of this country is like—immersed in files; writing voluminous notes; collecting enormous documents.

After I had finished with Malaviya I had a long talk with Jinnah. Of course we are now discussing matters with men who are interested in Government of India politics and not local government politics, and naturally our schemes for provincial responsibility do not interest them so much as to know what their powers are going to be in the Government of India, and I fear these for the present are going to be very small.

Then a very pleasant dinner at Tony Grant's, where Cleveland and Major and Mrs. Ross were guests, with a little bridge afterwards, but mainly occupied with talk with Grant about my suggestions made from Aden about the Middle East. He likes them very much.

Thursday, *February* 28. This morning, after breakfast, I drove down to the Secretariat and had a long talk with Vincent. So far as the Government of India is concerned, if Bengal will agree with them, they propose to treat Bannerjea's resolution about internees as I would treat it. That is all right. Vincent seemed to agree with everything I suggested, but I tremble to think what would have happened if I had not been here.

Then I had a talk with Chelmsford, who came to see me about Persia; and then I went to see Marris and gave him the contributions to the report which I wrote yesterday. I found him very miserable. He had been working all night and looked tired out. He said he could not get done working up my notes by March 17. I asked him what the hell that had got to do with it—that nobody could work at a thing like that against time. He must go on as fast as he could, and I was responsible for the time at which I went home. But it is becoming increasingly clear that I shall not get away on March 17. I do not think it will be a matter of more than a week, or, at most, a fortnight, and I cannot spoil the thing for lack of a few days, and I must finish the job, unless I am recalled home, which I quite anticipate. Well, there will be one result: Tilak, who has taken a passage for home by the same ship, will be disappointed. I cannot describe the weariness of my flesh. I am tired of conciliating, cajoling, persuading, lobbying, interviewing, accommodating, often spoiling my own plans to quell opposition first from Basu, then from Nair; first from Meyer, and then from Vincent. I have been counting the days to get home, and it has been borne in upon me that I am going to spend a longer time here than ever—here where there is no war and where people do not feel it; where a long sojourn is obviously sapping of vitality; where I am fighting every day against the inclination to let things go; while every telegram that comes from home makes me more anxious. It may be that I am losing my patience, that I am a little bit sore that the Government on whose behalf I came, as a member of which I have been working night and day, has never sent me, in answer to my telegrams, one little line of encouragement. If I have failed, what have I done? I have kept India quiet for six months at a critical period of the War; I have set the politicians thinking of nothing else but my mission. I have helped the Government of India, day in and day out, in the discharge of their ordinary functions. That I have done, and if everything else fails, I think I am entitled to some message of encouragement.

Then home, and some talk with Kisch about the India Office reforms, and then some talk with Duke about Indianisation and the date of departure for home. I have practically made up my mind to telegraph to Islington to say that I deeply regret I cannot catch the boat on the 17th, but that

I have got a transport by which I am leaving immediately the report is signed, say, a fortnight, probably, afterwards, but this must be conditional upon a promise being made that I can get a transport. About this I have to interview the people, otherwise nothing will induce me to remain.

Then dinner at the Gymkhana Club—a dinner given by Donoughmore and myself, fixed for February 28, at a time when we thought and hoped and prayed that after dinner we could leave Delhi for good on our way home. Alas! the dinner took place with none of the other hopes. The only absentee was Duke, who, poor fellow, had just heard of the sudden death of his brother from pneumonia on the frontier. It was a melancholy reflection that we had endeavoured to arrange a dinner which would give fun to the Viceroy's house party and his staff and those who had been kind to us at Delhi. But when the arrangements were made, alas! all the people that we could ask were the same people that had dined nightly together; the dinner had to be cooked by the Viceroy's cook, and the music had to be played by the Viceroy's band, so that it looked as if we were going to have another dinner comparable only to the usual dinner party at Delhi. However, things turned out to be better than was to be expected. In the first place, we dined at small tables; in the next place, we had given the guests champagne, which made the things go. Then Alan had taken a lot of trouble about choosing the music, and a lot of trouble over the menu. Lady Chelmsford wished that he would order her dinner and choose her music every day! We had a quite successful Indian conjuror after dinner, who unfortunately confined himself to Indian tricks, with one or two exceptions. The mango trick he did vilely. Then we had a cinema film, and left, everybody having obviously enjoyed themselves, at midnight, for Alwar.

XI
ALWAR

Friday, *March* 1. After an uneventful night's journey, we arrived at Alwar, at the Maharaja's private station, at a quarter to nine, and were met by the Maharaja, who had motored in from his country house. We motored out there to breakfast at ten, Charles Roberts remaining behind in Alwar to look at the library, and we having to undergo what is practically a ritual in Native States—a tiger shoot for the distinguished stranger. Nothing thrills me so much as these shoots. The excitement and the arrangements make the day pass like lightning, but what I hate about them, which destroys the happiness, is that I am expected to shoot the tiger. I have now shot five, and I never want to shoot another. But I want to see it done. I agree that it is essential to shoot them, for the damage that they do to the villagers' cattle, and sometimes to the villagers themselves, is infinite, but I would prefer that somebody else took the responsibility of the climax of a shoot, upon which so much depends, and upon which so much trouble has been taken. Never have I seen the ritual conducted so marvellously efficiently as here. We did not go out until news had been definitely received as to where the tiger was. We left at about a quarter to one; we motored some seven miles, and then got on to pad elephants with a most awfully comfortable air-seat that the Maharaja had designed. He and I went to a tower, to reach which, without disturbing the jungle, we had to climb over a hill. I had never seen an elephant climb a hill before, and it would not be tolerable on an ordinary pad, but it was quite comfortable on the Maharaja's specially-designed seat. It was quite exciting. We got to our tower, which was roofed from the sun, for it was very hot, and we were very comfortable. The others were on elephants, Donoughmore and Raoji Saheb of Bharatpur behind me, and the other three on the flank. There were some spectators on the top of the hill. The country is quite gloriously beautiful, rocky and hilly, and we were in a sort of valley. Then ensued a long wait whilst the beat came up. The tiger was in it, and Alwar was able to tell me at intervals where it was from the signals which reached him. After about three-quarters of an hour the tiger broke out of the beat between the beaters on foot and the beaters on elephants, and went away to our left. Just at that moment, on our right, there came out of the jungle and across one of the rides that are cut down the side of the hill, like pheasant rides in Scotland, a fine sambhur. As the tiger had broken out of the beat, I was allowed to shoot at it, and got it. It was a good beast, with 38 ins. horns. It was not quite dead, and Alwar sent a man to shoot it. He climbed the hill and got up to it, and then fired seven shots at it before he hit it. Then Alwar left me ; he said he had news by signal where the tiger had been found, and he went back to get it. Then ensued another very long wait. The tiger had nearly crossed the road where the motors, camels, horses, and elephants were drawn up. By everybody making a noise, it was sent back ; finally it got back into the beat, and Alwar rejoined me. After some little time, when the beaters were quite close to us, the tiger broke out high on my left. One could see it crossing the open space quite distinctly. Alwar shouted directions to the beaters, and the tiger came down, and came at a gallop right past the bottom of my tower. I should have preferred, if I had been alone, to take it before it got there, because it is always difficult to shoot perpendicularly downwards, and also, I am ashamed to say, that I had forgotten to take the 200 yards sight down which I had used when shooting the sambhur. Well, I fired once at him, and missed him, and a second time, when I thought

I hit him, just as he was disappearing into a clump of bushes. Alwar assured me I had not hit him ; that he was lying there and would come out and be shot. I said : " Supposing he is hit ? " " Oh," he said, " that does not matter." I said : " What about the beaters ? " " Oh," he said, " they are all on elephants." Alwar is a most marvellous man, and the way in which he arranged this beat himself was quite wonderful. The elephants were brought round this small bush, but the tiger did not come out as Alwar had predicted. It charged back through the elephants and through the beaters. Again Alwar left me ; reformed the line some quarter of a mile off, and they came forward again. Every now and then one could hear the tiger roaring and charging the elephants, which it did five times. Finally, they could not get it to move. So we left our tower, got on to howdah elephants, and joined the line. They then said they had discovered tracks of blood, and what I had always suspected was disclosed—and what, indeed, Alwar had recently confessed, that no tiger would have behaved like this and refused to go forward if it had not been wounded—that I had wounded it with my second shot as it disappeared into the clump of trees. Now began the most exciting thing I have ever seen. A stone was pointed out to us, behind which the tiger was said to be. It was not more than 20 yards from the elephants. Our elephants crashed forward desperately—Alwar's, mine, Donoughmore's, and Raoji Saheb's. Every moment I expected to see the tiger on my elephant's head. But he was not there ! Then suddenly Alwar told me that he could see it ten yards in front of him ; my elephant was told to join his, and just as I joined him there was a terrific roar, and I saw the heaving of the grass and bushes in front, but I could see no tiger. Then he tried to get through the bushes at the elephant. Twice he paused, and then, turning, sprang back away from us. We could not see him. Donoughmore and Raoji Saheb fired, and then all was still.

G. E. F.   Raoji Saheb of Bharatpur   E. S. M.   H.H. of Alwar   D.   A. P.

ALWAR

[*To face page* 292

We then saw the tiger going away. We crashed on, over rocks, up hill, down hill, over another 150 yards, when suddenly I saw the tiger under a tree, close up against it, about 20 yards in front of my elephant. He was passing us. He saw me as I saw him ; he opened his mouth with another growl, and his tail was moving. Another spring was imminent, but I had time by then to bang in two barrels of my rifle, and the breathless five minutes was over, and the tiger lay dead. It was a tigress, 8 ft. 3 in. long. Then we went home, very tired after our long day's excitement, and we would have been very happy except for the mauling of a man, which I am assured is incidental to this ritual. I cannot ascertain news of his health.

In the morning, before starting out, I had a long talk with Alwar about the Native States, and he gave me a book of his which he had written on the problem. I agree with his arguments ; I do not agree with all his conclusions ; but it is a clever book, and it is extraordinarily well written. There is no Indian as intelligent as he is. I would rather have him at the Imperial Conference than anybody else, but he has taken no interest in the War, save to send his Imperial Service troops. His pamphlet shows a man of imagination and of industry, of knowledge and of reasoning power ; while with regard to his conversation at dinner, when we discussed the Hindu religion and the sanctions in Holy Writ for a certain custom, the Aryasanaj, and its relations to idolatry ; the Jains and their respirators out of mercy to the bacteria ; the fact that Rama is recorded as having eaten peacock—nothing could have been more interesting. His defence of his drinking liquor because it was not the sort of liquor mentioned in the laws of Mannar—all was Alwar at his best. Then the conversation switched off to most wonderful stories of leopards and tigers ; one leopard that was so tame that he could drive a motor car up to it without disturbing it at its kill ; how it had been caught, let out of its cage close to this house, killed a goat at once, and then walked into the house to sleep two or three nights in succession, the house then being empty ; of a tiger and panther that had had a fight ; that you could shoot them without disturbing them at their kill, and so on, all leading up to the argument that animals had characters just like men had. We went to bed early.

Saturday, March 2. I spent the whole morning talking to Alwar about the Native States and in dealing with the report in my own room. We did not leave until nearly half-past one, just before which a photograph was taken of the house party. Then we left on elephants, and proceeded for an hour's journey through the most beautiful country imaginable to the base of a rocky hill, up the side of which a perpendicular ride had been constructed. The journey was very comfortable, but very hot, the sumptuous armchairs which replaces the pads on the elephants here making all the difference to comfort. Alwar had announced that it was a general beat, as no tiger had been located, and that everybody would get an equal chance of fun. He placed Halliday, Parsons, and Franey on their elephants at the base of a ride ; Donoughmore and Raoji Saheb of Bharatpur at the base of the next ride on the ground, and he and I went to another ride nearest to the beaters. I felt that I should have first chance at anything, which was not according to plan, and I determined that if a tiger should by chance cross the ride I would either refuse to fire at it or miss it flagrantly and obviously, so that Donoughmore should get a chance. I enquired whether there were any guns on my right, and was told that Franey, Parsons, and Halliday were there. As I had left them on my left, the other side of Donoughmore, this news astonished me, but I found that they had been moved, and were coming along with the beat. This form of shooting in the Native States fills me with disgust, because it means that my host will do anything to provide me with shooting, but expects that those who accompany me are to be spectators, and to have no fun at all. It is not in accordance with British tradition, and I continually struggled against it, as the future account of the day will prove. When the beat reached the ride on which I was sitting, we got on to our elephants and went and stood behind Donoughmore, to watch him have his turn. This was to the good. No living animal had appeared. As we watched, four animals new to me, a little horned antelope, crossed the ride. Donoughmore, not realising that they wère to be shot, let them pass. Then an enormous blue bull appeared high up. Donoughmore fired at it twice, and missed it. We went on to the third ride and sat down at the base. The blue bull appeared first, and I shot him. It was an enormous animal. Then one of the four-horned antelopes appeared at full gallop, and with extraordinary luck I killed him with one shot, a very fine gallery performance that I cannot possibly account for, for I am no more good than a rabbit with a rifle. It turned out to be a male, but so young that it had no horns. Then Alwar informed me that the best climax, which was to be full of animals, was the fourth beat. This pleased me enormously, because Donoughmore would get the shooting. He said : " We will go and take up our position at the end of the ride ; it will take then an hour to do." I said to him : " But it is Donoughmore's turn this time." His face fell with displeasure, and he said : " All right." Then we started off. It was a long beat, looking most promising—very jungly, with water at the bottom. I cannot describe the beauty of the scenery—great rocks, the trees, the high hills. To my astonishment Alwar suddenly stopped and announced his intention of having tea. We sat down in the shade and had our tea. Suddenly we heard the beaters quite close to us. Instead of finishing our tea and going to our position, Alwar sent a bugler to stop the beat. There were poor Halliday, Parsons, and Franey, on their elephants in the beat, waiting for something to shoot at and not being able to understand in the least what had happened. He lazed over his tea, and when it was all over announced that there was no time to finish the beat; that Franey, Parsons, and Halliday could now have tea, and we would go home, when he and I would put on slippers and go and sit in his cage to wait for a leopard which would probably kill. I said nothing, I was so angry. I suggested that Parsons, Halliday, and Franey should remain behind to finish the beat. He refused this on the ground that he did not wish to disturb the tiger which was probably in this beat. No mention had been made of this before, and as the next day was going to be our last day, and we were not going for a tiger, I did not see the merits of this suggestion. If it were so, he could easily have started an hour earlier in the morning, which he never seems inclined to do. When we got to the palace I told him that I could not go after the leopard because I was too busy; that it was Donoughmore's birthday, and I would be grateful if he would take him instead of me. I was overjoyed to find that Donoughmore returned in half an hour with the leopard. He had seen the kill; he had watched the panther feeding at about ten feet distance; was highly delighted and in the best of spirits. We had a very merry dinner, during which Alwar announced his intention of making us stay over Monday. This, of course, I cannot do, but if Donoughmore does not get his tiger on Sunday, I shall suggest his remaining. I tried to arrange some fun for Parsons, Halliday, and Franey, and suggested that they should go into Alwar and shoot black buck. Alwar assented, but something seemed to go wrong with the arrangements, for Franey did not go and Halliday returned, not having found the black buck shoot. I am hoping that Alan will bring some black buck home, otherwise I am certain he will not get a shot. However, Franey had a shoot with Verney at Faridkot a week ago, and I hear there are four panthers to sit up for to-night, so I shall try and arrange that Parsons and Halliday, Donoughmore and I go for them. The Maharaja insists upon going himself, and will not hear of my not going.

I am writing to Chelmsford, for Marris's use, a criticism of Sir John Wood's contribution on the Native States, which I feel more and more will not do.

Sunday, March 3. This morning was spent by me working on the report, while Halliday and Parsons went into Alwar to look at the city, and to see if they could shoot some black buck. My whole time is spent in trying to get some shooting for my companions on these week-ends, but I do not meet with much success, although they had nothing to complain of at Kheri, where Halliday had his chance of a tiger and everybody else got stags, and Parsons got first shot at a leopard. It is the Native States that are so difficult. I am staying on here another day, because it is not an ordinary week-end visit. I work in the mornings much more uninterruptedly than I can in Delhi, and am making real progress, with which I am satisfied. Alwar has given me many new ideas, and his power of organisation is so splendid that I like to talk things over with him. A small trifle came to light yesterday. I asked him about bees in the jungle, and he told me that the jungles are gone through before a shoot with a view to getting rid of the bees.

Then came the tiger shoot, which was a marvel of successful organisation. We went a short distance by motor, some distance on the pad elephants, and then got on to our howdahs. I had a hasty consultation with Alwar, whom I am beginning to teach, after many conversations with him, that I want the shooting equally distributed. He told me that only two howdahs could get a chance at a tiger, and that the others would not see the fun at all ; it was for me to arrange who were to be the people to see the tiger, but I must be one of them. He said that he could not tell whether it would come to the right or the left, but he knew I wanted Donoughmore to be in the best place, and he would put him to the right. I felt he might be at his old games again, and I was half inclined to say that I would go to the right and Donoughmore to the left, but then I felt that he would have the laugh of me if the tiger came to me, so I abandoned this. I then conceived the great idea of having Halliday in my howdah with me, and told Donoughmore to take Franey ; Franey might get a chance at the tiger if Donoughmore missed it, but anyhow he would stand a better chance there than anywhere else. For Parsons I could do nothing, so my suggestion was that he should go with Alwar to a place where he would be a spectator of the whole proceeding. As a matter of fact, Parsons assumed that when Donoughmore was posted he was to stop with him, and therefore there was no opportunity of his seeing anything. I wish that I had a pen capable of describing the scenery, which was finer than anything I have yet seen, I think, anywhere—thick jungle, a deep ravine, tremendously high rocks on all sides. The tiger had indeed delivered himself into our hands. He had killed and walked straight up the ravine towards the high rocks. Where I stood, facing me was a precipice of enormous height, at least a thousand feet high, on the top of which Alwar's staff was sitting. Away to my right, at the top of almost as high a range of hills, began the beat. I was posted watching one of the rides, Donoughmore, on my right, watching another ride. Between us was a pad elephant to prevent the tiger breaking out where neither of us could see it. On the top of a rock 200 or 300 feet up the hillside sat Alwar, with a bugler, who could see into the jungle and everything all around. When all was ready, Alwar ordered the beginning of the beat by the sounding of the bugle, and the usual shouting, fireworks, blank shots, smoke bombs, and so on began. I had arranged with Halliday that if we were out of sight of Alwar he should sit in the front of the howdah, but, alas ! this went astray, because Alwar could see everything. I then arranged where Halliday was to get first shot, reserving to myself the first shot only in such a place that it was impossible to put the elephants where he could get first shot. I stood facing the ride, Halliday behind me, rifle ready. Soon after the beginning of the beat the Maharaja yelled to me that the tiger was coming behind me. I told Halliday to move to that side of the ride and to be ready to fire. The tiger apparently came down from the high hills in front of the beat, right across some thin jungle, and sat down in the thick jungle close to the pad elephant. Halliday would have got a nice shot if he had broken, but, alas ! he did not. He went right up again, almost straight where he had come from, and then down, and came to the edge of the jungle within about fifty yards of Donoughmore, who did not fire at him, because he thought either that it was not safe, as he would have fired straight into the beat, or that it would come closer—I am not sure which : perhaps it was a little of both. So far everything had gone well. It had looked as if Halliday was going to have a shot ; Donoughmore might perhaps have had a shot. Then a curious thing happened. The tiger came straight across from Donoughmore into the nullah, and right down through the nullah where I could shoot and Halliday could not. I fired, and the tiger rolled over. I fired again as it was rolling, and Halliday fired. It got up and went back along the same nullah ; was fired at by Alwar from his rock, a long shot which missed, and the tiger lay down in the thin jungle. The beat was stopped. I was in agony lest somebody again should be hurt by a wounded tiger. We went into the jungle on the elephants, and found the tiger lying stone dead where Alwar had seen it last—a very satisfactory performance, but, alas and alack, I had got the shot !

We then went home quickly ; had an early dinner whilst Parsons and Halliday went into Alwar to sit in cages for two leopards. I have to record that, alas, again it was a failure: I do not know why. I had the most entrancing night of my life. We dined very hastily at six in the most weird costume I have ever dined in, and then went out on a shikar expedition, which was not to end in bloodshed from our point of view, and not designed to do so. My costume consisted of my pyjamas, a felt hat, a silk muffler, a pair of felt slippers, thin white socks against the mosquitoes, a silk dressing-gown, and a rug. Alwar and Donoughmore accompanied me. We then went to a ravine, thickly jungled, about 400 yards from the palace—a short way in the motor car, and then about 100 yards across a stream on elephants, until we arrived at a tower. This tower had a spiral staircase up it, and at the top was roofed with windows, most of which were open, circular, of course. Under the windows, at a convenient height from the ground, were square loopholes screened with black silk. On the floor was a thick mattress, covering the whole floor space, with small pillows, where we sat. We made ourselves comfortable. On the ground in front of us, quite close to us, a buffalo calf was tied to a post; a little beyond it was a bowl of water. To the right of it, and quite close to it, was fizzling away a bright incandescent arc lamp, with a gasometer attached. Donoughmore and I sat so that we could part the hangings and look through the loophole at the buffalo and the surrounding country. Alwar sat at the far end of the circle, or rather lay, and there was an A.D.C. sitting motionless and cross-legged. We were told that we were free to move, but must make no sound, except the sort of sound that was likely to be heard in a jungle: a cough, a breath, a sneeze, a chink of stone or glass would be fatal. It was opined that the tiger would kill at eleven. I asked Alwar how he knew this. He said that it usually killed at eleven. I asked him how he knew this, and he told me that a buffalo made dung about four times in a night; that there had always been in this place two piles of dung, and therefore it was about midnight, or a little earlier, when the tiger came. Everything was still. A sambhur doe barked in the distance ; some night birds, a night-jar and an owl began to play about ; the stars shone through, and the moon got up at about twenty to ten. The buffalo showed not the slightest signs of alarm ; for the most part it slept ; sometimes it stood up. I was troubled with a cough which I thought was going to ruin the whole experiment, but whenever I had to cough I threw my rug over my head, and, as events showed, I did nothing wrong. Donoughmore slept fitfully, and we kicked him to prevent him snoring. There was no reason why I should not sleep, but I could not ; the excitement was too intense. At about a quarter to ten my attention was attracted by the buffalo rising hastily to his feet and looking in one direction. In the faint light I saw the tiger pass right across our front. I kicked Donoughmore, who rose and looked too. The tiger came straight on, a most glorious sight, right up to the bowl of water, and began to drink noisily. This aroused Alwar's attention, who came over and sat between us. The tiger remained with us for about three-quarters of an hour. The excitement of it is almost indescribable. By drinking first, it clearly showed that it knew the buffalo was tied up. How had it this reasoning power ? How on earth it explained to itself that there should be a buffalo tied up for it there I do not know. It did not mind the noise of the night in the least. After drinking, it wandered all about, looking in every direction. Then it came up to the buffalo. The buffalo showed no sign whatever of alarm ; it faced the tiger as a rule and was perfectly placid. There was no spring, and Alwar tells me that the idea that a tiger suddenly breaks its captive's neck is ridiculous : it does it by sheer pulling. It came right up to the buffalo, which snorted in its face at a distance of six inches ; then going behind it, as the buffalo danced round, and making a great deal of noise, the tiger playfully hit it low on the hind leg, quite softly, with its paw. The buffalo danced round, and he hit it again with the other paw on the front leg. Then it caught it by the neck, and a short struggle ensued. The tiger never left go, but lay down, dragging the buffalo's head on to the ground. Some minutes elapsed; the movements of the buffalo got less and less. Finally, with a swift shake of its head, the tiger let go. The buffalo lay still on the ground, with its neck broken, and the tiger walked right away and disappeared, just nosing at the bowl of water as it went. Alwar whispered that it had gone to the water to get another drink. After a time it came back from the opposite direction, and then began to feed. It never looked at the tower, but occasionally it stood up and looked away in the direction from which it had originally come.

All was over by twenty-five minutes to eleven. The tiger, who had eaten noisily, crunching and cutting with a loud noise the skin with its teeth, walked away from the tower and disappeared in the jungle. We had some supper and a drink and lay down to sleep. I do not know whether I snored; Donoughmore's snores were awful, but the tiger, which was not hungry, never came back. I kept on kicking Donoughmore when I woke up, but I slept most of the night, always when I woke looking out to see what was happening, but all was still.

In the morning, the first birds that appeared on the kill were the fawn-coloured Indian magpies. Alwar told me that if the tiger had been on the kill, then you would have seen the magpie sitting on the tiger and eating bits from its mouth—really picking its teeth for it. Then came the crows, and finally the vultures. As the most beautiful dawn in the world began to spread we went home at about six and slept till breakfast. Nothing could have been more beautiful, and I appreciated to the full Alwar's delight in it, without any desire to shoot the animal, although I was a little sorry for

Donoughmore, who has not got his tiger yet, and had this marvellous chance. Donoughmore pathetically said in the morning that I had kicked him to stop him snoring three times when he was awake ! Poor man !

Monday, March 4. This morning I have been busy on the Government of India proposals for a full-time Solicitor-General. I think that a Parliamentary draftsman is wanted. I should like not to use the Advocate-General at all, but to have a separate law officer.

I spent the whole morning on the report and on work generally. At half-past one Franey and Parsons went into Alwar to shoot black buck, to sit up for panthers, to dine in Alwar and to join us on the train. We heard by telephone at dinner time that they had got no panthers, but that Alan had shot a small black buck. We went out, no tiger having been marked down, for a chance beat which was to be full of samburs, to that part of the hill which we shot on Sunday that we had left over unshot. It did not take us long to get there. We sat on the enormously steep rides going up the sides of these hills. It is marvellous to see the elephants climb an almost vertical hill. For the first beat, Donoughmore, Halliday, and Raoji went to the ride nearest to the beaters. The jungle was very thick along the lower slopes of the hills half-way up them, and they sat on some rocks, leaving their elephants at the bottom of the ride. I and Alwar went to the next ride behind them. As usual, men were up on the top of the hill all along, to watch what happened. The beat went at right angles to the top of the hill, and on the other flank were some low hills on the other side of the ride by which we had come. A dried up river, with a little water in it, was there too, and at the bottom of the ride on which Alwar and I sat a tiger had killed a buffalo, but he had not been marked down. Very soon Alwar began to get restive where we were sitting. He said that a tiger could be within ten yards of us before we could see him, because of the configuration of the ground. I said I would not then shoot at him. He said supposing it were wounded by Donoughmore, when he came we should be in danger. He hauled up the hill two pad elephants, which did not give us much confidence in where we stood, and waited. Very soon a tiger was announced on my side of Donoughmore's ride. The beat took a very long time, as the hill was very precipitous, and there were gullies running along it thickly wooded. The tiger seemed to be very reluctant to come out. Alwar saw it once coming back towards the elephants. Donoughmore, Halliday, and Raoji came back and stood at the bottom of the hill. I begged Alwar to let him change places with me. He said he could not ; it would take too long ; that I should probably not get a shot, and Donoughmore would get a better shot afterwards. Eventually the tiger, after some charges on the elephants not pressed home, and after threatening once to come out above me, came out well below me. I had a glimpse of him as he passed behind a hillock, and fired intentionally a snap shot, because I did not want to get him, and missed him. He was galloping hard, but one could just see that he was a fine male tiger, the first male we had seen. Then we moved to the next beat, and I, suspecting that nobody got a shot at a tiger unless Alwar was there, insisted upon Alwar going with Donoughmore. The tiger came out and crossed their ride far above them ; Donoughmore did not get a shot. Then Alwar joined me, sending Raoji with Donoughmore to an open space just behind. He said the tiger having come out first low and then high would now come out low and go to Donoughmore, where I could not see it. Half-way through the beat he altered his mind and took me up on a howdah to the highest and steepest climb I have ever had, almost to the top of the steepest part of the hill. Then a casualty happened. Suddenly the tiger appeared almost on a level with my howdah above me. As soon as it

E. S. M. and H.H. of Alwar

Their Highnesses of Bikaner, Patiala and Dholpur

ALWAR

[*To face page* 304

saw us it opened its mouth with a roar and charged straight at my elephant. He was only about twenty yards off. There was no miss possible here, for in another second he would have been on the elephant, and the elephant would certainly have been mauled if he pressed his charge home. Drawing a careful bead on the tiger with great coolness, I knocked him down with the first shot. He lay for a second, and then crawled back into the jungle, but not before I had got three more bullets into him that left him dead. So I got my third tiger. It was a highly exciting finish, and it was the biggest tiger I have ever seen. It does not compare well in measurement, as it had a curiously short tail ; it therefore only measured 8 ft. 11 in.

We got home fairly late, and then went to sit up for a leopard which did not come ; we dined at nine. Alwar made a little speech of welcome ; and we then motored into Alwar, reaching there at midnight. A hyena came out from the beat, but nobody shot at it, and we saw it in the road as we motored into Alwar.

XII

DELHI X—JAIPUR—DELHI XI—BHOPAL—DELHI XII

Tuesday, March 5. Most of to-day I have spent on the report. Various disturbing incidents have occurred. Chelmsford is on the track of indefiniteness again—affirming principles and leaving everything to be worked out by a committee. I told Chelmsford that the reference to the committee I proposed was limited.

Harcourt Butler came to lunch. He looks very ill and tired ; he has had fever and is very lame. What he says about his Province fills me with hope. He told me that he realised that he was not in this business and that he was going to accept anything which came, but that he is bound to say that he likes our proposals. This is all so much to the good. He says also that Willingdon will be very pleased at the new ideas, because he was much alarmed by the old ones. That is to the good. He tells me that he found Hewitt in England admitting that everything we do now must be a real reform without too many safeguards. I do hope it will turn out to be so. He tells me also that the changes in the atmosphere in Calcutta from an Ilbert-Bill-like attitude when he went home, to the President of the Chambers of Commerce saying that we had got to co-operate with the moderate Indians was a striking testimony to the success of our winter's work.

Then dinner at Viceregal Lodge in the gardens outside ; it was quite cold ; then a few excellent charades for our entertainment ; and bed.

Wednesday, March 6. We had a long and wearying discussion between Lowndes, Duke, Roberts, Chelmsford, and myself, as to how to carry out provincial decentralisation, and how to ensure that this is an unalterable policy. This needed the examination of American, Australian, Canadian, and South African precedents. I entered into the controversy in a very bad temper. The need for a clear definition becomes increasingly apparent as isolated individuals crop up who do not believe in the doctrine of political autonomy. But there is no doubt that statutory demarcation of territory must lead to litigation as to the validity of statutes. I am the last man to want this. What politicians have suffered at the hands of lawyers and parliamentary draftsmen need not be described. Further than this, I do not want to find that there is no authority in India capable of dealing with a legislative situation which requires action but in which the local government will not move and the Government of India cannot. On the other hand, if I leave the statute unaltered, it gives to the Government of India concurrent and overriding powers on all subjects comparable to the power of the South African supreme Government, and what is to happen when a Curzon returns to India who does not believe in provincial autonomy? A convention of a few years growth will be swept overboard. The more like Curzon the Viceroy is the more impotent the Secretary of State will be. The deadlock which Chelmsford refers to as justifying the intervention of the Government of India can always be created. Circumstances can be described as a deadlock to suit the will of those who want it. I am perfectly prepared to give the Government of India power to interfere when a Province trespasses on the affairs of other Province or upon the affairs of the Government of India, and I am perfectly prepared to preserve their power of Ordinance. Further than this I do not like to go. But, as I have told Chelmsford, I am quite prepared not to say that I will deprive the Government of India of its universal concurrent and overriding rights provided that he will not say that he will not deprive them of these rights, and leave it to be discussed at home with eminent constitutional authorities such as Haldane and Bryce. I am not competent to do battle as a layman with lawyers like Lowndes and Chelmsford ; and if a little learning is a dangerous thing, a little law is a particularly dangerous thing, and little lawyers are particularly dangerous people. Anybody who has the right to describe himself as "an honourable and learned member" thinks he has a right to expound law. I have suffered from this on income tax things in the House of Commons at the hands of people like Lancelot Sanderson, Hohler, and Phipson Beale, and I want my Reading, Buckmaster or Simon to put against my Lowndes and Chelmsford.

In the afternoon I had Bingley to lunch, and we went through Army questions.

I talked to Bingley, too, about the I.M.S., or rather he talked to me, because he spontaneously made this suggestion. There ought not to be two services in India. If the Indian Army becomes united to the British Army in an Imperial Army, the I.M.S. should be absorbed in the R.A.M.C. ; if the Indian Army remains distinct, the R.A.M.C. ought to be absorbed in the I.M.S. I agreed with him, and said that I did not believe in the absorption of the Indian Army in the British Army, but I did agree that there should be some greater control by the War Office. But in any case, whatever the combined service was called, we ought to set to work to combine the two medical services, and this he agreed to.

In the afternoon we had a long discussion with the Government of India on the Council of State and the affirmative powers in the Provinces. We reached general agreement—complete agreement on the Council of State, although many of us regret that there should be in it an elected element ; and complete agreement on the affirmative powers in the local governments, with the exception of Nair, who was bad in argument and who aroused the anger of all his colleagues. I tried to argue with him, but it was no good, and all that is left is that he is coming to lunch with me to-morrow. He objects first to the affirmative powers given to the Grand Committee. I do not agree with him, but I see the force of one argument—that the Government of India despatch of 1916, if ever published, would show that we are going back on what they were willing to do then—forfeit the affirmative powers in a Legislative Council which was to have a substantial elected majority, and their proposals were agreed to by all local governments except Madras and the Punjab. To-day all local governments agree, including Madras, except the Punjab, and even in the Punjab O'Dwyer—and it is his personal opinion—would take a non-official majority. Now, although it is true that we are going much further than 1916 in B subjects, in A subjects we are preserving a non-official majority, but unelected in the Grand Committee, the O'Dwyer policy, and not the Government of India or the rest of the Provinces. It is quite true that the despatch of the Government of India was a bad one ; it is quite true that Chelmsford admits that he is wrong ; it is quite true that our policy is sounder ; but Nair is right in describing it as less liberal on A subjects than was originally intended. I could not argue it freely with him, because the Grand Committee as it is to be constituted is much more liberal than he thinks it is, and as Basu, who is far wiser, realises. They would have tightened it up if I had pointed that out. Then, too, although Nair admits that my new formula for the right of the Governor to restore his A provisions is better than the old one, he does not accept it, but he announced yesterday that he would be willing to do so and to waive all his objections if the Indian member of the Executive Council was compelled to be an elected member of the Legislative Council. This is a concession which it would be difficult to make to him, for two reasons. First, I am never sure that I have got him when I have made a concession to him, and he may find some other point on which to ride off. Secondly, it is a matter of principle. The Governor ought to have the right to select the colleague that he likes best, and we do not want to import at present any responsibility to electorates for A subjects. That will come. It will come under our scheme by transferring the A subjects to the B category, but it ought not to come by making the member of the Executive Council responsible for A subjects responsible to the Legislative Council. I suggested that the Governor should be required to take such steps as possible to ensure that the man he recommended is not unacceptable to his Legislative Council. This does not satisfy Nair. When he comes to lunch to-morrow I am going to try a new formula—that the Governor is to be expected to look, in the first instance, for the man he wishes among the Councillors of State from the Province or the elected members of the Legislative Council in the Province, or the members of the Imperial Legislative Assembly elected by the Province, and only to go outside these if there is some man of high standing and repute who enjoys the reputation and esteem of the Province but whose other advocations have not led him to seek election to any legislative body.

Thursday, *March* 7. This morning I have had a talk with Chelmsford, and am engaged upon the report, writing a few essential letters, and so on.

I have finally had to telegraph home that I am not coming on the 17th. I cannot help it, but it is a very severe blow to me.' A matter of this kind is far too important to rush, and new points are continually cropping up. Chelmsford has been at me daily to decide, and I only decided when it became obvious that I could not help it.

I had Sankaran Nair to lunch, and he was very frank in criticism of my scheme. He told me that he thought in practice we were giving to the Indians everything they wanted, but in theory we were withholding so many powers that it would make the scheme unacceptable, because the extremist would point to the theory and not to the practice. This arises, of course, from the insatiable desire of both sides to see everything down in writing, so that nothing is left to chance. Numbers must be jerrymandered ; statutes must be made in order to assure the Indians that a knavish Government will not " do them in the eye," and in order to assure the civilians that the Indian extremists will not spoil their game. Until somebody has the courage to risk, nothing will be satisfactory. But I am not justified in taking a risk which might prevent, if it went wrong, more ordered progress. I sent Sankaran into the seventh heaven of delight by suggesting a Standing Committee of the House of Commons to be associated with the Secretary of State. He said he would accept anything if that were done. I am sure it is right. We want to train Parliament, and not have the spasmodic and ridiculous procedure which is now called " Parliamentary control."

In the evening I had a very satisfactory talk with Jinnah, who gave me an assurance of his support, subject to liberty of amendment. If the Home Rule League supports us, I think it ought to be arranged that action against the Home Rule Press and Home Rule members can only be taken after consultation with the Home Rule Committee.

Chelmsford is very stiff about my suggestion that the Grand Committee procedure should only be used in exceptional circumstances. I must insist on that, or I will never get it through the House of Commons.

In the evening a State dinner was given to the Legislative Council. The Legislative Council has been in session for a month. In no house in Delhi have I yet met at any meal a member of the Legislative Council. In the party for the investiture which Chelmsford gave at the beginning of the session they were not included. They have not been to Government House. This dinner, to which they are all asked in a block to meet nobody but themselves and the Executive Council, is the only substitute, and then the seats are arranged—would the gods believe it ?—in order of precedence, so that Chelmsford sat between Sir Claude Hill and Sir Sankaran Nair, and I sat between Lady Chelmsford and Sir George Lowndes. It really is the stupidest thing imaginable. They tell me that when the garden parties are given, when there is no war, they come, but why do not they come to lunch, breakfast, and dinner? Why does not Chelmsford see a man who is going to move a resolution? Why does not Chelmsford talk and argue with a man who is going to do something? Ye gods, I cannot speak too strongly of all this; and political India will never work if it remains.

Friday, March 8. The whole morning was spent discussing our scheme with my *adlati*, and making improvements in our draft conclusions. Of course new points emerged which will lengthen our discussion, and everybody is now in a mood of hesitating to improve, lest it may delay by a day our departure from this place; added to which the tents are becoming stifling.

After lunch I had a few words with Chelmsford. He does not see any objection to my alteration, which makes the Council of State the real germ of the Second Chamber by giving it power to promote legislation. He does not like the limitations of the affirmative powers committee to things essential to their responsibility for A subjects, but as we have got a formula like this in every connection, I propose to insist upon it.

I have just had a telegram from the Admiral saying that he will put his flagship at my disposal on April 7. This is almost a month hence. Good God, how can I stand it! But Chelmsford assures me it is no use making other arrangements, because he is quite certain we shall not be ready before then. This means leaving Delhi on April 5, and even if I could get away two or three days beforehand, any other way of going home other than the flagship would not land me home any sooner. I shall decide definitely on Monday.

Chintamani came to see me, and finding that he already knew so much by leakage, I took him into my confidence. He gave no expression of opinion, and said he would come to see me again on Monday.

Then we began again at three in a stiflingly hot tent, and succeeded by six o'clock in getting all the way through our draft conclusions, improving them and tightening them up. I also got their approval to the Standing Committee idea. It was the most strenuous day I have had. Nothing is so awful as going through a draft with six other men. You have first of all got to see that the draft expresses what is agreed, and then you have to see whether you want to alter that agreement, because I cannot regard my proposals as final until I can make them no better. Charles Roberts was at his worst. He could not see this dual work that we were trying to do. He kept on objecting to new proposals—that they were not agreed, and he always tries to draft everything as if it was a statute. He is the most meticulously-minded man I have ever come across. I believe if you asked him to stay with you for a week-end he would not take the proposal in that form ; he would understand it to mean that I was proposing a statute which would say : " Be it enacted that, on the appointed day, Mr. Roberts, Member of Parliament for Lincoln, shall proceed, save as mentioned in section 10 of this Act," etc., etc. My method of working is so different—forming conclusions and training myself to discard them, without prejudice, for better ones. This cautious phrasing makes us in dialectics miles apart. However, there it is : we emerged ! I think my Standing Committee of the House of Commons, which everybody seems inclined to adopt, will go far to save the situation.

In the evening I had a very long talk with Chelmsford while walking up and down the garden. His temper was nearly as short as mine. We went all over the ground together, and I think there is still no divergence of opinion.

I adopted the depressed attitude very much, partly because I was depressed and partly because I want him to get a little courage. I can always talk to Maffey and be quite certain that Maffey will repeat it to him. My suggestion for a Standing Committee of the House of Commons pleases him more and more.

I then dressed for dinner, at which Chelmsford did not appear. He was going off fishing and had dinner in his own room. So we dined on the verandah, Lady Chelmsford saying he was very depressed. I took the opportunity of seeing him before I went off and soothing him a little bit, but I had to put my point of view.

At half-past ten we left for Jaipur. I had never much wanted to go there, but Chelmsford had insisted, because, he said, Jaipur had made such a point of it, and was, after all, the premier prince in Rajputana. I am bound to say I do not regret having come. The party consists of Alan, Franey, Donoughmore, Seton, Halliday, Verney, and old Basu, who was asked by Jaipur. He has been quite a delightful companion, telling us stories of his life. He gave one account of how he had been libelled in a newspaper because he had called a friend who was occupying the same tent with him by his first name of "Ramani," which means a woman. Here is old Jaipur, the oldest of Indian princes, and in many ways the most conservative, asking one of the most prominent of the *intelligenzia* as his week-end guest. It does at least, I think, show that the idea that the Native States are outside modern developments is a belief which has now no foundation in fact.

Saturday, *March* 9. We were met at the station at seven this morning by old Jaipur and his Chief Minister, Sir Mumtaz-ud-dowlah Nawab Mohamed Faiyaz Ali Khan, and immediately got into motor cars and drove off to a small pond to shoot the little sand grouse and a few duck. The amount of water about this year made it a poorer shoot than it usually is, but we collected six duck and sixteen sand grouse, of which ten sand grouse and three duck fell to my gun. It was very hot, but very pleasant, and at the little pond at which we were shooting I saw no fewer than 28 different kinds of birds. We drove back to breakfast, a very big and heavy meal, at eleven, and at twelve started for the day's shoot. I ought to have mentioned that we were not at Jaipur itself, but at a shooting camp of His Highness's called Siwai Madhopur. It has characteristic Indian scenery--perfectly flat ground covered with thorn bushes which are just bursting into beautiful red flowers, and occasional sudden ranges of hills with precipitous cliffs rising sheer out of the background, the lower slopes being covered with jungle. Old Jaipur is a dear old thing, the soul of hospitality, and he has built for us quite a delightful camp. He must be 70, and his white beard is very conspicuous. He is very fat, and was dressed in a gauze thin brown sari, covering white clothes, with bare fat legs and bare feet. He has given me a royal reception. He cannot speak a word of English, which is rather a bore, but he is continually interjecting pleasant remarks. When I am haunted day and night as to whether my expedition has failed or not, whether my plan will be rejected by the Indians and howled at by the English and laughed to scorn by constitutional historians, I do take satisfaction to myself at finding how excellently I have got on with the Indians, be they the Indian politicians or the Indian princes. The same method is wanted for both—a sympathetic desire to find out what it is they want, and a perfectly frank expression of your own opinion. The terribly strained relations between the Government and the people now seems to me to be due more to the Government always talking to the people with reservations, which show they are founded on distrust than anything else ; and if you do not trust a man, he will not behave as if he ought to be trusted. We drove in motors to the foot of a cliff, and then mounted 20-foot high machans protected from the sun, each built to hold five or six persons. On the one nearest to the beat were old Jaipur, Donoughmore, myself, Seton, and Basu, who enjoyed himself thoroughly, never having seen a tiger shoot before. On the other machan were Halliday, Parsons, Franey, and Verney. The beat began at one and lasted till quarter to three. It was an easy place to drive, particularly with the 1,200 beaters that were employed, and the tigress which was in the beat came out into the clearing high up on the side of the jungle, about 100 yards from Donoughmore. Donoughmore at last got his tiger. He drew a careful bead, knocked down the tigress, and with two other shots finished it. My attention was distracted from subsequent proceedings by suddenly seeing two cubs coming out of the jungle close to the machan. Seton, who was to have second shot, missed them both. They went on across the clearing at a hand gallop. I fired and killed one, and the other was killed from the other machan, as it subsequently turned out by Halliday, which was again good, because Halliday had never got a tiger. Then I looked up and saw another tiger walking in the jungle, on the far side of the other machan. I fired two shots—it must have been 300 yards—and thought I knocked it down, but apparently I was mistaken. There was no blood and no hair, and no sign of the animal has been found. So that we got three dead tigers. Afterwards a small sambur came out past us, accompanied by two does. Verney killed it. Then a hyena broke out far below me. I had to wait until it was clear of the men waiting behind, and did not get it. Two blue bulls came out slowly right across the clearing, and passed both machans before the tigers arrived ; of course we did not shoot. When we got down from the machan to inspect the bag, very many curious incidents have to be recorded. So far as I know, nobody fired at the tigress except Donoughmore, who fired three shots at it, but

D. R. Verney F. C. T. H. B. N. Basu

M. C. S. A. P. E. S. M. H.H. of Jaipur G. E. F.

JAIPUR

[To face page 316

Donoughmore asserts that another cub broke back past our machan into the jungle from which he had come low down. This cub is also said to have been seen by Verney. High up above where the tigress had been killed, at a subsequent moment I saw what I thought was a cub or a leopard, and pointed it out to Seton, who then said he could see it still after it had disappeared from my sight. I told him to fire. He fired, and then I said that was not where I saw the cub last. When Donoughmore's tigress was inspected, she was found to have at least four bullet wounds in her, so that Seton must have fired at the tigress lying dead on the ground. What, in that event, happened to the cub I do not know. The second mystery was that when we met the party from the other machan, Verney and all his companions were firmly under the impression that they had killed the cub that I killed. After the tigers had been killed, news came of a panther which had been marked down in another small beat, and we went to it. I told Seton and Parsons to toss as to who should shoot it : Seton won. We then went to sit on a machan—Seton, Parsons, Franey, and I. Seton and Parsons selected the positions they liked best. Donoughmore, Verney, and Halliday were on elephants. The beat began. I have not recorded that it has been stiflingly hot all day, very cloudy, with one torrential downpour of rain, which, fortunately, lasted only a few minutes, and there was a good deal of thunder about. As I say, the beat began. High up as we faced the clearing on the edge of the jungle, on the hill opposite us, almost on the top of the hill, there came a whole lot of sambur with a few small stags. Then a pig appeared in the middle of the jungle below us, and then Alan spotted the panther. Seton tried to see it, and could not, so I told Alan to fire. It must have been nearly 350 yards from him on the side of the hill, nearer the top than the bottom. He made a marvellous shot and broke its back. We could see the panther moving, and we had the most agonising time, because we could see the beat coming on and could not communicate with it, and I was dreadfully afraid that somebody would get mauled. Seton did a little shouting in bad Hindustani. Parsons and he had other shots, which missed it, but finally, as it crawled about, Seton got in another shot, and hit it. But it was still moving. The beat was too near to do any more shooting from our machan, so Verney and Halliday came forward on their elephants, which were terribly frightened of the panther, which was occasionally growling. However, at close range they eventually stopped all motion in the poor brute. Alan was highly delighted with himself, and I am delighted that he should have got it, and not unnaturally he was in agony at the amount of heavy ammunition which was being poured into his only panther skin. It has certainly been blown about, but that is better than having a beater mauled. Thus ended a wonderful day's sport—sixteen sand grouse, six duck, three tigers, one panther, and one sambur. Nobody is clear whether we saw four or five tigers, but I think there must have been five. We also saw blue bulls, hyenas, pigs, and countless birds. The Maharaja is the soul of hospitality, and promises us after dinner, when we are all tired, with a demonstration of ventriloquism, some juggling, and a nautch. When one of his ministers was asked how many nautch girls there were going to be, he replied : "One each," so that we are all excited to see what is going to happen.

We had an enormous dinner, prepared by some contractor, which, fortunately, we were able to discard in favour of the more than ample food produced by the Maharaja, cooked by his own cook. Indian food is excellent when well done, and nothing else was necessary. Dinner was assisted by a ventriloquist on the verandah, who gave us excellent imitations of Indian birds, animals, and noises ; but after dinner we had an entertainment which was more than boring, and to tired men anything that lasted till twelve o'clock was hard to bear. It began with a protracted nautch, danced by hideous women heavily clothed in stiff, gold embroideries. Their idea of dancing seemed to be the slow movement of the feet, accompanied by awkward gestures of arms, to a din without end or beginning. I am told it was a bad example, and it certainly was a boring entertainment. At a late hour a woman conjuror took the stage. Some of her tricks were excellent, but they were accompanied by a wealth of patter which to us was meaningless and which was unceasing. The tricks took a very long time to perform, and some, such as the famous mango trick, has too much paraphernalia to commend itself to me. Anything can go on inside a tent large enough to hold a family.

Sunday, March 10. Verney, Seton, and I got up at seven, and started off to shoot partridges. We saw a black buck or two, which none of us wished to shoot, and then we started looking for the partridges, but it soon became apparent that there were none. We got back into our motors, and went back to the scene of the activities of the morning before. On the way I killed quite a nice chinkara. He was on the edge of the crops, and provided an interesting shot. At the water we killed twelve sand grouse and a couple of duck, and then had to leave, in order to get back in time for the sport arranged overnight at half-past ten. We were very disgusted to find that there had been an alteration in the arrangements, and that we were not starting off until 11.30. No news of tigers, which I had anticipated, but we drove through an old city into a huge gorge of entrancing beauty, and sat on a high machan, waiting for what the beat might bring forward. Nothing came out except one bear, which I killed, without incident or event. I saw him for about a quarter of an hour before I could get a shot at him. He just appeared for a second, and then disappeared into some thick bushes. He came out again, and I killed him with three shots at about 200 yards. The occupants of the other machan got nothing at all. Six sambhur does and two very tiny stags came out, and were not fired at. Jaipur said he was now quite satisfied. I had killed plenty of birds and a very fine bear, and I had also killed a tiger, but he was unable to understand why I did not accept it. To-day was all right; yesterday he was disappointed with. In Jaipur the man who killed the beast possessed it. He told all this to Basu, and I told Basu that I should not discuss yesterday. The point was that he thought I had killed it, and another member of my party genuinely thought he had killed it. I was not going to make a dispute about it, as I did not want the animal. He and I were both satisfied that I had killed it: what did it matter to let the other man think that he had killed it. All the Maharaja said was "Hukm," and then relapsed into silence.

In order to occupy the time I discussed with Donoughmore, Seton, and Basu what they thought about a bet I had made with the immaculate Charles Roberts. Charles Roberts undertook, before I left England, to drink his first whisky and soda if the Congress accepted my proposals. I believed that there was a chance now—I would not say more than a chance—that the Congress would pass a resolution accepting my proposals, and then add a rider to say that they proposed to insist upon certain amendments: would that involve Charles drinking his whisky and soda or not? Donoughmore suggested that he should be allowed to arbitrate, with a result, he alleged, which would be dangerous to Roberts's virginity. Seton said that he feared the decision would be, or ought to be, yes, he must drink his whisky and soda, but he was entitled to amend it, if the Congress amended it, by leaving out the whisky. Then Basu said that he thought the Congress would pass a resolution accepting, leaving all amendment to subsequent negotiation, so as not to provide their enemies with a handle for saying that they had been captious.

E. S. M. and H.H. of Jaipur

[To face page 320

After the first beat I begged for another one : it was only three o'clock, and I must say they moved the beaters on elephants with lightning rapidity to another beat on the side of the main hills facing the railway. We got into the most jerry-built machan I have ever seen ; it was only supported at three of its four angles. Donoughmore, Franey, and I sat there, the Maharaja and Basu going home, and Seton and Verney going up to sit on some rocks above us. We sat there from about five until quarter to six, when the excitement began. We had been warned that nothing might come out, because it was purely a chance beat, but the end was amazing. The first thing that emerged was a hyena, an animal I had long wanted to kill, as I had never killed one. It came slightly below us, and I knocked it down with my first shot and killed it with my second. Then high up on our right a bear suddenly appeared, and was shot at by Verney. I sent a shot after it afterwards. I think we both missed. The bear tried to get back through the beaters, and we heard it growling. Then we lost sight of it, save that something passed under our machan which we could hear but could not see. Behind us a line of stops had been placed, and if we had been more expert, I think we should at this stage have turned round and faced the other way ; but there was always a chance of a late sambhur, and we had not the certainty that the bear was not immediately in front of us. Shortly afterwards a rifle shot rang out from these rocks above us, and we saw that they had shot something coming from behind. It turned out afterwards to be another hyena which Verney had shot within ten yards of the rock on which they were sitting. Then our attention was attracted to a fusilade from the rock, and we saw that the bear had come round from behind us and had advanced straight on to Seton. He fired at it at a distance of about twenty yards, and then Verney fired, and the bear came rolling down between us and the rock, and finally died above our machan. We then turned round and looked back, and were rewarded by getting a pig. When the bear was examined, only one shot was to be found in it, and I am afraid Seton missed it, but Seton's first introduction to big game shooting was pretty exciting, for if Verney had missed the bear, they would have been in a very awkward predicament on their low rock. We could not have failed to see the bear if we had been looking behind us, for the ground was bare, but we lost our chances. Indeed, it now appears that although they had taken up an admirable position for animals coming from the direction of the beat, Seton and Verney had planted themselves in the only path of egress for animals coming from behind. We drove back, thoroughly well satisfied, and we ended our two days shoot with three tigers and a panther, two bears, two hyenas, a chinkara, a pig, a sambhur, 22 sand grouse and eight duck—the most successful shoot in the time that had ever been held at Siwai Madhopur. The Maharaja was delighted. After dinner, at which the ventriloquist again assisted, we had a series of pretty little speeches. I buttered our host, his shikaris, and his arrangements; he garlanded us all, and gave me a dressing-gown and a large photograph of himself. He also gave Donoughmore and Basu photographs.

Monday, March 11. We have had a short conference this morning, and then I spent some time on the report. At 12.30 Chintamani came to see me, and his comments on the scheme showed that he accepted it so far as he understood it. He does not like the Affirmative Powers Committee, and he wants all members of the Government to be paid the same, Rs4,000 a month, the salary of a High Court judge. Except for that, he made very little comment. I hate the affirmative powers, which I do not believe are necessary, but I cannot go back upon them.

Then Hogg came to lunch, and I found him, although he did not express many opinions, not startled by the scheme.

He told me that Welby had been making a speech refusing the announcement of August 20 ; that he was afraid that he and Wardlaw Milne were in a minority, but he believed that if only a man would appear who would organise they could carry any scheme. They wanted some capable organiser to devote the next few years to getting a European and Indian force behind us.

Then a conference with the Government of India, at which we ratified my suggestions about the Secretary of State, and came to an agreement on the difficult subject of the A and B list on the lines of my most recent note. Marris is not satisfied with this, but I am quite prepared to be as definite as I like about what they want to do. I cannot be definite here as to how they want to do it, because I am not a parliamentary draftsman, and I do not believe in them.

After the conference I had a very long talk with Sinha and the Viceroy about the proposals. Sinha said very little, but I think he is all right and will be very useful on our side.

Then I saw Kapharde, who assured me that he was going to England to see people about why India wanted Home Rule, and so forth. He is an extremist, they tell me, associated with criminal undertakings in the past, but he seemed to me to be a sensible old man.

Then I went to dinner with Mahmudabad. Roberts, Basu, and I were the guests, but there were various members of the Legislative Council present, including Sapru and Jinnah. Mahmudabad did not seem to me to be very good-tempered. By the by, he told me that he was only 41, but he looks much older. Jinnah was very pleasant. The food was excellent, mainly vegetable, and entirely Indian. After dinner the most marvellous dancer in India, for whose services Mahmudabad had paid 1,000 rupees for the evening, was the chief entertainer. The dancing was in short spasms ; the music was the usual doleful wail of instruments ; the man was hideously ugly, misshapen in body, dressed in heavy gold embroideries with bare feet. Most of his dancing consisted of brass-god-like gestures of the arms, slow movements of the feet, with occasional ecstatic whirls, well executed. He yowled a sentence and then danced it. To me, I could see no more resemblance between the dance and the sentence than between the hollow boom of a monkey and the movements of an ant. This is the sort of thing that would occur. He would say : " Now the fiery glance of your eyes has stolen the heart from my bosom." Then a few jerks and a twirl. " Stop drawing water from the well ; I want to talk to you." Then a few twirls and a jerk. But he was imcomparably better than the nautch which followed, when hideous women repeated the spasm-like movements of arms and feet, grotesquely dressed and howling like jackals. They tell me that our music is as incomprehensible to them. So it is to me, but then I do realise that our songs have some sort of beginning and some sort of ending, and I can distinguish between lively music and doleful music, heavy music and light music.

Tuesday, March 12. This morning I spent with Marris, and the afternoon with the Viceroy. We made progress. With the Viceroy our conclusions at last took shape. He will not move on the Grand Committee point.

Wednesday, March 13. I slept badly, because I have been thinking all night of Marris's chapters. I have not written in my diary anything about them, because I am going to write a letter to Marris embodying my views, which I shall append ; but it is interesting to note that Vincent last night after dinner confessed what I had suspected—that the chapter to which I took the strongest exception was one in which he had had a very substantial share.

Sir William Duke came to breakfast, and we went through his recommendations about Indianisation and the pay of the services. I told him that to give alternatives to the local governments meant two or three years delay. We went through the Marris chapters, and then he left.

Then I had a series of interviews with Indians. First came Sastri for three-quarters of an hour, but nothing happened, because I spent the whole of my time expounding my scheme.

He was followed by Malaviya, who showed himself discontented with the scheme. He did not like the proportion in the Council of State of officials to non-officials, and reminded me of a more liberal recommendation of Minto's that it should be half and half, including non-officials nominated in the half. He also wanted three Indians, and not two, in the Executive Council.

Then Marris to lunch. He seemed to me very obstreperous, and very much wedded to his objectionable chapters as they stood. I brought in Duke afterwards to help, and I think I made some impression on Marris. Of course this is one of the matters upon which I must win, but it was worth while trying to convince Marris.

In the afternoon Duke and I had a long conversation with the Viceroy upon Indianisation. He proved quite tractable. I talked to him also about a few other things.

I dined at Government House—a small dinner party, and played bridge afterwards with Donoughmore, a man in the Political Service called Durand, and Tony Grant.

Thursday, March 14. I breakfasted alone; read Austen Smith on the Medical Services, and spent the morning going through Marris's chapters with Kisch.

At 12.30 Ainscough, the new trade commissioner, came to see me, and I discussed with him the difficulties of his position; how he must not see Europeans to the exclusion of Indians; how he must try to keep on the right side of the Indians, and prove that we were not developing British trade with India

Bosanquet, Davis, the Agent, the Nawab Saheb, the eldest son and heir, and so on. We were kept waiting some time for the Begum, who finally arrived, and I drove with her, followed by the others, to a guest house, where we had breakfast. I found her very difficult to talk to, because her English is so bad and her voice is so muffled in her white veil. She was very pleasant.

Davis, our host, was extremely nice to us. But it seemed to me quite clear that Bosanquet was the real Agent for Bhopal. Davis spoke with great pride of the people trusting him. He was actually asked to find a wet nurse for the impending child of a Bhopal Thakar, but when it came to a question of Hamidullah's position, he was incapable of doing anything or exercising any power : I should not think he interfered at all. When I was looking for somewhere to spend this weekend, it was Davis, who happened to be in Delhi, who suggested he should run the shoot for me, and we were told to go to Salampur, the station on the Delhi side of Bhopal, and motor 20 miles to camp. On the day we left, no real working plan had been sent to us, but a wire had been received to go to Bhopal. We came, and everything began to go wrong. Our luggage was not sent straight from the station to the camp, but had to be brought up to the guest house ; the 20 miles run in the motor turned out to be not an inch less than 50 miles over a road so vile that the average number of punctures per car was about two and a half ; I had four. We took five hours to reach our camp. Davis was completely ignorant as to distances and localities. We then had a beat, which was to produce cheetal and sambur, and which actually produced one tiger, killed by Halliday, and one leopard, killed by me. Both animals disappeared into the beat after being shot at. There was no instrument of any sort or kind to stop the beat. Men were walking to certain death. I never yelled so much in my life or talked so much incomprehensible Hindustani. Davis was powerless. There was no control over the beaters.

Providence alone is to be thanked that no calamity occurred. Both animals, fortunately, were found to be dead.

We got home to camp after dark, to find that the dinner had not yet arrived and that there was no food ; and then I was kept up very late talking to Bosanquet.

Sunday, March 17. We started at six on Sunday morning, in order to have plenty of time, and then had to wait an hour when we got to the place of the beat, because the coolies had not arrived. Kisch and Franey tossed for the chance of getting a tiger, and Kisch sat with me. Our machans were such as ought never to have been used for a tiger beat : a wounded tiger could walk into them. The tiger came out of the beat, and had to cross the bed of a river deeply grown with grass at intervals. It was coming straight for Franey and Verney, when a misplaced stop drove it back into the beat. We saw it, but I prevented Kisch taking a chance shot. It then appeared again, moving through the grass, where one could not shoot at it, on our right. It came out of the grass some 150 yards off in such a position that the gun had to decide whether to shoot it before or after it reached a tree. Kisch decided, quite rightly, to wait till it passed the tree. To my consternation, a shot was heard, and the tigress began to gallop. Kisch naturally missed it. Another shot was fired behind us.

Then followed two half-grown cubs out of the grass. I am sorry to say that Kisch missed. I killed one cub, and missed the other. Thus a thoroughly "mucked" beat ended ; and we went off on an interminable walk to another beat, which resulted in my getting a 31 in. cheetal, and Franey a magnificent sambur, 38 ins., with very thick horns.

We then came back to Salampur, the station that we ought to have got out at yesterday. The impassable road proved to be better than yesterday's road, and the journey two and a half hours instead of five and a half. What a week-end !

Monday, March 18. I got home to Delhi early this morning to find that my correspondence with the Viceroy had been futile. It looks pretty bad.

An interesting point seems to me to ensue if we are going to differ, even on one point out of very many. That does not mitigate by any means the possibility of writing a general report. Am I to write the dissenting minute to the general report or is he ?

The morning I spent with my colleagues, and as the result of a very dispiriting conversation, I have got to acknowledge defeat. Not one of them, including Basu, would support me in my row with Chelmsford. Of course it is not of prime importance ; it is doing a thing honestly rather than dishonestly, but it is the same thing. It is done, however, and I had the humiliation of going to see Chelmsford and telling him that I was abandoning the proposal.

The afternoon I spent on the report. In the evening I dined with the Commander-in-Chief. It was a very cheerful little party, consisting only of General Scott and his wife, the Commander-in-Chief and Lady Munro.

Tuesday, March 19. I had Claude Hill to breakfast ; worked on the report ; and went to see Marris. I had a dismal time with Marris, who seemed to be in a funk about everything, and had been so impressed by Vincent's arguments as to actually say that he did not feel justified in writing the report unless he was allowed to write what he thought fit. I never heard such nonsense. I told him he was a hack, and had got to express only our views ; but when I get both from him and from Vincent the same sentiments I feel a little bit tired. It is a pure question of funk. Looking on the thing as a whole, he wants to go back on everything. Vincent, he told me, was going to dissent, and all the rest of it.

Meyer came to see me at lunch. I found him in a very pleasant mood.

I must chronicle that, just before lunch, I went with Sir George Barnes to see the Government printing press at the Secretariat, and thanked the printers for all the printing they had done for me. I think Meyer and Duke, who are going to meet to-day, will arrive at a compromise about Indianisation which will cut short the deliberations to-morrow considerably.

And then a tragedy happened. I had been feeling pretty seedy all day, and, taking my temperature after lunch and finding it 100, I went to bed. Austen Smith was soon round, and I have been ill ever since. (I am writing on Friday morning.)

I never come across a doctor without feeling profound contempt for the profession that I once examined. On cross-examination, a doctor is always at his worst. He has no science ; a few empirical rules for diagnosis ; brilliant skill in directing appropriate nursing ; and an optimistic desire to await events. Cross-examination he cannot stand. I have had great fun with Austen Smith about this disease. When the temperature went to normal, the first night he said he knew it would go up again, because it was only due to aspirin. The second night he said that it was now normal for good. When I pointed out to him that I had already taken aspirin, he said : " Oh, yes, but I can see the difference." When it went up again he said : " I always expected it would ; it is quite normal." " Normal in what disease ? " say I. " I do not know," says he—" an ordinary fever." He is busy enjoying himself by keeping a temperature chart. I suppose that will be a good thing to produce at the coroner's inquest ! But a more ridiculous supposed scientific document I have never seen. He takes my temperature when he happens to come in, and refuses to accept my readings of the thermometer. I employ my time in taking my temperature, and I find it fluctuates as violently between Austen Smith's readings as it does at other times. There is no account taken of this. Occasionally he remembers to put in that he has given me a dose of calomel or aspirin ; sometimes he gives me doses and forgets to put them in. Poor man, he is much worried ; I simply worry him off his head. My latest form of torture is to say to him : "Well, doctor, what do you expect to find ? What has happened since you were here last ?" As he is always wrong, it makes it all the worse for him.

I have now been in bed, off and on, since Tuesday—to-day is Friday. I went to bed to please him, but in bed I am bound to say that nothing has happened which could not happen up. He tells me that one puts people to bed to keep them in an equable temperature ; but the trouble about India is the equable temperature. You cannot catch cold by getting out of bed now that it has got so hot. The one danger is the draught. Last night there was a series of about eighteen thunderstorms crashing round my tent. These storms are always accompanied in this country by howling gales. The wind whistled through my tent ; I was in a draught all the night. Six of these thunderstorms I should have missed if I had been dining at Government House.

Another of his arguments is that in bed one can apply treatment ; but he applies no treatment. He gives me no aspirin except at night ; and he gives me, merely when I demand it, a wishy-washy medicine, the taste of which is strangely familiar to me. I remember it. Up to the age of six I was doctored in London by an old man whom I regarded with great veneration because he was just approaching his eightieth year. He must then, therefore, have been qualified for nearly 60 years. I am now 39. This potent drug, which has not the slightest effect on me, was, I suspect, the acme of scientific knowledge no less than 90 years ago. I put all this down because it will be easy to see afterwards how that poor man, worried to death, with a wild look in his eyes, must funk the dread hour when he has got to come to my tent. It gives one certainly a fresh glimpse of the troubles of this country, because what I suspect is that sun, wind, exposure and fatigue produce a series of blood ailments in this country which nobody has ever really diagnosed. It is said by Clutterbuck that all the people in Kheri, including the doctors, believe that mosquitoes are not the only source from which you can get malaria. Well, perhaps what they call malaria got without mosquitoes is a non-bacterial malaria comparable to what I have got now. At other times I think it is a touch of the sun, as it began with backache, and it is a curious symptom that my temperature is always highest in the late afternoon and has a tendency to go down late at night. But it is no use ; I certainly do not know, and Austen Smith does not know either, what it is or what to do. Meanwhile, the sands are running out of the glass. I am trying to do what work I can, knowing that every half-hour's work sends up the temperature ; that is indisputable ; and I want so awfully to get home. Since Friday's row, Chelmsford is a complete convert to that desire. He told Donoughmore on Tuesday that whether we got away on the 7th or not rested in my hands ; and he told Verney that he hoped, for our sakes and his, we would leave on the 5th from Dehra Dun. I could not stand his remark to Donoughmore, so on Tuesday night, when I wrote to him and told him I was ill, I asked him what I could do to assist matters as I heard he had said the date of my departure depended on me. The result was that he came running down to my bedroom with a volume of short stories by A. E. W. Mason, which he said I would find helpful on a bed of sickness.

Wednesday, March 20. I got up on Wednesday morning and went to the conference at Government House. Everything went smoothly. We sat from the early morning till five o'clock in the afternoon, and we nearly finished, but I felt awfully ill at the end. I went to bed at once.

Thursday, March 21. I got up again on Thursday morning and went to the renewed conference. Result : we actually finished, finished, finished ! The main incident was a fearful row between Basu and Nair and the rest of us on the proportion of Indians that were to be admitted into the I.C.S. Chelmsford lost his temper, and I lost my temper, and tried to be sarcastic, Basu plaintively remarking that hard words broke no bones, and then he went on droning away about the Manu and the Bengali, and all that they had suffered. In the end we gave him an extra three per cent., and he expressed himself satisfied, Nair, however, saying that he would not hear of it. The consequence is that I have lost Nair's support for the whole scheme. It is a great pity, but I was too ill to fight. Nair had promised me support for the whole reform scheme provided I gave him a Standing Committee of the House of Commons, but this Indianisation proposal had not then been considered, and it cannot be held to bind him.

We got back before lunch, and whilst I was sitting in my room along came Basu. " May I come in ? " I heard his soft voice say. " Yes, Basu, I think I have recovered my temper," says I, endeavouring to be polite. " I forgot to give you these," said the poor old man, with his peace offering in his hand. " These " are three silk bands that have been made by his wife and girls for keeping up one's pyjamas ! This was too much for me, and the crisis was over. He said he was afraid that the Viceroy was very angry with him, but he was used to it.

Now there remains nothing at all but to hammer away at this old report, and the trouble is that nobody seems to be doing anything on it but myself, and I am in bed.

I went to bed immediately after Basu had left, and spent the remainder of the day there. I slept very little because of the thunderstorm.

Friday, March 22. I have been in bed all day. I had a meeting in the morning with Roberts, O'Donell, of the U.P., and Thompson about the drafting of the A and B list, and they are hard at it now in my tent, coming in to see me occasionally.

Chelmsford came to see me in the evening ; reported to me the absurd decision of the Home Government about the Imperial Conference, under which the representative of the Native States would not only have a lower status than the representative of British India, but a lower status than the representative of the Native States had last year, and we agreed to draft a protest. He then told me that he had discussed the names of the representatives with the Council this morning, and that they had unanimously determined to recommend Scindia as the representative of the Native States, and, failing him, Patiala.

Saturday, March 23. This morning my temperature was normal and I felt better. The good doctor, on hearing this news, looked miserable, said that his anxiety was enormously increased, and told me that he had a doubt lest it might not be a mild case of paratyphoid, and he wanted a second opinion. I told him I thought that now the crisis had passed we ought hastily to consult the best doctor we could find to lay before him the astonishing and astounding fact that a patient alleged to be ill had no symptoms. He said he was going to get a certain Dr. James, who is civil surgeon in this city, to come at half-past eleven. According at 11.30 there entered Dr. James, and they went all over the weary business again. By that time my temperature was soaring up, and had reached the dizzy and alarming height of 99.2, where it stayed for the rest of the day. Paratyphoid, which had come out of its cage because I had told Austen Smith yesterday that I had only been inoculated against typhoid itself, was put back again, and the weighty decision was taken that I was well enough to move to Dehra Dun. I asked for soldier food : I was told that slops would do me no harm. I said I did not wish to be as weak as a kitten when I got up. I was told that my pulse showed I was very strong.

I did a little more work on the A and B list, and, after a talk with Duke, Marris came in and said that it was impossible for us to leave on the 7th, and that the 17th is the earliest date on which we can go. I see the Mission staggering home, Duke and Basu having found, at a ripe old age, honoured tombs in New Delhi, then completed ; Seton and Kisch having fulfilled their term of service, prolonged in their absence year to year by order of the House of Commons ; Parsons imitating the Mohammedan practice of using henna to die his white beard red, accompanied to the *Northbrook*, then a very fine old ship, by a wailing lamentation from Marris that he wants five more days ! I did my best to soothe him, and to tell him that if we were not done on the 7th we would wait till the 8th, and then till the 9th, and so on, but I suppose that we shan't leave before, as I think, the 12th. This will not in effect lose us more than two days in time. The Admiralty telegraph that the 22nd is the earliest day that they can conveniently transport us across the Mediterranean. As we were due at Port Said on the 19th, there is no reason why we should not reach Port Said on the day that we are going to tranship.

I then said good-bye to Bannerjea, who will support us. He let loose a most unblushing assertion. He told me that Mrs. Besant owed her position partly to religious and partly to political reasons. I said : " Yes," and also to the eloquent words spoken on her behalf by a reputed moderate who was rated high among the orators of India. He perked at the compliment, and then said : " You are a politician, and you know that when you are in a minority there is nothing to be done but side with the majority." There's a noble sentiment of Indian statesmanship for you !

Then I saw Nair, who confessed himself highly delighted with our scheme. He points out that it gives opportunity for advance in a way that he never saw a possibility of before. The Legislative Assembly of the Government of India can introduce laws to mitigate the horrors of caste ; the Government of India can then judge whether they are going to make a row or not, and accept them or refuse them in the Council of State. This enables them to get a move on without forcing the Government to depart from its neutrality in religious matters. Nair confessed to me that he always came to the Council and asked for at least 100 per cent. more than he wanted, because otherwise he would never get what he wanted.

I asked him whether this was really the best method, but I could not move him ; he said it was the only method which would prevail with his colleagues. He ended by saying that he was prepared to come to England to help me whenever I liked, although his horoscope told him that he was not due there until July 12, 1919.

Then came Basu, also very happy. He has told Maffey that if India wants anything more than we are going to give them he will come and live in London permanently. He tells me that Nair has gone down to Madras to tell Mrs. Besant that she promised to accept anything which he accepted, and that he is accepting this scheme.

Then a final talk with Wood, in which I urged him to get a move on, to get rid of his characteristic slowness. Basu brought him a journalist of a name that I cannot remember, who has been lurking in Delhi for two months, and who is going to run a moderate newspaper, who assured me that the extremists in Bengal will have nothing to do with our proposals. I asked him what he had been doing in Delhi, and he said that he was political adviser to the Raja of Cosimbazar ; so his business is to write his speeches for him and to organise the victory of the landholders over the Government on the subject of income tax for agricultural land. What a system !

Then a long talk with Mahmudabad. I got into his mentality at last, and liked him enormously. Meston must have got across him. He will accept what we recommend, and come out into the open and fight for it. He is sick of the Mohammedans who prefer Pan-Islamism to their Indian citizenship, and so on. It was an affecting talk. He appealed to me to advise him what to do and when he was to take the plunge, and I gave him such guarded advice as I could. They must choose their opportunity, but they must get rid of a system which is only comparable to Redmond making a Home Rule speech with Carson on the platform. Extremists who do not mean well to the Government must be separated from those who do.

By this time I was pretty tired, and I went to sleep, and slept well. The doctor came, and finally consented to my getting up. The temperature, tired of soaring upwards to the dizzy heights of 99 odd, was racing in the other direction, and was 98.

Sunday, *March* 24. I did nothing in the morning except to have a long talk with Maffey.

After lunch Chelmsford came in, and he and Duke and I spent the afternoon over the first six chapters of the report, which we got through without disagreement. But there is rather a horror over us all. The news of the German offensive makes one realise, as one has always realised, that in all work for after the War one is building on what may be the sand. Are we going to have an Empire after the War ? I can honestly say that my work this six months has helped, because it has kept India quiet. But what is happening in France ? A suppressed German wireless claims 16,000 prisoners and 200 guns. The newspaper correspondents in the published Reuters seem optimistic enough.

Is all going well? The Commander-in-Chief, who came to say good-bye, is quite optimistic. After all, so far as I can judge, the German wireless is full of lies of the German-lie kind. The Commander-in-Chief tells me that they always count among their prisoners all wounded that they pick up. Well, if they are advancing over our first line, this must account for a considerable number; but even without this, an offensive on a 50-mile front as successful, let us say, as the Somme offensive (which was no great success) ought to have produced 50,000 prisoners. And as for the guns, how can there have been guns in the furthest advance that they claim—2,200 yards. Machine guns, yes; trench mortars, yes; but guns, it is impossible.

When our work was completed I was a thorough wreck, with a splitting headache, incapable of going to bed, in fact I had practically to be led there; and Austen Smith, that great prophet after the event, knew how weak I was, knew that I would be weak, despite his assurances that slops were all that I required. Well, it cannot be helped. I have got to find some means of picking up strength. At present it is quite clear that three hours' work knocks me up. Sleep is impossible in my tent. People run in every minute—first a chuprassi to know if I want anything; then a khitmagar to know when I want dinner; then another khitmagar to know for how many; then a chuprassi with a Reuter telegram; then a chuprassi with a telegram addressed to Lord Donoughmore; then a chuprassi to know if Mr. Parsons is there; then I ask for a glass of soda water, and Kisch comes in to say that I sent for him. Then Roberts comes in with a suggestion that I should that evening see Ghandi to try and persuade him from going on a hunger strike until Mahomed Ali is released. So I went to bed, after making the announcement that anybody who came into my tent would be hanged. Guard was mounted at every door, and I got two hours' sleep. My head was better, and

I was able to sit up and see Grant, who came to say good-bye, and stopped for two hours.

Monday, March 25. This morning I have received two more chapters from Marris, about which I have much to say.

I spent the morning in bed, including lunch time, and saw during that time Vincent, and said good-bye to him.

After lunch I got up and worked with the Viceroy till dinner. Donoughmore turned up about five o'clock, after having an awful day in getting home from his mugger shooting, owing to a breakdown on his car. He seemed highly delighted with himself; he got three muggers and had seen jackals called out to be shot and eaten.

XIII

DEHRA DUN

Tuesday, *March* 26. We arrived at Dehra Dun this morning. It is one of the prettiest spots I have ever seen. The bungalow in which the Viceroy lives is a low, one-story, thatch-roofed house, cool and nice, with a pleasant, small garden. Seton, Parsons, Franey, and I are in another bungalow some 150 yards off—all very pleasant, with the 4,000 feet hills away in the distance, and Mussooree on the top of them. The lights of Mussooree at night make the whole thing look like the back cloth of a theatre.

I worked hard at the report all the morning. The Viceroy was closeted with Sadler and Ashishtosh Mukerjea, who had come about the Calcutta report. They seemed awfully pleased with themselves. Their report bids fair to be unanimous. Sadler tells me that he is not going to complete writing it till June or July. Marris is delighted with them, and wishes we had the same amount of sense. They came on to talk to me—old Ashishtosh, wily, quiet, looking like a cross between a walrus and 'Ole Bill, of Bairnsfather's cartoons, watching Sadler orating as if he was watching one of his own children.

After lunch, to my astonishment I discovered that the Viceroy was going off fishing as soon as he had finished with Sadler. This is a nice method of revising the report against time! However, he promised to work when he got home in the evening. I had a foul headache after lunch, and went to bed for the rest of the day. The Viceroy returned very late for dinner, having got one fish. We were to work after dinner. Maffey came in and said that he thought the Viceroy was too tired to work; I said I was quite agreeable.

partly due to a fearful amount of work, and partly due to the fact that I could find little that it was useful to record. We have spent almost every day without exercise continuously from ten in the morning till eight at night in revising the report—Chelmsford, Duke, Marris, and I. Chelmsford has sat through the whole proceedings, taking his turn in reading out aloud the paragraphs, and confining himself to such speculations as to whether the Government of India is a plural or a single noun. Marris has fought consistently for the right to say disagreeable things about people : I have fought to avoid it. Duke is very slow ; he wants three or four minutes to express an opinion on anything, but when he does, he is usually right. There have been long arguments, and I have had much to suffer from Marris's temper, which culminated on Friday by my determining that I could not go on under a situation in which I was left to argue with him, Chelmsford sitting in judgment or being appealed to as a sort of judge, as to which of the opposing counsel was right. So I lost my temper, spoke violently, received apologies from him, and things went better thereafter. I wish I had done it earlier.

The report is much better. We have knocked out the alternative suggestions of joint sessions between the Council of State and the Legislative Assembly, the will of the Legislative Assembly prevailing. I do not know whether Nair will object to this, but Basu wrote to me that he had no dissent. We have also much improved the drafting.

There was a terrible incident on Thursday, which cost us, I take it, three days in concluding our labours. Vincent was invited to make his comments on the report. He began to complain about suppression of truth, and it soon became obvious that every alteration in the report which we had made to which Marris did not assent had been reported to Vincent, and Vincent had been asked to fight the battle over again. Chelmsford lost his temper almost immediately, with the result that Vincent put up his papers and left, saying that he had no responsibility in the matter and would do no more. I had to make the peace, and it took me some time. We are in this position because we have to take opinion with us, and if Vincent dissents, Nair will also dissent.

There is nothing much to record of other matters. Our gloom and depression have been increased by the steady postponement of our departure for home, but it is no use now avoiding the necessary steps for completion. Lowndes turned up ; he was to have gone fishing with the Viceroy, but, of course, that was postponed in the altered circumstances, and he was most useful to us in assisting in the drafting. There was one afternoon during which scribblers were scribbling and printers were printing, and there was nothing to do, so I went to Mohand to shoot, and the Viceroy went fishing. Mohand is a very beautiful place in the Siwalik hills, with glorious flowering trees and creepers, mainly bohinias—very hilly. Our plan consisted in driving cheetal into the dried-up beds of rivers, where we sat on machans to shoot them. There were few good ones, and I was not successful in getting anything worth having. It is run by a subhadar of the bodyguard called Jaffar ; it is much over-shot.

I paid a hasty visit one afternoon to the Forest Research Institute, and had dinner with Osmaston, whom I also met at dinner at Kisch's.

Three events have got to be recorded. The first is that Tilak and company, who were proceeding home on a Home Rule mission, were stopped at Colombo by the Home Government. The second is the appalling financial crisis in Bombay. The third is the Prime Minister's appeal for further effort in the War. With each of these, and the events that follow therefrom, I must deal in detail.

The Tilak incident was very characteristic. Passports were issued to him and his friends without reference to me, but in issuing them, it seems to me that the Government were clearly right. Tilak had to go home to fight the Chirol case ; and to stop his expedition at the time that the papers are full of Lord Sydenham's activities would have been a fatal mistake. But, having allowed him to go home, either out of sheer malice or crass stupidity, the Home Department, without reference to the Viceroy, sent home a telegram containing so black a picture of Tilak's antecedents and probable activities that I do not wonder the Home Government were nervous. It seems a little strange, however, that they should have cancelled a passport given by a duly authorised authority without consulting him. However, it was done. I drafted for the Viceroy a telegram of protest, which was ultimately sent, with a request for reconsideration. It has failed ; the Home Government refuse to let him sail, mainly on the ground that the General Staff will not have it ; so that it seems that Henry Wilson is governing England. I asked them to telegraph home accepting the Government's decision, and suggesting a stop being put upon Sydenham's organisation. This they won't do, and the only thing I am confident about is that they will handle Tilak stupidly when he returns.

The incident at Bombay was equally serious. The first lesson to be drawn from it is the extraordinary disadvantage of governing India with no permanent staff, and with at least two capitals. I am not disposed to think at this juncture we can move again from Delhi, but nothing could illustrate the inconvenience of the present system more than what occurred. The permanent Finance Department was at Simla ; Meyer was touring Madras and Bombay, and was, as a matter of fact, in Madras. The Viceroy was in Dehra Dun ; the Controller of Currency was in Calcutta. Suddenly a telegram comes from Howard, the Finance Secretary, saying that there has been a run on silver in Bombay ; that 45 lakhs were drawn out on Tuesday ; that the run is continuing ; that the Controller of Currency is sending all that he can from Calcutta ; that if it continues they have not the coin to meet it, and the only thing to do then would be to close the banks for three days, and to issue an Ordinance of inconvertibility. Chelmsford passed the telegram on to me to deal with. I pointed out that the telegram contained absolutely no reference to the causes of the run. Is it due to panic because of the German successes on the Western Front? Is it from large holders or small holders? I pointed out that they had not informed the Secretary of State, who is responsible for currency. They even suggested not saying anything for two or three days, when the people ought to be told at once. I suggested the issue of an appeal from the Viceroy to the people not to withdraw silver, and to bring their silver to the Government. Telegrams fly about, but nothing is done ; no suggestion is accepted, and I have nothing further to record in this connection until yesterday (Sunday), when I saw Meyer. Speaking from memory, the run was 45 lakhs on Tuesday ; 36 on Wednesday ; 27 on Thursday ; 27 on Friday ; and 28 on Saturday. The banks then closed till Monday, when 57 lakhs would be available, including the 10 lakhs a day coined by the Mint ; and, in anticipation of India Office sanction, Meyer was going to coin 15 rupee gold pieces with his own raw gold, which might relieve the situation.

The run was due to the rotten system of cotton speculation in this country. They buy cotton forward ; the settlement is annual, on April 25. The man who is "caught" either has to produce a substantial sum of money, or, having made his forward contract for purchase of cotton, produce the cotton. The silver is wanted for the ryot. No sort of indication seem to me to be forthcoming to prove that currency notes have been attempted for the ryot. Meyer was very hysterical. He pointed out, which is quite true, that increased financial assistance from India to the War could not be considered until we knew the effects of probable inconvertibility, which I, for one, think would be very serious. People may refuse to sell their goods for paper, and you may have riots and revolution, because all these long months no single word has ever been spoken to anybody in India about the necessity of husbanding silver. We made appeals in England *ad nauseam* about gold and silver at a time when I know full well it looked as if we were in sight of inconvertibility every hour, when we received the banking returns at the Treasury every night, when we shook our heads and resorted to all sorts of desperate expedients for meeting our obligations in America. Meyer complains that we did not send him specie from England.

Well, the Committee of Enquiry that will come from this horrible event will prove that the India Office did everything it could. It was the Treasury that stood in the way, and the Treasury were right in standing in the way. Inconvertibility in India is serious; inconvertibility in England meant the end of the War. But what I can never forgive Meyer for is that he never explained the situation to any Indian. Again, ample telegrams and despatches from me at the India Office will prove that I pressed this on the Government of India until I was tired of doing it, and even last night Meyer had the effrontery to say it was now too late. At the moment of writing (Monday) the warning that the Ordinance is coming has gone to all local governments. The situation is worse. The demand for silver has spread to the United Provinces, and there are only two lakhs left in Calcutta. It now seems that nothing can be done; but I say unhesitatingly that the Government of India has never made a single effort to avert this crisis, except to ask for money from England, which anybody who was not completely parochial would realise could not be done. Why it was only the other day that Meyer was touring and calling for money for the loan, without mentioning the financial stringency. You must take people into your confidence in war time.

This brings me to another point. Last week-end a telegram arrived from the Prime Minister, pointing out the gravity of the situation at home, and asking for more assistance from India. Reuters were full of descriptions of what the Colonies were doing. There was nothing coming from India. I at once told the Viceroy that, in my opinion, he ought to hold a conference to see what, in every department, could be done, and suggested his summoning the heads of departments to Dehra Dun. I told him that I wished to be in a position to explain at home that I was satisfied that India was doing everything possible. What was the result? After a consultation with Vincent, he said he was holding a meeting of his Executive Council when he got to Simla on the 20th; that he would immediately send to the heads of local governments and to the members of his Executive Council, asking them to consider what was practicable; and would I prepare the sort of points that I wanted them to consider. There you are again; they can do nothing by themselves. I am not here to do this work; I want to go home and away from these people altogether. I prepared a plan. At last it dawned upon the Viceroy, after I had dropped strong hints, that if I was to go into the matter at all, and if the conference were to be held at my suggestion, I wanted to be present—that I ought to be present, and he then asked me to come to Simla with him; it might entail a certain delay in the report. Accordingly, I agreed to come, and to leave Dehra Dun on Saturday night for Simla. We hoped then to get the reprint of the report to read on Saturday and Sunday, finally to revise it on Monday, to send it to the printers, who would take one and a half days to make the corrections; to hold our conference on Tuesday, and for me to leave, thank God, for the ship on Wednesday afternoon. The whole of this arrangement has been upset by the interposition of Vincent into the report, so that we shall not get the revise of the report until Tuesday morning, the day on which we have fixed the conference. On Tuesday we shall be busy all day ; we shall have to read it on Wednesday, revise it on Thursday, and leave on Saturday. This is the timetable, to which I mean to adhere.

XIV

SIMLA

On Saturday night we left for Simla. We had an excellent train journey to Kalka, which we reached at eight o'clock in the morning. We had breakfast there, and at nine o'clock we started up the hill on a motor trolley on the railway line. The scenery is, of course, gorgeous, but four hours round hairpin curves is very tiring, and I had quite enough of it when we arrived on a perfect, though cold, day at Simla, with the glorious hills stretching all round it. I myself am not fond of hills ; they obscure the view ; and the sight of snow-capped mountains does not please me. I cannot say anything about the appearance of Simla, which I have seen before, because I have not left Viceregal Lodge since I arrived here. We went from Summer Hill station up to Government House in rickshaws, a form of conveyance which I, personally, find most distasteful. One would never allow a pony to take one uphill, and to make men do it, puffing and panting, seems to me quite horrible. Hill stations ought not to exist.

Viceregal Lodge is exactly like a Scotch hydro—the same sort of appearance, the same sort of architecture, the same sort of equipment of tennis lawns and sticky courts, and so forth. Inside it is comfortable, with suites of apartments comparable to those of the Carlton or the Ritz, with the usual mountain scenery from the windows. Since arriving here I have been at work without ceasing, continuously, without exercise, from two o'clock yesterday afternoon until the moment at which I write, considering the report. Is it to be believed that, after bringing me up here, the conference is to take the form of a meeting of the Executive Council, at which I am not to be present, and then I am to meet them after they have confabulated together! This is the sort of step they take to preserve their little dignity. They have not been able to do without me, but they do not want it to appear that I am giving the lead.

I had a long talk with the Commander-in-Chief yesterday. He thinks he could do with more recruits. There are indications that the Punjab and the North-west Frontier have reached the possible limit; but Sir Michael O'Dwyer, although he wanted to slack off, in the new crisis is prepared to go on at the same pace. Officers are forthcoming both from home and in the young officers that we are training. Any number of recruits could be obtained. The Commander-in-Chief was rather stiff about commissions. He said that the demand for commissions was political. I pointed out to him the difficulty of asking men to come into the Army merely as sepoys, with no prospect of advance. We were not making a similar request to any other part of the Empire. He admitted the difficulty. He was willing to have officers' training schools in India, provided that vacancies in the schools were, in the first instance, allotted to men already in the ranks. I have no objection. He does not approve of an increase of bounty for recruiting, because he thinks that people will hold back, thinking the bounty will get still larger. The reason why he is able to send a telegram home offering to send Indian divisions to Egypt and Mesopotamia to replace all the British divisions is because the sick returns have so greatly improved. He is quite willing to allow Indian princes to raise troops of their own and officer themselves, with the assistance of British officers to lead them in the field. He would be willing to extend this principle to people who are not actually native princes, but who are comparable in status. He said the lead must come from the Viceroy.

Then followed Hill. He thinks we can send as much wheat as they can ship. After the recent rains, he is quite prepared to agree to send the two million tons which the Home Government asked for, and although he thinks it would necessitate the fixing of prices for wheat, and probably for wheat substitutes—and this would be very difficult—he is quite prepared to do this, too, up to another 500,000 tons, if the Home Government want it.

This morning I have had the Adjutant-General to see me. He talked of the difficulty of building depots in which to put the troops, but agreed that this ought not to be the limiting factor, and that both the Army works and the civil works ought to assist them in building.

I forgot to say that Barnes thinks that something more ought to be done to get men out of the commercial community, although obviously the difficulty of compulsion for them, when compulsion for their Indian fellows is not attempted, is very great.

Hudson, the Adjutant-General, is quite willing to give everybody a prospect of rising from the ranks. He does not much like the Chief's idea about princes.

Then I saw Holland, who satisfied me that he is doing everything he can. He says his aim ought to be, after the War, to make India self-supporting in five years, in which period it can be done, but, unfortunately, there is no available material and tools. We cannot smelt zinc, we cannot roll copper, we cannot roll steel in this country. The Home Government have just refused permission to put up a rolling mill. He does not think he has anything new to suggest. He is working every day, and all day, to increase output. He is having the same struggle about inspecting and designing staff with the War Department that we had in the Ministry of Munitions at home. He is very keen on an appeal to Indians generally, and told me that Malaviya had said that he could not appeal to stop political agitation, because the Southern Indian and the Mohammedan would not listen to it; but if counter Indian agitation, like Lord Sydenham's, was stopped, he thought Indians in India would stop too. Holland told me that Ghokall would have done it, but he was a big enough man not to be misunderstood. But the great point, in my opinion, is to get India behind you in this thing, and I have been agitating and struggling for an all-India conference. What I have suggested will be clear from the letter I wrote to Chelmsford at Dehra Dun and the letter which I am writing to him to-day. Hill is the opponent. He wants a caucus to elaborate proposals and to lay them before the Legislative Council. Chelmsford is not in agreement with him, and I think I have won, but the whole thing depends upon the speech that Chelmsford makes to them, particularly as the conference will probably take place after the suspension of specie payment.

It is a gloomy day. The whole fabric is spoiled by this financial business and the way in which the Government of India have dealt with it. Our report and all the work of the winter seems to loom so small now in all these matters. I therefore end up with a good story I heard last night. When the Viceroy goes on tour it is the practice to allow local officials to know what is likely to be required. The Controller, therefore, sends out probable dinner menus, with the suggestion that any alternative can be used if the things suggested are not readily available. Whilst he was on tour in Burma it was suggested that ox-tail soup should be provided for him one day. Afterwards he received a bill for 500 rupees for the oxen that had had to be purchased to provide him with the soup!

I forgot to mention that this afternoon I had an interview with Vincent. He thinks that 200 officers can be spared from the Government service, and I found him fully in accord with the idea of an all-India conference, and anxious to do something about temporary commissions. His one anxiety was about Tilak. He said that Cleveland had told him that he must swallow Tilak, because bigger men than he had had to swallow worse things than that ; and he went on to say that he would follow it by a big amnesty, including Mahomet Ali, but I do not suppose he will stick to his guns when the question arises. However, to-day, for what it is worth, he was full of beans.

Tuesday, April 16. This morning, Duke, Roberts, and I went hammering away at the report—pruning, altering, changing order, explaining more clearly, avoiding misunderstandings, and so on. Every day it gets better, but this work from ten in the morning till twelve at night, with also some work before breakfast, is very, very wearing. Roberts has been most useful, in fact I wish I had brought him in at an earlier stage ; but I feel the awful responsibility, because none of them notice anything until it is pointed out to them, except in a few trifling instances ; and Duke, whose judgment remains, as ever, sound, seems to contribute less and less.

The Viceroy was all the morning in session with his Executive Council. They were discussing War contribution. They all stayed to lunch and went on afterwards. In the afternoon I was sent for, and invited to attend. The Viceroy told me the decision about 400,000 men, 100 commissions, entry for Indian Indian civil servants into the I.A.R.O., combing out of Europeans, and, instead of co-operation for Indians which he had accepted from me at Dehra, an "Our Day" celebration of the War crisis. These were absurd and inadequate decisions ; but to my astonishment and amazement, he said, as I came in : "These are what we have decided," with an emphasis on "decided"—"and what I have asked you to come here for is in order, as you yourself suggested, that you should ask questions, so that you should thoroughly understand the situation." This is exactly what I had feared at Dehra—what I had told Maffey that I feared, and what I had been assured was not the case. I should never have come to Simla under these humiliating circumstances. I came to the conclusion, although I had not much time to think, that they had decided that they would rather stand on their own legs than have my assistance. I confined myself to what the Viceroy confined me to ; I asked a few questions, which had this effect :—the 400,000 became 500,000, a pretty considerable jump, showing the carelessness with which they had come to their decisions, and I think that they felt pretty much ashamed of their "Our Day" suggestion. However, I determined that I would take no share in the responsibility, and that I would say what I thought of them in London.

In the evening we went back to the report. I heard that Sinha had agreed to go to the Imperial Conference, but that Bikaner had refused. He has asked Scindia. When I get home I am going at once to lay down that future appointments to the War Conference shall be by the Secretary of State, on the recommendation of the Government of India. They cannot choose men in this country.

Wednesday, April 17. On Wednesday we again worked on the report. The financial crisis is better, and they will weather it, I think.

I came to the conclusion that I could not criticise the Viceroy's schemes in London without informing him that I was going to do so, because, in particular the newspapers, at any rate, had imagined that I was a party to the decisions. I therefore wrote him a letter, telling him very clearly what I thought of him.

Thursday, April 18. This morning the Viceroy came in before breakfast and spent an hour by my bedside. He was very indignant, or said he was, at my letter. He complained that I had completely misunderstood the situation ; that he had thought at Dehra that all I wanted to do was to understand their decisions. As I had put in my letter at Dehra

H.H. of Jaipur B. N. Basu Prime Minister Jaipur State H.H. of Jaipur

FOUR CARICATURES BY E. S. M.

[*To face page* 356

that I wished to join in their deliberations, in order that I might understand their decisions, I told him that this was quite wrong, and that I had told him that I would be in a better position to defend them if I were a party to them. I told him that he had published in the newspapers that I was coming to take part in the conferences, and that I thought I had been very badly treated. He assured me it was entirely a misunderstanding. I told him that I had no choice but to accept his explanation. He then went through the decisions one by one, and explained that I was completely mistaken in thinking they were decisions; they were going to meet again that very morning to discuss them. I told him that I could not be responsible, and that if I had misunderstood, it was he who had mislead me. He told me that he resented very much my writing to him when he would have been very glad to discuss the matter with me. I told him that his words, which I had carefully noted, could only have been interpreted as meaning that I was not to discuss them with him, and that, therefore, I had no choice but to put on record my views. He told me that he had only meant to carry out my wishes. I told him that I could only conclude they had come to the conclusion that they did not want my assistance. He assured me that this was not so. He began very much by blustering, always with the same courtesy that characterises him. I took the opportunity of telling him that the attitude of Colonial Governor which he adopted towards a very weak Government seemed to me to be wrong, and that he ought to lead them. We parted the best of friends, and he ultimately went back to his Executive Council. Much to my joy and satisfaction, the Executive Council modified their alleged decisions, and the proposals are now more or less satisfactory, although Claude Hill has run away from his proposal to increase the wheat supply. I have protested to the Viceroy, and I think that will be met.

I do not care in the least that they should still be in a position to claim the credit for what is done. I have done my duty, and everything now depends upon the way they handle their Durbar. Letters come pouring in from Indians to me, pledging themselves to assistance, but naturally pointing out, what I think they have a right to do, that they want commissions, and that they want the publication of our report.

In the morning I went through our alterations with Marris. He showed signs of the most tremendous overwork. He said that in ordinary circumstances he would have been proud of the thanks which the Viceroy and I proposed to offer to him, but that we had so altered the report that he was ashamed of it ; he could not face the men whose opinion he valued most in the world—Meston and Curtis. I did not argue with him ; I merely asked him what his allegations against the report were. He said that we had deliberately suppressed the truth. I asked him if he would be kind enough to suggest any amendments, and we spent the whole morning on them. With the utmost patience I listened to his complaints ; argued with him ; shifted him in some respects, and agreed with alterations to meet him in others. But his complaints were so ridiculously small. His points merely amounted to the alterations of words, and I attributed the whole of his outburst to overwork. Of course the strain has been immense. I then dressed him down and spoke quite straightly to him. I told him I had never met a man with greater devotion to duty and greater industry ; I had never met a man with a better natural style and a more real command of language. But he failed, like everybody else in India failed, from having no political instinct, of despising political science, and I told him that I did not think he was capable of making the best argument he could, or of intelligible exposition ; that the I.C.S. had been so long accustomed to state their conclusions without reasoning them. I therefore told him that, whilst leaving him to do the drafting, I must insist that I must be the judge of whether what I wanted to say was brought out or whether what was said was intelligible. I asked him to go through the report chapter by chapter, and I challenged him to find a single argument which he wished to use that was not there in some form or other, provided that it had been accepted as a true argument. I had inserted words in the introduction to say that it was definitely not my purpose to criticise individuals, classes, or communities; that I would not sit in judgment on my fellow men, nor would I accept his judgment on matters that I had not investigated: it was a report of what I believed, and not what he believed. Straight talks of this kind do no harm, and he went away much more cheerful; and we spent the afternoon with Chelmsford on the report, Chelmsford's share, as usual, being meticulous.

I definitely fixed the day for going home as Monday next.

I had a letter from Nair agreeing to the proposals about a joint session, a variant from what we had agreed, and a much better arrangement, and as I have also had Basu's agreement, that is all right. One could not have better offers of help than from Basu, Ramaswami Aiyar, Jinnah, and Tilak, but, of course, these men here spurn them, because they are based on the assumption that national wishes will be respected as they are going to be in Ireland.

In the evening I went to dinner with some old Cliftonians who had invited me to dine with them at the United Services Club—a beautiful drive through Simla by moonlight, and a most excellent dinner. General Edwards was in the chair, and my health was proposed by General Vaughan. Barstow was there, and I sat next to him. He is a very decent fellow. Edwards talked of our meeting at Calcutta, when he knew he was being "vetted" for the position of Director-General of the I.M.S. Kisch made a most excellent little speech. I only recognised, as a contemporary of mine, one man there, an officer called Vanderghugt, who was in School House. We sent a telegram to Sir Douglas Haig, which included, at somebody's brilliant suggestion, the school motto, "Spiritus intus alit." Edwards could not read it or understand it; the Indian telegraphist will maul it; and Haig will never realise that it is not the school motto of his time, or, indeed, of the earlier part of mine.

The Viceroy came in to see me with a problem: was his name or mine to appear first on the report? He told me that it was my scheme and my report; that the reforms would always be known as the Montagu-Chelmsford reforms, but that it being in India, he felt he must sign first. What an interesting problem, fraught with what consequences to a great Empire, requiring our serious attention! I told him that it was too early yet to say that there would be any reforms arising out of the report, that that depended upon the action taken by him in India and by me at home. We had only begun our difficulties. I might be out of office in a few weeks; he might have done some internment affair which would upset the apple cart. I might find my colleagues would not accept my suggestions. Well, he said he did not care about the order; I said I did not; let us see what the principle was. There was no doubt about it that the Viceroy was under the orders of the Secretary of State; there was no doubt about it, either, that our relative precedence in India concerned functions, shooting parties, railway stations, salutes, dinners, lunches, and not to State documents; that I was sorry to say that I could not permit him to address the Cabinet except through me, nor could I address the Government of which I was a member through him. He looked rather sorry for himself, but agreed. As a matter of fact, I made up my mind to reconsider the situation and see what could be done.

Friday, April 19. The whole of Friday was spent on the report.

The financial situation continues to improve, and they will soon have to consider a financial contribution to the War.

I dined in the evening with Vincent, and was able to do a little business with Marris after dinner. Vincent seemed to be very happy and cock-a-hoop. He has, on the whole, behaved very well, and has been the best member of the Council on the question of the War contributions. He lives in a charming house. I was glad to see Donoughmore again. He loathes Simla, and says that one lives one's time on the point of a hill, and that you cannot lie down anywhere without the danger of rolling back to Kalka. The scenery is, however, magnificent, and it is so jolly to see daffodils, lilac, wisteria, pansies, banksia roses, but, oh, the rickshaws, I hate them more and more.

Saturday, April 20. Marris has been much happier since Thursday, and we practically finished the revision of the report by Saturday night.

Lady Chelmsford arrived from Dehra Dun with her two daughters, and we had a considerable party to dinner.

Before dinner I had a long talk with the Commander-in-Chief. I think he feels the change from Robertson to Wilson at the War Office very much ; he does not get the same information, and he feels a little lonely. He presented me with an excellent memorandum on the history of the Indian Army. I wish I had got it sooner ; I might have persuaded Chelmsford to include it in the report. It is a valuable document.

I also saw Colonel Longhurst. I am so fond of Longhurst in London that I wanted to bring him news of his brother. He is a very nice fellow, and is shortly going to rejoin his battalion. He gave me the first news I had heard of the serious air-raid on St. Pancras station. He also interested me by saying that military opinion in India was divided between Robertson and Wilson.

Sunday, April 21. After breakfast we finished the report. We are all rather pleased with it. It seems to me to be well and closely argued, and it is now, I hope, free from everything that could offend anybody. I can at least say that it ought not to be disregarded, and it has a principle. The main principle, so far as I can see, is that instead of founding the Indian Government on the confidence of the people of England, we are gradually to found it on the confidence of the people of India. We are beginning in the Province, maintaining the Government of India as now, but subjected, I am glad to think, to more criticism, and future progress will depend upon the creation of an electorate. I do not see how any reasonable man can find fault with the principles. There is much room for improvement in the workmanship and the proposals, but the report certainly cannot be disregarded. It will be, however, completely out-of-date unless we proceed with the schemes quickly. At the last moment we were able to make substantial improvements in the order, and added a new paragraph to the introduction which, I think, improves it greatly.

We are all feeling rather happy, and I went off to say good-bye to Mrs. Verney, at a lunch given to me by Colonel Verney at his pretty little house in the garden here. I had, strangely enough, never met Mrs. Verney, although Colonel Verney has done so much for us. He has been an excellent companion on many of our week-end trips. He is a keen sportsman and extraordinarily good with the arrangements he has to make, which have never once broken down. A military secretaryship cannot be an easy job, but he is, I suspect, possessed of a very good staff.

I forgot to record that this morning I made the suggestion to the Viceroy that our two signatures should be attached to the report side by side. It seems ridiculous, but it made him much happier, and, after all, it is a unique occasion which demands a unique form of signature. The report will be signed, let us hope, to-morrow at one, and at three we leave. We have now nothing more to do. Hurrah for home!

Just a few words of retrospect. It is good to be going home, but six months of India must make one regret their coming to an end. I love this country; it is where I am happiest. The circumstances are cheerful. We have got an agreed report. There is no difference of opinion, except, perhaps, on details, among my delegation. There is no difference of opinion, I hope, in the Government of India. We have kept India quiet for six critical months. When I came out, moderates were rushing to join the Home Rule League; on leaving, the succession of moderates from the Home Rule League is making marked headway, particularly in the United Provinces—Mahmudabad, Chintamani, Sapru, etc. Further than this, the War news seems a little better in the last few days. I am glad to think that Chamberlain is in the Cabinet, where, I think, he will be of real help to us. As regards Chelmsford, I have had to record many criticisms of him, but I, as I know only too well, am not easy to work with. We have been associated day in and day out, in circumstances of the most fearful and frightful fatigue, and of almost unequalled responsibility, for nearly six months, and I believe no two men could have quarrelled less. I believe that to be entirely due to his personality, to his patience, to his self-control, and to his receptiveness. He is also a gentleman, if there ever was one. However, we should certainly have clashed if he had been constructive, and perhaps quarrelled, although I am painfully conscious of the shortcomings of my proposals, and wish to goodness I could have had some constructive assistance. The comfort of life has alone made it possible to do the work. Secretaries and A.D.C.s relieve one of all the trouble; no worry about travelling; no worry about arrangements; no worries about interviews. It is a wonderful thing to be head of the machine in a country like this, and the rebound to the mundane conditions of a private individual in England will be very great. It is curious how every position has its penalties. In a subordinate position the limitations imposed upon one by one's superiors hamper and confine ; in a supreme position the instrument through which one has to work thwarts one's purpose. The Government of India is really not adequate. Goodness knows how it can be made so. I am not at all sure that we shall not have to reconsider Delhi and take some other place like Dehra Dun. I have been convinced on the awful penalties of the migration to the hills. If Dehra Dun were the capital, one and a half hours would take one to Mussoorie, and the two places might be almost one. Nasik would be even better, where one might stop all the year round. But how are we to leave another unfinished capital at Delhi ? How can we undo the city that the King-Emperor founded ? Are we still to spend our six millions on a mistaken capital ? What can be said ? I must consider this more at home, Then, too, in the future this report, the principles of the report, are dead unless they are acted upon, unless they animate the Government. Will they do anything when I have gone ? Will they think about it again ? Do not they want someone to drive them before they will move ? These are the anxieties. Shall I be allowed to carry out the proposals ? That is another anxiety. On the other hand, I have gone through the winter feeling that I exercised a very great influence with educated Indian opinion. Certainly I have got out of them what nobody now in India could have got out of them, but the question which I go away with is : Have I done anything to establish the confidence of the officials, or led them to agree that I have influence with the Indian ? The events of the past week lead me very much to doubt it. It is quite true that I have no business to stay in India a day longer than I need ; it is quite true that they have first to consider their position. If the Government, as it now stands, loses its prestige, it has nothing else to rely on. But, after all, it is a little astonishing that it has never been suggested by a soul that I should speak at this Durbar. I had assumed that they would ask me to, and I had already made up my mind that I could not, consistently with my duty, do so, but that I could have written a short message for the Viceroy to read. I have been working among them for six months, and it does seem to me a little surprising that I should leave the country without any message four or five days before this great event in India's history. Is it attributable to their lack of perception of what is fitting or what might be expected, or is it attributable to lack of confidence ? If it is the latter, I have only myself to blame. I have pressed them very hard, and I should not blame them if they were glad to get rid of me. I am not sure, even now, that I shall not offer to Chelmsford six or seven lines of farewell, and ask him whether it would be of assistance at the meeting. It will be interesting to hear what he says. I could then have a shot at drafting, and give it up if I felt I could say nothing worthy of the occasion.

The Barnes have a very nice house not far from Government House, with beautiful views and quite a nice garden. High up on the hill above them is Sir Sankaran Nair ; next door to them is Peterhoff, where the Hills live. Peterhoff is the oldest and the most beautiful of these residences. It really is an awfully nice half-timbered house, with a glorious garden and a beautiful panelled hall and dining-room. It was Government House before Lord Dufferin's time, and Lady Dufferin comments in her diary upon the impossibility of ever filling the new Government House. Since then Lady Minto has added a new wing. Such is the growing luxury of life in India that it is now incredible to think that Government House could ever have lived in Peterhoff. I wonder whether anybody will say in future how comic it was that we should have said, as we do say now, how will it ever be possible for a Viceroy to live in Government House in New Delhi ?

In the evening Maffey came to see me. I talked to him about the very difficult position that I thought I was in through leaving India just before the Durbar. I offered to write a letter. He objected, first on the ground that they were asking for a message from the King, which ought to be the only message, and, secondly, because it was the Viceroy's own show, and nobody else ought to intervene. Just as I thought. After a long talk, Chelmsford came in in a very cheerful frame of mind and much pleased with my presents to his daughters. He asked me to send him a photograph for himself and a large one to hang in Viceregal Lodge.

Then we all went down to dinner. I had asked that a dinner party might be given to the members of his Council and Grant, to meet my delegation and to say good-bye. We had a very pleasant evening.

Monday, April 22. I was sent for by Chelmsford. I found three copies of the report spread on his table, and Lady Chelmsford in Red Cross uniform standing by him, and Maffey, tall and silent, next to her. There was one copy for the Cabinet, and two bound in blue leather, one for him and one for me. He had already signed all three. I signed, and we shook hands. I wondered whether he was still thinking of the order of the signatures and had determined to sign first.

Booth Tucker, the head of the Salvation Army, came to see me. He was strangely dressed in khaki trousers, white socks, black leather slippers, a red tunic, and a white pugaree with a red band across it, with the words " Muhkti Fanj " on it. It is a strange life for a man who has been in the I.C.S. He talked to me once again on the criminal tribes. He told me that he had been lucky in a continuity of policy in the United Provinces, despite changes in the Lieutenant-Governors, but there was no harmony between the Punjab and the U.P. Criminal tribes wander all over India ; they require a separate organisation to deal with them, because they bribe the subordinate police to testify that individuals are in their homes during raids. They have ample funds, because in the U.P. in one year 34 lakhs were stolen by them, of which only four lakhs were recovered. He showed me some silk cocoons grown by the criminal tribes reformed by him ; he pointed out that 4,000 criminals in Madras made 60,000 rupees honestly in one year. They must steal or starve, unless looked after, and they prefer to steal. I do not wonder that they do. But, just like the fox at home that does not raid the pheasants while it has its cubs, so if they are leniently dealt with in a State or a Province, they go over the borders to maraud. He wants a special secretary appointed in the Home Department, and an annual conference to see that the excellent law is uniformly and steadfastly administered. He told me that in Madras, when Harold Stuart was there, they did better work among criminal tribes than in any other Province. Now the Madras Government had said that they had too much to do to bother about them, and each Collector must do what he could. By the by, I heard only yesterday that Pentland had said that he would disallow a resolution which was to be moved in the Legislative Council on the subject of the migration to Ooty, because it was not in the public interest. How can one expect the Morley-Minto reforms to work well in this sort of way ? It shows how necessary instructions to Governors are. While he was talking about silk, I reminded him of Lefroy's slashing report on the Salvation Army's work. He said he did not mind in the least. He told me that Lefroy had no knowledge of the silk industry from a commercial point of view ; that the Government of India ought to have employed MacNamara, who has been so successful in Kashmir, where they make a net profit of 25 lakhs out of their silk. They distribute eggs free to 50,000 families ; they receive from them 36,000 maunds of silk at 15 rupees a maund—small profits, a pound a year, but, nevertheless, enough in the hideous poverty of the country. He said that silk ought not to be left to the Director of Agriculture, where it is a by-product, but it ought to be specially dealt with. He gave instances of Lefroy's lack of knowledge ; that he had used the expression "raw silk" to include both the waste and the cocoon ; that he had given statistics of the export from Bombay and Sind without realising that all that left Bombay and Karachi came from Kashmir. As usual, I suppose the wrong man was selected without a right appreciation of the circumstances. He tells me that every Director of Agriculture says that mulberry trees will not grow in the plains. He knews of a forest in the Punjab which was intended for sisal, but where mulberry trees only had come up. It can be grown in the plains as it is grown in Japan, with great care, on the best ground. How valuable it would be to meet the land revenue if it was done in British India proper. But when I see rickshaws and coolies, showing that the water power has never been used, how neglectful we have been of the industrial improvement of India ! Every village in Norway has its electric light. I twitted him about his joining Sydenham's organisation and attacking the Viceroy and myself.

He said that he had not ; all that he had done was to say something about the old woman that sits on the roof of Government House and tells the enemy aeroplanes where to drop their bombs. By the by, Mrs. Besant is going to issue a telegram asking Indians to help in the War. It is a clever document which has roused the fury of the Services, because it uses the Prime Minister's words about Ireland. Why should not they ? She wants to get interned, and if she fails to accomplish this, she is going downhill so fast that she will disappear. But she is too clever for them, and they are too stupid to avoid her game. They are already beginning to consider where they shall deport her to, if they took power to deport under the Defence of India Act. Horniman is a different story, but if they touch Mrs. Besant, they are doing a very foolish thing. Her influence goes day by day, and nothing can save her but their action.

Afterwards Maffey came in, and brought a letter from Sir Claude Hill to the Viceroy, saying that Sir Dorab Tata had said that Indians would expect me to be at the Durbar, and that at least a letter would be necessary from me. He said that if I wanted to write a letter, the Viceroy would be glad of it, but he thought it would be better if he was authorised to give a message from me in his speech. I told him that the matter was one of considerable difficulty, which could only have been really met if I had remained for the Durbar. If I was absent, it could only be deduced that I had left India, which would give away my departure, which ought to remain secret. If a letter was read, it would do it still more. I thought a letter would not meet the purpose, but I would draft him a message. We then had a very frank talk, Maffey and I. We went over Chelmsford's good qualities—his receptivity, his patience, his lack of prejudice, his loyalty ; but also his refusal to give a lead and his lack of constructive ability are very obvious. I begged Maffey to get him to make a speech this time. As I have said before, Indians can be swept off their legs by speeches. They never hear them. But the trouble is that they are holding a Durbar without anybody who has ever made a speech. They all read documents, and read them without troubling to learn them first. The result is that the documents are merely departmental hashes, often revised, reviewed and cut about by the Council. You cannot stir a crowd by this sort of thing. Maffey was in agreement with me. I told Maffey that I was going to write a letter to the Viceroy from Aden, telling him what I thought remained to be done in India, and we went through some of the points. I then wrote to the Viceroy, saying that I did not intend to draft a message, but the sort of thing I wanted to say was this—that having carried the work with which we had been jointly entrusted as far as it could be carried in India, he and I felt it to be my duty to return to England, to discharge my responsibilities as a Minister and Secretary of State, and to lay our proposals before the Cabinet without delay. As the papers had announced, I had shared in the preliminary deliberations, and was a party to his appeal. I felt confident that India would do her utmost, united and steadfast, for the Empire and her own future. I pointed out to him that such an announcement would show :

1. My reasons for going.
2. That we were going on with the report and it was not to be allowed to slumber.
3. That I had helped in deciding on War policy.

I wonder what he will really say. I am sure they have made a blunder, but that is the end of that !

We lunched together, and, after lunch, the Viceroy and I sat and talked till three o'clock. We came to the conclusion that Sly should be the next member of the Viceroy's Council ; that Robertson should succeed O'Dwyer, and Cleveland should succeed Robertson ; that Willingdon should go to Madras, and Hopwood to Bombay. I wonder how much of this will be done ? I told him earnestly that he had got to govern India in the next few months not as if the report was already carried out, but as a country for which he wished the report to be carried out ; that it was a matter of some difficulty, and that he should take no action against anybody unless he had done his best first by persuasion. I urged him to lead and not to follow, and so on. He took it all very well, and in his turn urged patience—an excellent piece of advice. I told him that I would try and get hold of Geoffrey Dawson, Chirol, Hewitt ; I would see Sydenham, but I thought it was impossible ; of course I would see Curtis. I made him promise not to publish the report until he had seen the newspaper editors. He told me he was going to send a private copy to each of the Governors and Lieutenant-Governors and to all his Council. He also told me that the

Amir had expressed his willingness to consider his moving against the Bolsheviks if a hint were given him by the Government of India. He would not even allow this story to be sent home, despite the military department, because it was against his policy.

Then Lady Chelmsford, Duke, Chelmsford, and I walked down the steep hill to Summer Hill station, and we left at half-past three. The whole of the staff and Mrs. Maffey were on the platform to see us off; there were all the members of the Council and Lady Barnes, Sankaran Nair, a solitary figure, with his head in the air and his tie creeping over his collar; Sir William Vincent very jubilant, but very distressed that I was not going to be at the Durbar, and blaming himself for never having suggested it; hoping I had written a strong letter, and very distressed when I told him that the Viceroy would not have one. I cannot get him to talk about the report, and I fear all the trouble I have taken will not mean his assent. He has shown himself at his best in arguing with the Commander-in-Chief and his colleagues about the response to the Prime Minister's telegram, and in the Durbar business altogether; but I am not sure what is behind it. The old Commander-in-Chief, bless him, was also there, very cheerful, and they were a happy crowd. Even Chelmsford looked happy, and Lowndes less woebegone than usual. As the trolley left, the band, at Verney's suggestion, but partly to show its devotion to Parsons, played what somebody fortunately told me was "Auld Lang Syne."

Then four hours down the hill on the trolley, winding in and out, varied only by a quarter of an hour for tea half-way down. The line is 56 miles long, and there are 100 tunnels. The scenery is much more attractive going down than up. We arrived at Kalka just as it was getting dark, and it was too misty and cloudy over the plains to get a really good view.

XV

SIMLA TO LONDON

Tuesday, *April* 23. Here we are, on the train. It is rather remarkable what a happy party we have been, and it says a great deal for the good temper of my colleagues. Our friendship has never been disturbed, and it has been a very happy family. We left Kalka at 7.30 on Monday night, and picked up Holland-Hibbert at 1.50 this morning at Delhi. We are now travelling through Rajputana ; it is fiercely hot, but they all tell me the season is three weeks late, and it is nothing like as hot as they expected. It certainly was very hot last night. Marris is the only one of us that nothing can make look cheerful.

Saturday, *April* 27 (Indian Ocean). I spent most of my time on the journey down from Simla in reading, writing farewell letters, and sweating. At one time the temperature in my saloon was 110, but my chief trouble was my growing insomnia. I do not think I have had a good night's rest during the time I have been in India, and during the two nights on the train I hardly slept half an hour. This did not matter when I had work to do ; I could always find something to read ; but I am sick of books, and the second night on the train, in particular, was just hell, in the slowness with which it passed.

We reached Bombay at 8.30 on Wednesday morning, and were met at the station by Carmichael, the Secretary to the Government, old Shaperji Broacha, Sasoon David, and " Uncle Tom " Chaubal. Rahimtoolah, for some reason or other, was not there. No one, to look at Broacha, would have thought that he had lost 25 lakhs by speculating in cotton, and I expect David had also been pinched a bit ; but there they stood cheerfully. The head of the police, Vincent, was also there. We drove to the Yacht Club, where we had breakfast, joined by the Admiral.

After breakfast Stanley Reed came to see me. He told me that Nair had been down to Bombay, and described our scheme as very satisfactory in almost every detail. He told me that Rahimtoolah had told him that the financial proposals, which had already been communicated to the local governments, pretended to set out to give autonomy to the Provinces, but made them appeal on all sorts of questions for the sanction of the central government. I read him from the sacred text the paragraph dealing with taxation and borrowing, and he confessed that Rahimtoolah's allegations were completely unfounded. I described to him the whole scheme ; he said we had accomplished a great deal, and I think we can rely upon his support and upon his being a good influence with Willingdon. They are sending up quite a good team to the conference at Delhi. They are not sending Tilak, but they are sending Sandavakar and Ghandi. Ghandi had written to Chelmsford to announce his intention of going to prison unless Mohamed Ali and Shaukat Ali are released. With regard to Tilak, if I were the Viceroy I would have had him at Delhi at all costs. He is at the moment probably the most powerful man in India, and he has it in his power, if he chooses, to help materially in War effort. If, on the other hand, he attached conditions of a political kind to his offers of help, as, indeed, he would, at such a conference things would bo said to him which would for ever destroy his influence in India, at least, so I think. If he is not there, it will always be said that we refused to select the most powerful people. Tilak is already saying that in his speeches, and it would have completely taken the wind out of his sails if he had been invited as one of the leaders of Indian opinion. Of course one can always say : " No help from such a source," but still, there it is. I read a speech of Tilak's on board ship, and it is quite obvious that he will not accept our report proposals. This seems to me all to the good : he is the leader of the opposition.

Reed and I had a great deal of talk about the necessity of political instinct and drama in connection with the Durbar, and I found that he agreed with much of my views on this subject which I have expressed before.

At twelve o'clock precisely we left Bombay (24th) on board the R.I.M., now H.M.S. *Dufferin*. I wonder if I shall ever see the country again ! Verney handed me a farewell letter from Chelmsford. It is cordial enough ; it describes me as impulsive and imaginative, which is certainly not my reputation at home, and he describes himself as prosaic and cautious. Prosaic, yes ; cautious, only because he is willing to espouse the resisting forces of his Government. He beseeches me to have patience, which is, as I have already confessed, good advice.

However, I am not going to describe, or attempt to describe, this journey. I have little or no work to do. The climate, although not hot, is depressing, and it is difficult to get any energy. The boredom is simply indescribable ; there is nothing whatever in the world to do. It was different coming out, because we had work, and had to get it done, and there were also the passengers. In this ship there is my own team ; there is Sir Archdale Earle, Mr. Justice Rowlatt, Admiral Wake, and Inigo Freeman-Thomas.

I am sleeping much better on board ship, but how slowly the time goes ! It is incredible to believe that we have only been three days on the ship. We shall get to Aden, unless we have an accident, the day after to-morrow, where we shall hear news, I hope, both from India and England, and learn more of what the future has in store for us in the way of arrangements for getting home.

The sea is dead calm ; it is not very hot ; there is no wind.

I think we have seen two ships since we left Bombay, and there is nothing to see over the side except perpetual swarms of flying fishes, skimming the water, streaking it, and sometimes going quite a long distance in the air, but, so far as I have been able to see, never very high.

Earle asked to see the report, and he has been sleeping over it ever since. Basu is also reading the report, and he cannot read two pages without sleeping. When I am arguing in favour of immediate publication, which is my great difficulty now, I shall be able to point to its pacifying effect on an Indian politician and a distinguished civil servant. Basu has read the whole of the first part, and is very pleased with it.

Sunday, April 28. At Aden, which we reached at five o'clock on Monday afternoon (April 29), we received the mail, from which I gather that food restrictions in England are not so bad as they sounded. My letters were full of accounts of operations and illnesses, but mails are wonderfully cheering things now that one is going home. The War news seemed good. Islington writes in great trepidation about the designs of the Foreign Office to take possession of the India Office. Of course it is a great nuisance to turn out of anywhere, but I cannot help thinking that we ought not to resist this. I can only hope it is settled by the time I get home, if I am to resume my office. The silence of the Prime Minister and the absence of all communications from my colleagues makes me very much doubt what is going to happen. A telegram from India announced that the King did send a message to the Delhi Durbar, and that Patiala has been chosen for the Imperial Conference. My advice on this subject has therefore been completely disregarded, and one of my first official acts when I get home will be to deprive the Government of India of the right of nominating representatives for the conference. It will have to be done by the Secretary of State in future, for they are not competent to do so.

Most of us went to dine on shore at Aden with General Stewart. Aden seems quite happy. They have got some aeroplanes now with which they keep the Turks very busy. They seem, however, to have many casualties, and the aeroplanes would appear to me to take too big risks by flying too low. Anyhow, the Turks have great success in hitting them with rifles. They have no anti-aircraft guns, only ordinary guns used for this purpose, and, at present, no aeroplanes of their own, otherwise Aden would be practically uninhabitable. Said Pasha still behaves like the perfect gentleman he is. On one occasion the Turks shot down an aeroplane, and Said Pasha wrote in to say that the two occupants had arrived on the ground burned to death ; that he regretted very much he had not the means to give them a Christian burial, but he had buried them with military honours, and that he would be glad either to send their bodies into Aden or to mark their tombs with any stone or inscription that the Resident chose to send.

Tuesday, April 30. We left Aden at dawn this morning, almost 24 hours before we expected. We had coaled. Our steering gear had gone wrong and was still a little wobbly, and Warren proposed to go at 15½ knots all the rest of the way, because this does not put such a tax on his compass ; the vibration is less. So, back to the weary round of novels, patience, picquet, " Slippery Jane," and hurried meals, the cooking being excellent, beginning with a strange naval grace—" For what we are about to receive, thank God."

Thursday, May 2. Earle has read the report ; he thinks that it has been amended to suit his views especially, and he is going to support it.

The War news continues better. I have been in a state of ebullient optimism about the War corresponding with my depression about India and myself, and I have a sort of feeling that in the next week or two the War will be over. As soon as the Germans are convinced that their offensive can achieve nothing more, it cannot be scientific or right or like the Germans to wait, as each month sees them more and more outnumbered ; but they may try their last remaining card, an attack on England.

This morning exciting news has come. There is an answer to my telegram from the R.N.O. at Port Said, instructing the captain of this ship to stop at Suez and not to enter the canal. We are to go up the canal on a canal yacht, apparently to save expense. There follows, I believe, a very long answer to my telegram, but it has arrived so corrupt as to be absolutely undecipherable. Therefore, there is still no news. There is also a strange telegram from Wingate, saying that he is sending Alexander to meet us at Suez, but, to my utter astonishment, he goes on to say that he cannot come to see me as he is too busy : Allenby will tell me all the news from Palestine. What on earth is Allenby doing in Egypt ? Is he going home.

It may save time if I spend a few minutes in just summing up now some of the principal actors in this drama. I begin with Donoughmore—a wholly likeable fellow, very broad-minded and extraordinarily good-tempered ; easily prejudiced and then obstinate, but with undampable spirits and very easygoing. He has never raised any difficulty about any point. I imagine he will be more useful to us afterwards than he has been during the trip ; and certainly always the best of travelling companions.

Duke, universally popular, as sound as he is slow in his judgment ; generous instinct ; conspicuous loyalty ; great caution ; no obvious originality, although I think he invented "dyarchy." He is a strange man. To look at him, with his big, light-blue eyes, firm lips, fierce frown, sulky expression, you would think he was universally bad-tempered and forbidding. He has a habit of staring hard, with a look of wonder and disapproval, but I think it is all manner: I hope so, at any rate.

Roberts, extraordinarily useful on details; the most conscientious of men, with a streak of suspicious obstinacy; great industry, never willingly letting a point go; as good as gold; full of principles and maxims; courageous, but sometimes hysterical. He has completely brought the Government of India to his side, and, although very detailed and niggardly in his mind, he has been a tower of strength to us.

Seton has really good brains, but a certain raggedness of mind which I think may stand in his way; but he is a very likeable fellow.

Halliday has been kindness itself, never losing an opportunity of being useful; considerate in the extreme; as likeable as it is possible to be; with the courage of a lion, undaunted by threatening death and the blight of all his hopes by ill-health. I hope I shall see much of him, and I shall never forget what he has been to me personally during these months.

Basu, wily, cunning, indirect, obstinate, a good fighter, a grateful fellow, a gentleman, with plenty of sporting instinct, a thoroughly good investment.

Kisch grows on one. With a thirst for information, often wrong-headed, often prejudiced, he is, nevertheless, a good fellow, with a consummate knowledge of many subjects, but little ability for drafting, and no tact. He has limitations which do not spoil the good points, which one learns to appreciate more and more, and he is certainly forgiving and tolerant.

Of course neither Kisch nor Parsons have the one ingredient which makes a really first-class private secretary. I know that when I was a private secretary I realised that not only had you to do what you were told to do, which in my case was often very little, but you had constantly to be thinking whether you could ease your chief's work or add to his pleasure in moments of recreation by inventing amusements, methods of greasing the wheels, and so forth. I failed because my ideas were always better than my methods of carrying them out. I suppose Drummond was the best private secretary I have ever known, and, of course, my chief was a much older man than myself, whom I had never known except as a private secretary, and for whom I had hero worship. Therefore I cannot apply the same standards to my people ; but although neither of them has ever made any difficulty in doing what I have asked ; although neither of them could have been excelled in their devotion and conscientiousness, this Drummond part of the business has never been applied.

Parsons is a very strange fellow—enormously likeable and affectionate, shy, with all the faults of very dark people. I could not have wanted anything better than he has given me, except what we have often talked about together—his lack of social conscientiousness. However, I do not believe I could have existed without him.

Tuesday, *May* 7. We are on the sea again, and, as I have nothing to do, I may as well take steps to finish the story of this great adventure in the same haphazard fashion in which I have carried it through to this point. I am too indolent to try and do it well, too indolent even to make it connect with what I have written before.

We got to Suez at dawn on Saturday, May 4. We had been told, contrary to expectations, that we were to save money, and, what is to us just as valuable, time, by leaving the ship at Suez. The *Dufferin* could not have gone through the canal at more than five knots per hour, and we should not have reached Port Said until Sunday morning. The Canal Company had placed their yacht at my disposal, and we were to embark upon this. Captain Betts, who had been the R.N.O. at Port Said and was now the R.N.O. to the whole canal, met us at Suez. I told him that I was going to take twelve people to Port Said, leaving the other four to await orders at Suez, because I was still determined to take three more if I could.

We went up the canal at 18 knots an hour. The banks were too high to see much. It was a very pleasant voyage, and quite cool, indeed, for parts of the voyage there were heavy thunderstorms. It is curious that it is supposed rarely to rain in Egypt, and that all three days I have spent there it rained. We passed the place where the Turks crossed the canal ; passed the disused defences—disused when Kitchener visited Egypt last and said : "I thought the troops were protecting the canal ; the canal seems to be protecting the troops" ; and ordered the defences to be moved into the desert. Now they are only used as bases for sweeping channels, as it were, across the desert, to see that nobody comes to try and lay mines in the canal. One ship was mined in the Bitter Lakes.

We got to Ismailia at half-past twelve, and were met by the Admiral. I told him that I proposed to take twelve passengers unless he told me that the presence of three extra would jeopardise the safety of the ship. Of course he could not say this, and it transpired that all the difficulty is due to the Admiral at Malta.

We lunched at Ismailia with the director of the Canal Company, the Comte de Serrionne, four of us—Kisch, Parsons, Halliday, and Franey—lunching on the *Grafton*. Serrionne was a charming old boy, and gave us an excellent lunch. My French had to be trotted out again, and was even worse than ever. We were shown the room in which Lesseps lived—absolutely unaltered, the furniture remaining as it was. The gardens at Ismalia are quite lovely ; they have some most beautifully coloured bougainvillia. There was a Frenchwoman there who had arrived from France two days before. She described the bombardment of Paris. There is a danger zone right across Paris ; a bombardment every twenty minutes ; nobody minded. Better without it, yes, but as it was there, what did it matter ? She had come on a French vessel because all British vessels refused to take her, and had had no adventure except a four days' sojourn at Malta.

We arrived on board the *Liverpool* at five o'clock on Saturday evening, May 4. Jackson's message that three more passengers were to arrive had not come, but I found the officers of the *Liverpool* quite delightful, acting as real friendly hosts. They did not mind overcrowding ; it was not they, the only people who had the right to grumble, who grumbled; and they soon stowed our huge mass of luggage and all our passengers away. Of course I am in the cream of comfort in the captain's cabin, with my bath opposite me. Donoughmore and Basu both have cabins of their own ; Roberts, Duke, and Rowlatt are in the captain's dining-room in swinging beds ; and the rest are in the sick bay, nobody complaining, as usual.

I had a telegram from Allenby saying : Could he see me at ten o'clock on Sunday morning ? Of course I said " Yes," and abandoned all hope of going to sea that night. The mystery deepens. We are going to take no less than 61 hours in going across, arriving at Taranto, if we arrive at all, on Wednesday morning.

I have had a most cheerful letter from my *adlati*, approving of the report, but strangely limited to British India, because they say they were not consulted about the Chiefs. This is Donoughmore and Roberts, not Duke and Basu. It does not much matter.

I have also had a telegram from Chelmsford, at last, giving an account of the meeting at Delhi. As I predicted, the exclusion of Tilak, who is, after all, the biggest leader in India at the moment, had a bad effect, and unanimity had been difficult. They had prohibited all controversial motions and resolutions. Why could not they let them have their say and attempt to get a real meeting? They could always have put up someone to answer any awkward question. However, I must wait, and suspend my judgment until I see the full account of the meeting.

We started off at six o'clock in the evening (May 5) without escort. It was rough, and the dawn broke on a sea probably too rough for submarines to operate in without breaking water. Everybody except Rowlatt, Marris, Parsons, and myself was seasick. I have eaten largely and kept as quiet as I could. The sea calmed down in the afternoon, and we passed to the west of Crete about midnight (6th). The presence of all the crews at the guns, the look-out of 20 people watching hard all day is most thrilling; but nobody seems to be anxious except myself.

We heard news last night of a submarine off Crete; we heard news of a submarine at nine o'clock yesterday morning right where we should be at ten o'clock this morning (May 7); but we have heard news this morning that at six o'clock last night that submarine was going west. Safety seems to lie in the speed of the ship, which is, however, only 19 knots; zigzagging; and that the submarines are lying nearer the ports; but to-day will be the most anxious, as we are right in the path of the submarines going in and out of the Adriatic Gulf, and to-morrow morning, when we shall pass them all lying at the mouth of the Gulf of Taranto.

Saturday, *May* 11 (on train from Paris to Boulogne). The time has now come when I must bring this series of notes to an end. The work of doing it has not been uninteresting. I am so conscious of its reflecting often contradictory moods of days and hours that I have never had the courage to read it, but it has, at any rate, served the purpose of keeping a record of events and opinions as they were formed, and of avoiding a series of letter-writing. I have been blessed with a shorthand writer who has made the work as easy as possible, and it has rarely occupied me more than an average half an hour at the most a day.

I have wished more than I can say that I had attempted something of this kind throughout the days that I have lived —the Budget of 1909 ; the crisis of the War ; the crisis of conscription ; Morley's resignation ; negotiations on Home Rule ; and, above all, the great crisis which lead to the formation of the present Ministry. I have known more of these things than almost any living man. I think during the last five years of Asquith's reign I knew him more intimately than anybody else, and I wish I could have put it all down in the same way that I have put down the uninteresting material of this journey to India. Perhaps one day I shall trust my memory and a few scattered notes to it, but it will never be the same thing, nor do I suppose that the future is likely to be so interesting from my point of view as the past.

THE END

INDEX

C

H

N

O

P

Q

R

S

Y

Z